PN
2012
. I6      International theatre
no.4          annual

## DATE DUE

| | | | |
|---|---|---|---|
| | | | |
| | | | |
| | | | |
| | | | |
| | | | |
| | | | |
| | | | |
| | | | |
| | | | |
| | | | |

# INTERNATIONAL THEATRE ANNUAL

Paul Robeson in the Stratford production of *Othello*

# INTERNATIONAL

# THEATRE
# ANNUAL

### No. 4

792#647

(1)

## GROVE PRESS INC.
### NEW YORK

Grove Press Books and Evergreen Books
are published by Barney Rosset at Grove Press, Inc.
64 University Place, New York 3, N.Y.

PRINTED BY MOUTON & CO.

IN THE NETHERLANDS

# CONTENTS

# ILLUSTRATIONS

# ILLUSTRATIONS (continued)

# INTRODUCTION

THIS, so far as I know, is the only publication which regularly sets side by side, for comparison, contrast and healthy rivalry, the annual dramatic achievements and the dramatic failures too of New York, Paris and London. It happens to be a fact that at the moment the theatrical future of the world depends on what takes place on the stages of these three cities. But it would be absurd complacency to suppose that this will always be so, except at the price of constant vigilance and experiment: and of keeping a wary eye on what developments are going on elsewhere in the world. That is why the *International Theatre Annual,* now published for the first time in America as an Evergreen Book, has in previous volumes reviewed the theatres of Spain, Germany, Scandinavia and Russia and now looks beyond the frontiers of Europe and America. We can never tell when some new and powerful artistic rival may spring up on the edge of the horizon; but we can at least be prepared to see him when he does.

HAROLD HOBSON

# LONDON

## J. W. Lambert

OF the hundred-odd pieces offered to the London public during the twelve months ending in the early summer of 1959 about twenty-five per cent were of no interest or value on any account whatever, and some ten per cent claimed attention on the highest level. This seems to me to suggest a rather satisfactory year. To expect these proportions to be the other way round would suggest the triumph of hope over experience to a ludicrous degree. As usual it was a shapeless year, its pleasures and catastrophes cropping up piecemeal, its splendours and miseries shared equally by the commercial managements, busy trawling the talent of the world with ill-patched nets and sheep for navigators, and the smaller theatres given credit for a policy, sometimes even a style, all their own.

The idea of a National Theatre remained an idea, the building a castle in Spain; but our campaigners may claim one victory. The Lord Chamberlain's Office, stern censor of the spoken word, has announced that it will no longer apply automatically the ban on plays dealing with the subject of homosexuality, but will licence any serious work on this theme. The immediate and predictable result of this enlightened dictum has of course been a rapid drop in the number of plays of this sort put before us. It can hardly be denied that several such plays have in recent years been put on by the club theatres despite the fact that, regarded simply as plays, they were to put it gently not very good.

Irene Hamilton and Dennis Lotis

*Murray*

'THE WORLD OF PAUL SLICKEY'
(Palace, London)

...ck Watling and Aidan Turner

Marie Löhr

On a broader front the year undoubtedly saw a spread into some quite unexpected quarters of Brechtian notions. In their concentrated form, shortsightedly applied by *dévots,* these are exceedingly tiresome in their selfconsciousness; but taken with a pinch of salt they can liberate the old-fashioned unimaginative production most helpfully. Most of Brecht's ideas, of course, apart from his silly little placards, must have come as no surprise to our lighter stage, just as they would have come as no surprise to Shakespeare; but there is still plenty of scope for aerating the stifled domesticity of many of our plays.

Most interesting of all visible developments has been that of the 'musical'. This may seem an odd claim to make of a year which has seen new plays—or plays new to London—from T. S. Eliot, Graham Greene, Samuel Beckett, Ionesco, Anouilh, O'Neill and Tennessee Williams. But nothing in their work has—with the possible exception of Mr. Greene's move towards comedy—marked any particular advance. The musical, on the other hand, develops steadily. The pattern traced by this particular form of entertainment is a curious one. When *opera seria* gave rise by reaction to *opera buffa* it was no surprise that, with the rise of the middle classes, the latter should turn into operetta—a field in which England, with Gilbert and Sullivan, struck out boldly by adding a strong dose of satire; next operetta declined into musical comedy, which in the first fifty years of the century became progressively feebler and feebler, clinging to life only by its tunes, which became more and more a pretty tinkle, and by becoming a vehicle for a popular comedian. Then from America came the sudden fresh impulse of *Oklahoma,* in which the music, though still 'pop' in character, approximated to that of the ballad-opera and the dancing, clearing under Agnes de Mille's drive the old Edwardian posturing and the intervening unison high kicks out of the way, became a highly expressive part of the structure of the piece, rather than a mere bosom-bouncing, thigh-beguiling interlude. And now two more American musicals have brought to London a degree of technical virtuosity which suggests that the wheel has come full circle, and that at long last something has been done to narrow the wearisome gap between the popular and the 'serious'.

I mean, of course, *Candide* and *West Side Story*. The most obvious common factor in these two shows is that both have music by Leonard Bernstein. Mr. Bernstein is a conductor of symphony orchestras in the United States; and as such his showmanship and skill have never been in doubt. Both qualities find more scope in writing for a less demanding ambience. Years ago, in *Wonderful Town*, Mr. Bernstein dazzlingly captured the idiom of 'pop' music; in *Candide* he provides with equal brilliance pastiches of half a dozen composers from Strauss and Strauss to Sullivan and Suppé; in *West Side Story* he uses the cadences and colours of jazz most expertly to enliven the strepitant sullenness of adolescent gang warfare. Of these three scores *Candide* is unquestionably the best, perhaps because in it Mr. Bernstein is being openly imitative—the romantic passages of *West Side Story* made it clear that left to find an appropriate idiom of his own he is at a loss. But the point is that, even though Mr. Bernstein does not trouble to do all his own orchestrations, his extremely successful music is more ambitious, more complex, than any that has been heard in this sort of entertainment since the latter part of the nineteenth century; it makes, for instance, the music of *My Fair Lady* seem all too clearly the milk-and-water stuff which in fact it is.

*Candide* requires singers of operatic calibre. *West Side Story* requires highly trained dancers; for here the emphasis is rightly on movement. The production and choreography of Jerome Robbins were, up to a point, remarkable. The menace of the

*Boys*

A scene from *Lock Up Your Daughters* (Mermaid, Lo

...ndra Church, Ethel Merman and Jack Klugman in *Gypsy* (Broadway, N

*Friedman-Abeles*

Ruby Dee, Claudia McNeil, Glynn Turman, Sidney Poitier and John Fiedler

'A RAISIN IN THE SUN' (Barrymore, New York)

Claudia McNeil and Sidney Poitier

Ruby Dee and Sidney Poitier

Pat Hingle, Christopher Plummer and Raymond Massey in Elia Kazan's production

*Friedman-Abeles*

U.S.I.

Raymond Massey and Christopher Plummer

two rival gangs swirling singly or in groups across the stage was conveyed with a sultry hip-swinging tension quite electrifying—for twenty minutes or so. But the same effects repeated over and over again must pall, and Mr. Robbins seemed not to have many shots in his locker, once he had exhausted the experience of Roland Petit and the New York City Ballet. Yet once again the point is that not for a hundred years—and then only in inserted *divertissements*—has such ambitious dancing been used in a popular entertainment.

All this seems to me most exciting—though it does of course cry out for the development of a race of supermen among performers, who can act like Gielgud, sing like Gobbi and dance like Somes by turns or even all at once. At the moment it is difficult not to be disturbed by inadequacy in one or other of these directions, or by the mediocrity which results from using a player of no particular mark who can make some sort of showing in all three departments. *West Side Story* suffered particularly in this way, for although the gangs twitched and sidled, loured and fought with finely disciplined attack, none of the principals was really equal to the situation. *Candide* came off a good deal better. Its hero, Denis Quilley, was stronger in both singing and acting than his opposite number in *West Side Story;* its heroine, Mary Costa, deployed an enormous sense of humour and a just sufficiently agile soprano for some extremely witty coloratura; and in Laurence Naismith's Pangloss—in the London version used as a narrator—it exercised a singing actor of invention and authority. On the other hand *West Side Story* had the best of it in the matter of sets—Oliver Smith's staging was exciting in conception and superb in execution; Osbert Lancaster's stage pictures for *Candide* were rather too 'amusing' and Robert Lewis's direction and—I presume—choreography not amusing enough.

There remains the actual substance of these pieces: *West Side Story* a version of *Romeo and Juliet* translated to contemporary New York, *Candide* firmly linked to Voltaire's original. We are growing accustomed to the use of Shakespeare in one form or another, and until the end, which petered out into a cowardly (and incomprehensible) softening up, *West Side Story* followed its original most intelligently. So did *Candide*, in which Lilian Hellman's was the guiding hand. Never yet has there been a more unlikely choice of subject for a musical—though after all it offers opportunities for a rustic wedding, scenes of high life in Paris, high jinks in South America, with rhythms to match and a great deal more besides. It also offers a comment on life not in the least cynical—and this was astonishingly well preserved in the musical—which, greatly to my surprise, having taken us through a disillusioning evening (described by Pangloss as having 'a happy beginning, a happy ending, and two solid hours of misery in between') made its closing scene not merely a conventional rounding off but a moving choral summary of the human condition.

So: under American impetus the musical has immensely advanced in its subjects, its music, its dancing—and the calibre of those prepared to concoct them with a degree of skill and polish which in this country we should reserve for a military tattoo. Bridging the gap between the American and the British musical came *Irma la Douce* from Paris, the engaging tale with bitter undertones of an amiable tart who so bewitched a simple young man that in the end he was reduced to being jealous of himself. Here the scale was smaller, and already the note of cheerful charade was allowed to creep in, not mitigated in Peter Brook's production by some heavily stressed oo-la-la impropriety. Only Clive Revill as a barman-narrator much resembling Harpo Marx seemed perfectly at home in this *bistro* world, for Keith

Michell, though pleasingly fresh, looked as embarassed as he was supposed to be feeling, and Elizabeth Seal, though enchanting, is in her dark mercurial way anything but *douce*. The music, too, though adequate, was no more than a compendium of all the accordion-based French *Schmalz* one has ever heard.

The music in all six British musicals to come our way was hardly even that. Leader of the field, I suppose, was Sandy Wilson's *Valmouth*—in which, as it happens, the principal hit was made by a new young designer, Tony Walton, who provided some pleasing extravagances for Firbank's absurd watering-place, but whose subsequent sets have been indistinguishable from anybody else's. The perverted preciosity of this twentyish lark seems sadly faded now; but its mishmash of homosexual and Roman Catholic jokes, strung together into a text, offered a veneer of suburban sophistication—curiously offset by Mr. Wilson's jaunty and nostalgic teatime music. Still, such as it is, Mr. Wilson's music is his own, which is more than can be said for the Tin Pan Alley anonymity of that for *Chrysanthemum*, a hearty, rather enjoyable old-fashioned frolic in which Pat Kirkwood strutted gamely, or *Mister Venus*, a disastrous entertainment which even Frankie Howerd, the Poplar Pan, could not begin to save. And down at the bottom of the class with *Mister Venus* must go the eagerly awaited entry of John Osborne into the field—*The World of Paul Slickey*.

After the universal obloquy with which it was greeted, it would be delightful to uncover true qualities ignored by my impatient colleagues. But the truth shall prevail, even at the cost of saying the same thing as everybody else. To bring real satire back to the British musical was a splendid aim. To select as primary targets the more vulgar sections of the Press, the shoddy parasitism of the gossip-writer, was an excellent idea— no feature of civilisation more desperately needs destroying.

To throw in some asides aimed at the Establishment in various aspects is always a worthwhile move. But to do, despite the talent we know is Mr. Osborne's, all this so badly ... In form, this was the old-style ragbag musical, halfway to revue. In the writing, Mr. Osborne's touch completely deserted him. The reason for this is not difficult to see. Mr. Osborne is not really a social commentator at all; he is a writer with a gift of rhetoric, an eye for anomalies, and a capacity for passionate involvement with certain characters. He is also a young man torn in two between a desire to see a brave new world and a deep attachment to the old one. All his plays have sympathetic seniors in them; and *Paul Slickey* is no exception. The dreadful evening warms to life only when Marie Löhr's Lady Mortlake or Harry Welchman's Lord Mortlake hold the stage—and hold it they do, with a presence and timing sadly lacking in their juniors. To see Miss Löhr merely watching a woman singing a song about capital punishment entitled 'Bring back the Axe' is to learn what acting really means; to watch Mr. Welchman's aged peer expand as the same silly woman sings a song about 'beautiful things' is to discover areas of dramatic experience seldom revealed to-day. Here, of course, the point is that Mr. Osborne, perhaps against his will, gives *them* the opportunities. His hero he has crippled from the start—making a mistake which *Expresso Bongo* avoided—by making his success-worshipping Paul Slickey a self-pitying wreck, longing to get away from it all; but surely he should be satirising the real thing? Then, having given Philip Locke the chance for a superbly sinuous interlude as a horrible priest, what softening makes him uncover this dreadful man as merely an impostor?

It remains only to say that he has no evident gift for writing lyrics, that Christopher Whelen's music was characterless, Kenneth Macmillan's choreography merely flashy, and Sir Hugh

Casson's sets understandably distraught. And then, too, Mr. Osborne was his own producer; but a hand at once more ruthless and more inventive was needed. The disturbing thing, perhaps, about this unhappy affair was not the assorted badness of the evening—which extended to many of the cast—but that it should ever have occurred at all. That Mr. Osborne's judgment, indeed his gifts, should have so far deserted him; and that no candid friends were at hand to tell him what was happening.

By and large, it remains gloomily clear, the British theatre has learnt nothing about musicals. Its own half-hearted step towards operetta, in the shape of pieces like *Bless the Bride,* have come to to less than nothing. Its gentle extravaganzas after the pattern of *Salad Days* have come to less than nothing. At best it brings to this exacting and exhilarating genre the tolerable high spirits of an undergraduate romp.

We lack the gift, it is painfully clear, of taking frivolity seriously, and while breast-beating is the order of the page it may be as well to cast a cold eye over some other departments of the 'lighter stage' in which we have only intermittently twinkled. Revue, for instance—and by revue I mean not those variety programmes hung on a necklace of nudes with a singing star for pendant, but a close-knit evening with a guiding spirit behind it such as used to galvanise the Little revues, or *Sweet and Low* and its successors, or more recently *Twopence Coloured* and *Airs on a Shoestring.* Their day, it seems, is done. The nearest approach to it during the period was *For Adults Only,* in which Hugh Paddick, haggard and spry, Ron Moody, a walking exuberant leer, and Miriam Karlin, flamboyantly crushed, injected a little genuine and welcome savagery into some topical jibes; and *Living for Pleasure,* in which Dora Bryan, the everlasting floosie (if the word seems dated, so does the type), Daniel Massey, a nice amusing young man, and George Rose, a crafty and slightly sinister comedian, made us laugh in a small way.

Here the saving grace, as in the plays of Mr. Osborne, was reserved for the veterans: the Crazy Gang came back to the Victoria Palace in *Clown Jewels.* They are past their prime, these elderly jokers. They move slowly; they hark back. But in their urchin glee there still remains the free spirit which runs through Dekker and *The Gull's Hornbook* and Wycherley and *The Beggar's Opera,* the Wellers and Little Tich. When they make television jokes they seem—or is it only a long-standing partiality that persuades me so?—really to be dancing round an absurdity which is a part of all our lives, not merely cashing in on a successful rival. And when they crack dirty jokes we tired of before our teens they seem to be sharing an exuberant boyhood, not—like Mr. Osborne in similar circumstances, trying to shock us with exhausted smut.

Back to breast-beating. The thriller, it is clear, is dead beyond recall. Eight appeared in London during the period under review: it seems hardly worth listing their names. None of them showed the smallest sign of doing what thrillers are doing in book form—that is, approximating more and more closely to highly intelligent character studies which happen, unlike so many highly intelligent character studies, to have exciting plots. A revival, with Betsy Blair, of *The Trial of Mary Dugan* showed us how far we have travelled from fustian.

Indeed, in some we have travelled so far that we have lost the knack; particularly, in farce. Farce, being the obverse of tragedy, should suit our national genius: and indeed it is clear that for centuries we had a flourishing farcial tradition. What has become of it? Have the actors lost it? or the audiences? or both? The answer, I am afraid, is that it is the actors whose courage has failed them. At the Whitehall Theatre a team led by Brian Rix and Leo Franklyn is beginning to rediscover the art of inventive clowning. A company from the North, appearing at the Victoria Palace in a piece sardonically called *Friends and Neighbours,* displayed considerable skill in deploying hyperboreal humours of a savagery fit to chill a southerner's blood. But our failings were brought home by the nearly simultaneous appearance of the Old Vic company in Pinero's *The Magistrate* and the Comédie Française company in Feydeau's *Le Dindon.* Pinero's is the earlier piece by ten years, and by that much the cruder; even so our lack of comic resource in all but the big moments was painful. Douglas Seale produced with a stunning lack of invention, seeming not to see handfuls of opportunities which the author had supplied for clowning. Michael Hordern, it is true, given the stage to himself and a long comic cadenza recalling the horrors of a night spent first in a most disreputable establishment, then in flight from the police, winding up at last in his own magistrate's court, confronted with a bunch of prisoners among whom is his own wife, produced a finely controlled piece of virtuoso anguish; John Phillips—looking like W. S. Gilbert—and Jack May—looking like Mr. Pooter—made an admirable pair of absurd Army officers. But where, in the company as a whole, were the discipline, the timing, the precise execution of exactly calculated effect which are the making of farce?

It was, as they say, to seek. It has no part in the reliance on inspired amateurism which is part of the English tradition. It was seen at its best in *Le Dindon.* It is only fair to remember that this piece has been in the repertory of the Comédie Française for at least four years; but then if I can trust my memory the performance has during that time not varied by a hairs-

breadth. Individual skill blends with teamwork to produce a
result which is not merely immensely funny but tonic. True, at
least two parts were inadequately filled—though I was apparently more irked than the rest of the audience at finding, as
a comic Englishwoman, an actress who could speak only with a
broad American accent. Yet it is more than a lucky chance that
makes us rock with sympathetic laughter when Andrée de Chau-
viron's deaf old wife sits, all unconcern, on an electric bell;
and more than cheerful improvisation leads us up to one of the
great comic scenes of the theatre—that in which Robert Hirsch,
as a sprightly but only human *roué*, emerges from a night with
a tart who takes her work seriously to find himself in demand
for further duties by a woman to whom he has been laying
siege for weeks. His despairing efforts to rise to the occasion,
hampered by lumbago and an untimely inability to keep awake,
are superbly done. There is not really much 'business' in M.
Meyer's production of *Le Dindon*; but every stroke tells.

Just as good musicals should be an essential part of a healthy
theatre, to be enjoyed by every height of brow, so the boulevard
comedy should provide a civilised evening's pleasure. Even in
France, saving my Editor's displeasure, this happy state of affairs is not always achieved. But though they are even more
preoccupied with the subject than we are, they don't, over there,
find it necessary to be quite so arch about sex as we are; and—
perhaps they have the advantage over us here—in their better
productions they generally feel able to trust the audience to see
a joke without slapping it across their faces like a custard pie.
If we lack invention and timing in farce, we lack finesse in
light comedy. I am not sure whether this is also true of Americans, never having seen an American comedy done by the sort
of people it was written for; but I suspect it is not. A dozen

light comedies have come our way, half of them imported. Those
from France, two in particular, have not been happily treated—
for, oddly enough, precisely opposite reasons. In one, *Hook,
Line and Sinker,* Robert Morley took Roussin's excellent *Le
mari, la femme et la mort* by the scruff of its neck and turned
it into a vehicle for his own extremely amusing brand of horse-
play, which we regret, I dare say, only if we remember that Mr.
Morley is in fact an excellent actor, that this is in fact also an
excellent play, and that two other excellent players, Joan Plowright and Bernard Cribbens, were all but submerged in the
process. Perhaps I should not speak of *Change of Tune* as having
come from France; Alan Melville, its English adaptor, refers
back to the Italian original but it surely owes its fame to its
existence as *L'heure éblouissante,* in which Suzanne Flon en-
chanted Paris. Geraldine McEwan, who played the part in
London, can stand comparison with Mlle Flon: no small compliment. She has less stature, but then she is less strident. She
is less well equipped to slide into the overlong drunk scene
which is the centre of the piece; but then she is rather better
equipped to catch the flavour of demureness poised, as it con-
templates the misguided self-importance of her absurd village
organist husband, on the brink of devoted derision. Miss
McEwan has all the charm of some small woodland creature—
at least some small woodland creature as drawn by Ernest H.
Shepard. But in this play she was supported by conscientious
and able actors who, no doubt at the bidding of their producer,
Vida Hope, underlined each joke and placed each *double
entendre* in unmistakeable inverted commas with a nerve-
wracking deployment of nods and becks and wreathed smiles.

Kay Hammond and John Clements snuffled and puffed more
or less effectively through Lionel Hale's *Gilt and Gingerbread,*
which again was, or became, hardly more than a vehicle. But

really only two light comedies call for comment, and one of those only because it provides one of our best actresses with some splendid chances. *The Pleasure of his Company* is an American piece coming some way after *The Philadelphia Story*. Nigel Patrick produced, and played an international playboy, in a jolly English way; the evening was made by Coral Browne, once the playboy's wife, now stodgily and, she insists, happily settled down in San Francisco. I personally, having seen her magnificent Lady Macbeth and Gertrude, should like to see Miss Browne made French, and in *Phèdre*; or as Millamant, 'for she is tall and stately'. She has the carriage of a queen but the allure of an Aphrodite and the mischief of an urchin (of course, of course—Cleopatra). Meanwhile, if I must, I will accept her in little old plays like this one.

Lastly, in this gallery of what should be grace and favour, a little work of all-round excellence—*The Grass is Greener,* by Hugh and Margaret Williams, with Mr. Williams leading an expert—and expertly chosen—company through its elegant paces. This is a nonsensical tale of an Earl with a stately home and a charming wife and a comic butler, of a malicious woman friend and a lankily unscrupulous American millionaire who pays his half-crown and walks off with the chatelaine. With Celia Johnson's wide-eyed schoolgirl grace and Joan Greenwood's siamese-cat strangeness to buttress his own suave solidity, Mr. Williams saves the day for light comedy.

If I have seemed to take my time in coming to the more aspiring prospects of our theatre, that is because these have been, though plentiful, not very exciting. A dozen plays by young writers, almost as many by established dramatists, and an impressive line-up of accepted classics in several languages testify to the vigour of our dying theatre; yet somehow I have found it possible to watch all but four of them with judicious calm, and have somewhat missed the sheer theatrical excitement which should have sprung from so much enterprise.

It has certainly been another remarkable year for young dramatists. And curiously enough one who had the misfortune to catch the attention of the Paul Slickeys (at least Mr. Osborne's gift for creating memorable type-figures has not deserted him) turned out to have real quality: the nineteen-year-old typist from Salford, Lancashire, Shelagh Delaney, whose *A Taste of Honey* was put on by Joan Littlewood at the Theatre Royal, Stratford, with the usual neo-Brechtian trimmings—jazz band in a box, direct address to audience, etc., but easily survived both this and a transfer to the West End which involved smartening up the production to a point where, at least early in the run the principals were torrentially incomprehensible. This strange little piece about a neglected girl, daughter of a trollop, her illegitimate baby and the flinching homosexual who helps her prepare for its coming proved to have its own flavour of youthful slum poetry, the predominant taste being indeed honey, not gall; charity, not anger. It also introduced a young actress who proved to have a talent at any rate for the *gamine*— Frances Cuka, dark, round-faced and quick to illumination.

Miss Littlewood's shoestring organisation continued as enterprising as could be, with varying success. Unpromisingly entitled *Fings Ain't wot they used t'be,* by Frank Norman, author of one of those prison autobiographies, another shot at neo-Brechtian social reporting misfired; it had its moments, but the roughhewn string of Soho sketches was altogether too loosely knit. Not so *The Hostage,* Brendan Behan's latest contribution to the stage—a rather engaging work, like a cross between *The Iceman Cometh* and *Salad Days;* familiar Dublin squalor (the Troubles again) being enlivened by some gaily offhand songs and a happily sentimental story about a harmless young English soldier caught in a den of eccentrics. Once again, for the record, the predominant taste was of charity, not anger.

We have come, of course, to look to the English Stage Company at the Royal Court Theatre in Sloane Square for our direction-pointers to the new drama; but in fact they have had little to offer. John Arden's *Live Like Pigs* presented most clearly the dilemma of the would-be free spirit. By contrasting the narrowness of the petty bourgeoisie with the freedom of a bunch of ruttish, diseased, filthy and thievish near-gypsies Mr. Arden perhaps did more than he meant to in the way of persuading us that the Welfare State is not so bad after all; and did so with a certain dramatic verve, occasionally sidetracked into unfortunate purple patches—the downfall of many a greater dramatist than he.

For the rest the Royal Court new playwrights' bold adventures proved to be homely plays of a familiar type thinly disguised by contemporary trappings—narrator, visible stage lighting equipment etc.—and in two cases hardly even that. *Moon on a Rainbow Shawl,* by a West Indian, Errol John, and winner of the *Observer* play competition two years ago, again turned out to be anything but angry: a neo-Chekhovian piece about a mildly picturesque group in a Caribbean slum backyard. Lacking passionate insight or beauty of language it remained a companionable little play with a kindly dying fall. So, in a way, was *Sugar in the Morning,* which sketched the foolishness and pathetic frustrations of a widow with social and cultural leanings reduced to running a boarding-house in a north-country town. By now a cliché of the contemporary serious play, the wandering Negro charmer duly strolled across the scene, but the remaining lodgers were acceptably roughed in in the manner of a slightly more sophisticated Dodie Smith. The play would I think have done

well in a simple conventional production, and with a less mannered and patronising performance than that of Margaret Johnston at the centre of it. *The Long and the Short and the Tall*
offered us a group of N.C.O.s and men in the Malayan jungle
surrounded by Japanese. The author, Willis Hall, handled his
jaunty dialogue effectively—and Peter O'Toole as a vicious
Cockney threw off his snarls (of course he had a heart of gold)
with immense bravura and a wide variety of accents. Mr. Hall
had the potentially interesting idea of projecting a strikingly
unmartial Japanese soldier into the bunch of dim-witted English-
men losing their nerve, but made his point—that war is a
brutalising process and that all men are brothers—only with
the help of the sort of sentimental contrivance which often occurs in real life but won't do in what should hope to be a work
of art.

Peter Shaffer, in *Five Finger Exercise,* produced an unmistakeable commercial success. I don't intend that phrase as an
insult, but I do use it on purpose. There was a blurring of
the edges in this tale of a family with a philistine father, a
pretentious mother, a sensitive son and a German tutor—fitted
into the household with some strain on credibility—which in
the end sapped one's confidence in, if the word is not too strong,
the play's integrity. Confidence in Mr. Shaffer's ability to write
dialogue with an edge, speeches with their own dynamic and
scenes which snap home their theatrical effect remains high;
and these aspects of the piece were finely handled by Brian
Bedford as the son—a difficult role, with the audience's sympathy always ready to slip away—Adrianne Allen as the foolish
frustrated mother, performing with tremendous effect her highly personal 'freeze', one of the most striking spectacles in the
British theatre today, and especially by Roland Culver as the
father, leathery, inarticulate, kind and wrong.

Denis Cannan is perhaps neither one of the new-style drama-tists nor an established middle-of-the-north-road-figure. This should mean a refreshing individuality—indeed does so; un-fortunately it also means that somehow his effects just don't come off. In *Who's Your Father?*, an intelligent farce after the French model, tingling with problems of identity, they cer-tainly didn't, so that the play all too rapidly did. A more res-pectful hearing was given to *The Hamlet of Stepney Green*, by Bernard Kops, one of a flourishing handful of post-Mankowitz Jewish writers who make good use of the tight-knit *mores* of their race—and bad use of an easy sentimental philosophising which casts over their family dramas a disagreeable patina of pawky pathos.

In terms of quantity at least established figures were led in London by Tennessee Williams. After a long battle with the Lord Chamberlain's Office on grounds which remain obscure to me Sam Wanamaker, pugnacious as ever, brought *The Rose Tattoo* down from the enlightened city of Liverpool. This relatively early play has a good deal to recommend it, being less desperately in search of sensation than some of Mr. William's later work. Its story of the blended sexual-maternal yearnings of a Sicilian widow in Florida and the lorry-driver she seizes on for satisfaction is told with a minimum of hot air, a certain directness. Mr. Wanamaker's production was modest in quality, though he himself rasped over his usual brand of angular bravado as the male animal in the case; the Italian actress Lea Padovani played the widow with a restraint at an extreme remove from Magnani's celebrated film treatment of the part.

In *Orpheus Descending*, at the Royal Court, another Italian actress, Isa Miranda, brought to another Italian-American a most impressive authority, a fine sense of a woman hardened beyond her true character; unfortunately her English, at least on the first night, was both muted and difficult to understand. Still more unfortunately Tony Richardson's production unerringly emphasised all the faults in this slow, congested play. A greater feeling for design as opposed to decoration might have made a good deal more out of this play, a refashioning of an early piece, *Battle of Angels,* which Mr. Williams says he has been working on intermittently since 1939. Perhaps it is no wonder that we seemed to be seeing an epitome of Williams —and perhaps this would have mattered less if the Orpheus, a deft young actor from the cast of *West Side Story,* Gary Cockrell, had been able to make this watchful wanderer into something more impressive than a sort of Christopher Robin in reverse. As it was the evening dragged itself along, and Mr. Williams's unfortunate flights of allegorical fancy, involving little blue birds with no legs and barren fig trees, slopped, an embarrassing treacly tide, across the footlights. The Arts Theatre, however, put on an excellent double bill, Mr. Williams's *Garden District;* that is, the two short plays *Something Unspoken* and *Suddenly Last Summer. Something Unspoken* was generally dismissed by the critics as of no interest. They were, of course, wrong. In this little piece there is a warmth and understanding missing for too long from Mr. Williams's work. There is also, of course, plenty of innate cruelty in the story of the apparently downtrodden companion-secretary who has for fifteen years exercised a far more dreadful power than any her *grande dame* could command: she has denied to the woman who loves her the opportunity to speak her love. Beatrix Lehmann was perhaps oddly cast as the little whip-hand; not so in *Suddenly Last Summer,* where she became one of those terrifying matriarchs round whom the family cringes—all save one, a girl played by Patricia Neal; the piece resolved itself into a series of arias for these two. Both displayed a rare mastery of the architecture of a long speech, and the result, balanced by the presence, amid all the torrid hate and hysteria, of a cool young doctor, and led cunningly on to a quite horrible climax, was an electrifying theatrical experience. Electrifying, but strictly meaningless: *Grand Guignol,* no more.

To go along with the English version of *Fin de Partie, Endgame,* Samuel Beckett wrote *Krapp's Last Tape,* a gripping and sentimental monologue in which a filthy, diseased and loquacious old man recalls with the aid of tape machine a moment thirty years past when he thought he almost escaped from loneliness. It was unwound by Patrick Magee with the prolonged football-rattle snarl which we shall soon be forced to assume is his normal voice, stirring but monotonous, and with some aimless phallic by-play with a banana which matched the equally aimless, all too Joycean smut of the title. *Endgame* proved in English even bleaker than in French, largely because only one of the cast in this relentless summary of human relationships possessed the gift of giving the sprung prose its proper music: Jack MacGowran as Clov, the bent and spiteful servant who hobbles from window to window, dustbin to dustbin, banging down the lids on the aged parents immured therein, and muttering the hopeless *Nunc Dimittis* of the servitors as Hamm the master, blind in his chair, parodies the Lord's Prayer.

*Endgame* indeed; by comparison a Ionesco double bill, designed perhaps as a sort of benefit for a more than promising young actress, Joan Plowright, seemed positively euphoric. Miss Plowright repeated her endearing picture of a doddering nonagenarian in *The Chairs,* and completed the evening with the spirited teenage innocent flirting with disaster in *The Lesson:* a feat of virtuosity—but it became clear, especially after a

Geraldine Page and Paul Newman in
'SWEET BIRD OF YOUTH' (Martin Beck, New York)

Eric Portman and Helen Hayes
in O'Neill's *A Touch of the Poet* (Helen Hayes, New York)

'ORPHEUS
DESCENDING'
(Royal Court, London)

Diane Cilento
with Catherine Wilmer,
Diana Beaumont
and Mavis Villiers

*Armstrong Jones*

Isa Miranda,
Fred Johnson,
Gary Cockrell
and Bessie Love

Crowder

Si

Murray Melvin

Frances Cuka and Murray Melvin

## EAST TO WEST END

Joan Littlewood's productions of *(above left and below)* *The Hostage* (Theatre Roya
and Wyndham's) and *A Taste of Honey* (Theatre Royal and Criterion)

*Crowder*  Robin Chapman, Eileen Kennally and Murray Melvin

revival of *Major Barbara,* also at the Court and with Miss Plow-right as Barbara, that if she were going to fulfil her promise it was time for her to expand her range. Bad luck, but perhaps good experience, that her first attempt at doing so should get her crushed beneath the comic weight of our own Leviathan of Levity, the One and Only Robert Morley.

A generation late, Anouilh's *Voyageur sans Bagages* at last arrived in London at the Arts. It does not wear terribly well, though Denholm Elliott judged the weight of the piece per-fectly in his tense but not tic-ridden performance as the young man without a name who doesn't at all care for the family which wishes to claim him, or relish the thought of resuming his former and unamiable personality. It is a short play, and wisely no attempt was made to make it fill the whole evening. On the contrary M. Anouilh confected a curtain-raiser from Louise de Vilmorin's *conte, Madame de* specially for the occasion: a pleas-ing little marionette-piece, pleasingly done by Elizabeth Sellars and Douglas Wilmer, it carried happily on the gradual return of the double bill—which, you will have observed, is getting more and more common in London.

Last of the year's more or less modern French imports, the first play by the French philosopher-dramatist Gabriel Marcel to be done here—*Les Chemins de Crète,* translated as *Ariadne,* also at the Arts. Rather modest dramatic action carried intel-ligent probing into the extent to which any of us can assess our own motives; but the adaptation rather muffled a strong Lesbian element in the original, and left us with a relatively straightforward portrait of an emotional vampire, most sym-pathetically played in fine-drawn aquatint by Helen Cherry.

Perhaps I should have spoken of O'Neill's *Long Day's Journey into Night* while dealing with Mr. Williams's brand of Americana; but the fact is that somehow I always think of

O'Neill's plays as coming from Sweden, where they are always being performed and where they seem perfectly at home. This was a painful experience, partly, or largely, because these chunks of autobiography, raw and bleeding, suggest confidences forced upon one; and partly because it is so badly written that only playing of genius could ward off boredom and the untimely giggle. The London production was respectable, no more. Anthony Quayle played Tyrone père, and up to a point played him well—with, as one would expect, great intelligence and understanding. But every time Mr. Quayle takes on, as he constantly will take on, these over-life-size parts he falls short; he seems to be, like Orson Welles, one of those players who can hold the stage superbly for say three minutes at a time, but for no longer; after that something is wrong, one has the impression of watching a film with the sound track switched off, or of being in a car which having run out of petrol is uneasily coasting. Thus, despite fine performances from Gwen Frangçon-Davies and Ian Bannen, each fresh outburst of spite and reconciliation seemed more simply tiresome than the last— and yet, alas, one could not dismiss it as rubbish, since one knew that it was, allowing for the wallowings of self-pity, all true.

One would not dream, needless to say, of dismissing Mr. Eliot's latest play as rubbish either—if only because in fact it is not rubbish. It is, however, a very pale, watery affair, *The Elder Statesman*. Lord Claverton is, we are gently shown, a hollow man, and Paul Rogers, another puzzling actor, plays him hollowly. It was difficult to work up any interest in the pale confrontations of a shabby—but not very shabby—past, or to feel the heart lift at the belated discovery that ordinary human love is a thing worth while. The language trickled on, a banal brook; only once or twice did the phrases begin to build up into those catalogues of little things with which Mr. Eliot conjures up the imminence, if not indeed the immanence, of disaster. Nobody in the play seemed to me at ease, and Mr. Martin Browne's hieratic production threw upon the cast a burden of meaningful speech which, with the exception of Mr. Rogers, they were unable to sustain. Yet can the work be quite as dull as it seemed? A doubt lingers . . .

No doubt at all about Graham Greene's *The Complaisant Lover*. There is not a moment of boredom in this entertainment, about a well-meaning husband who establishes a *ménage à trois* in order to ensure the happiness of his wife. Some of the pleasure of this play, especially in the Amsterdam hotel scene, is illegitimately attained; but Ralph Richardson, when he crumples up on learning of his wife's infidelity, reaches one of the highest points, of his, or any other player's, acting career.

Among the near-anonymous, the plays that come and go, only a professionally-turned American piece, *Two for the See-saw*, calls for a mention, since its story of a middle-aged refugee from the puzzles of marriage, fleeing in his turn from the inconsequent delights of a more Bohemian love, managed to retain some contact with human nature. A little actress from New York, Gerry Jedd, brought a taking breath of that kittenish charm combined with a daunting capacity for suffering which is a recognisable hallmark of the twentieth-century witch; and Peter Finch concealed with some dexterity the flabbiness of his role. Another American play, *Dark Halo*, offered us Mary Ellis as a faith-healing spiritual *Gauleiter* but allowed its point to escape in the mechanics of its plot. An English play, Ted Willis's *Hot Summer Night*, took trade unionism and the colour problem for its framework, diverted its attention to the misery of the frustrated wife of a trade-union leader and

finally came to nothing because in spite of a splendid performance by John Slater, and a melodramatic one by Joan Miller,
the quality of the dialogue was too low to raise the piece above
the level of homely journalism. In a study of ... but no, let a
kindly oblivion bury the rest, in whom somebody no doubt
believed.

The giants of the past must never be allowed to overshadow
the pygmies of the present; and besides, the whirligig of time
brings in his revenges. But it remains true that the major experiences of the months under review have come from the past.
Not, for once, from Shakespeare, who has been thinly represented by *Macbeth* and *Julius Caesar* at the Old Vic; these were
homespun performances, not at all disgraceful but hardly
calling for comment. Their neo-Shakespearean interlude, with
Shelley's *The Cenci,* gave everybody an opportunity to answer
the question 'Why don't they revive *The Cenci?*' Because, the
answer comes clear, it is not worth the trouble. Seldom have
actors as actors so totally engaged my sympathy as here, grap-
pling with characters so preposterously self-contradictory, so
ludicrously motivated or unmotivated that the effort of ration-
alising their roles must have driven the players mad. Not that
the evening was dull. Michael Benthall's production, like most
of his work, made the most of the narrative. Hugh Griffith,
his nose sweeping the stage like a harvester of death, his eyes
spinning in their sockets with evil, could hardly resist the
temptation to make this monster a pantomime figure, but all
the same did distil something of the dedication to the dark that
is a twentieth-century commonplace, as it was a sixteenth-cen-
tury commonplace, but towards which that longwinded intellectual innocent Shelley was only groping. And at last Barbara
Jefford received the recognition she deserves; an actress of

power, she develops her range slowly; in *The Cenci,* as the
much-enduring Beatrice, she added several notes to her compass at both ends of the scale.

Earlier the Old Vic did Stephen Spender's version of Schiller's
*Maria Stuart,* with Catherine Lacey as Elizabeth and Irene
Worth as Mary. In one splendid scene these two viragos, one
black, one red, spat anger at each other as they circled the
stage, whips flourished no more fiercely than tongues. Elsewhere Miss Lacey finely carried off Elizabeth's not ignoble
posturing, but Miss Worth was unable, so to speak, to rise to
Mary's final fall, so that her last confession, a scene of great
though quiet power, went for little. On almost all counts,
however, the Old Vic's performance was evidently superior to
that of the company from Düsseldorf who played it in London
at the same time. The work of this company was not negligible;
by the standards of our own provincial theatre it was much to
be admired; but it was very dull, informed by a kind of plod-
ding earnestness, hardly relieved in Lessing's highly topical
mockery of pride in race and faith, *Nathan der Weise,* even by
an actor whose reputation had preceded him, Ernst Deutsch,
but whose fluted irony hardly carried beyond the first few rows
of the stalls. Their rendering of Hauptmann's *Michael Kramer*
was so leadenfooted that a version of the same author's *Der
Einsame,* given at the Arts Theatre as *Garden of Loneliness,*
came as something of a shock. It is true that Richard Du-
schinsky, the translator and producer, has been reproached for
taking undue liberties with the original; and indeed he is I
think guilty—but I should let him off with a caution. His
version carried very strongly the stuffy atmosphere of late nine-
teenth-century Prussia which Hauptmann was at pains to create
—and if the result was closer in feeling to *Look Back in Anger*
than seems fitting, it is perhaps not so far out after all.

For real unrelieved stupor, however, we were indebted to a visit from the Swedish company directed by Ingmar Bergman. Mr. Bergman has acquired a great reputation with his mannered but brilliantly focussed films. In Sweden he has an even higher rating as a theatre director. I can judge only by what I see. Goethe's *Urfaust* was not perhaps the most sensible choice, when Strindberg was available. This early version of his *Faust* is no less tedious than the later expansion. Translated into Swedish (a language which appears to consist almost entirely of hard consonants and furtive, flat vowels; acted with a very modest degree of skill; and produced, against a permanent background of three gothic arches and a coloured backcloth, sometimes red, sometimes green, sometimes a lurid purple, at a pace recalling a slow motion film, and with a minimum of gesture, it provided an evening of jawbreaking boredom and no evidence of any feeling for the theatre at all.

Yet Scandinavia gave us the best things of the year ... what, not the Comédie Française? No, not the Comédie Française. Playing safe in London (as, for the most part, in Paris) the company brought with it two farces, a comedy and a bagatelle. Of *Le Dindon* I have already spoken, and warmly. Molière's *Les Femmes Savantes* was disappointing in precisely those respects in which we expect the Comédie Française to set us an example —in the speaking of the verse, the use of the spoken line as itself an instrument. Only Lise Delamare spoke it as it should be unfurled, making each point with great clarity within the framework of a fine legato line; though to be fair I should add the name of Jacques Sereys, working in a smaller compass as a snake-like little pedant-poet. And just as Mlle Delamare later illuminated Musset's tiny boudoir joke, *Un Caprice,* so M. Sereys strengthened Molière's Commedia dell'Arte piece *Les Fourberies de Scapin* with a superb outline of twittering senility. On the face of it M. Sereys did nothing that a hundred, a thousand other impersonators of comic old men have not done before; but somehow the true spirit of humanity blew through the caricature—as it does in the best Aguecheeks. Here too we could admire one of the most difficult of all stage feats finely executed: Micheline Boudet's exhilarating delivery of a long laughing speech (and it may be as well to point out, since one of my colleagues has rashly observed that these diamond-bright giggles are all very well, but 'nothing to do with Molière', that every outburst in the speech was written in by the dramatist himself). As Scapin Robert Hirsch deployed his ballet-dancer's training to good effect, as they say—to slightly too good effect, I would say; quite quickly all this prancing and tumbling becomes tiresome for want of variety—mere movement, however dapper, is not enough.

And when it came to the celebrated mock fight with a dozen invisible adversaries, assuming as many voices, Harold Lang did the job rather better in a production of Otway's version of the piece at the Lyric, Hammersmith. Elsewhere, alas, he lacked the technical address and the personal appeal to carry off the evening successfully, though he hardly deserved the hostile demonstration with which he was greeted on the first night. Altogether more successful were the Old Vic's two Molière productions of Miles Malleson's translations. These are of course in prose: one dimension was inevitably lost, and with it something of the quality which lifts these plays out of the ranks of standard bourgeois satirical comedy. But, as such, how much was left! In Sganarelle Miles Malleson himself, dewlaps aflutter, happily chunnered away through the old gentleman's highly sceptical observations on the subject of honour. Tartuffe, dressed up to or beyond the nines, with an infinity of gleaming bare white shoulders and a firework display of diamonds, produced what I thought an extremely interesting performance in the name-part by Derek Francis. There are two sides to this notorious character, the hypocrite and the crook. Most actors make no attempt to reconcile the two, but focus on one or the other. Not so Mr. Francis, who gallantly attempted a synthesis —with, I thought, considerable success. But, perhaps because familiar aspects of caricature were almost entirely missing, his conception as a whole seems to have been found a little dull.

The performance of *The Cheats of Scapin* at the Lyric, Hammersmith was part of another double bill in the season given by a small and welcome body calling itself the 59 Theatre Company, and artistically led by Caspar Wrede. Their first— I hope not their last—season's programme was unfailingly interesting; not least because, while still charging sixpence for their programmes, they filled the little booklet with useful and well-written information—a revolutionary step among our backward theatre organisations; even the Old Vic has apparently never thought of offering more than ten lines or so in a special case (e.g. *The Cenci*). The 59 Theatre Company led off with Buechner's *Danton's Death,* a young German romantic revolutionary's view of the figures of the French revolution— and were generally damned for doing so, I'm not clear why. True, the piece is wordy; but it is also relevant to our own time. True, the production was perhaps excessively sombre; but then I thought it rather well acted, not least by Patrick Wymark, hitherto known as a successful Shakespearean clown, as the sardonic Danton, a man of flesh and blood among the ideological shadows (though it is a pity he was not balanced by an adequate Robespierre).

The company then took a long trip to Scandinavia. First came Strindberg's *Creditors*: a spider-wife, an ex-husband escaped from the net but returned to play with fire and bring to his knees the already tottering second husband. A cruel little *pas de trois,* expertly stepped by Mai Zetterling—so good an actress when not imprisoned within one of those wilting little girls— Michael Gough and Lyndon Brook—two craggy young actors who command a nice line in neurotic tension. To follow this gaunt work with one even more bleak was asking for trouble; but then Ibsen's *Brand* turned out in a devoted performance to be not nearly so depressing as most of us feared: turned out, indeed, to be positively uplifting. To all intents and purposes never before seen in London, this harrowing chronicle of self-defeating fanaticism fascinatingly changes front as it proceeds —at first adoring the man with a fire in his belly, heaping scorn on the dim people of everyday; then, though hardly exalting the humble and meek, turning a blinding light on the dreadful pride of the moral campaigner. It was never intended by Ibsen for the stage, and in translating Michael Meyer has, mainly by omitting a great deal of dated satire directed at specific Norwegian situations of the time, reduced the play to reasonable length; and he has made it over into a rhythmic prose—the octosyllabic verse of the original being impossible in English—which sounds nobly without ever slipping into false poeticism. The problem of staging was at any rate adequately solved, and the problem of acting the giant role of Brand himself rather more than adequately. Now that we have seen the piece, we must scratch our heads in wonder that none of our leading players—if one excepts Sir Ralph Richardson on the radio—has dared to try this part. Patrick McGoohan, who did, rose to its climax finely after a start in which, anxious to establish Brand's intensity, he did not trust himself to project it from within himself, but fell back on a harsh and abrupt speech which sounded both peevish and monotonous. But as the trials increased, as the doctor's humanity undermined

Brand's paranoia for a moment, as he chose the death of his
son rather than the abandonment of his mission, as he demanded
even worse sacrifices from his wife, as she preferred death to
life at his side, as his parishioners at last turned upon him (as
well they might), and as he saw himself for one terrifying
moment in the eyes of a mad girl as Christ recrucified, then—
in recoil—for what he was, Mr. McGoohan expanded into the
part until, as the avalanche roared down upon him, we were
left with an unforgettable image of spiritual hubris, and a truly
tragic fall.

*Brand* was written when Ibsen was in his late thirties and
had escaped from Norway to Rome. The plays we know came
later, were still more closely linked to the circumstances of the
time. But genius will out. Shakespeare's plays, and Molière's
were all intensely topical, and have turned out to be universal
as well. Gradually Ibsen's are doing the same, though there are
still foolish voices raised to call them 'dated'. Well, after the
Old Vic's production of *Ghosts* there can be no reason for
anyone to suppose that this is a play about inherited disease,
rendered obsolete by salvarsan. It is a play about the failure of
the human spirit, about acceptance as the easy way out—acceptance of irrelevant moral conventions allied to material social
conventions, of the refusal of love, even the refusal of charity
in its true sense. And it gains its power because it shows the
growing awareness of this failure in a fine woman, not in an
obvious weakling. In the eyes of the world Mrs. Alving is a
noble creature, bearing with exemplary fortitude the burdens
laid upon her by circumstances; and so she is, but she comes to
see, and we with her, that she has brought her fate upon herself. I cannot imagine this inner dawn of understanding being
more exquisitely painted than it was by Flora Robson. It was
in itself a pleasure to see Miss Robson in a worthwhile part;

her talent for sympathetic suffering is all too often exploited in humdrum little dramas; here once again we saw it flower. Her Mrs. Alving was gracious, self-controlled, very much the lady of the manor—too much so, some thought; but to my mind every nuance of feeling was there. And this in spite of the fact that originally the producer, John Fernald, and the actor, Michael Hordern, had hit upon the unhappiest possible approach to the difficult character of Pastor Manders: he was played for laughs, as though he too were a character in a Pinero farce. Later, when the piece was transferred to the West End, Manders was taken over by Sir Donald Wolfit, in whose hands he remained a figure of solemn silliness, true, but gained also the stature of a not quite ignoble failure. And throughout Miss Robson was helped by the splendid Oswald of Ronald Lewis, his kind, broad face paling and narrowing as madness closed in upon him. And at the final curtain, as he lay inert in the darkness of the bright room, Miss Robson left us, as she stood above him, with a heartrending image of a woman for whom, at last, there was no easy way, no convention, no guide. What became of Mrs. Alving, after the play was over?

# BROADWAY, NEW YORK

## Richard Hayes

At midpoint in the arbitrary interval of time—from May to annual May—that by some curious formality constitutes the New York theatre season, a certain melancholy frosted the native scene. Only one play of indisputable excellence, and that an import—the wiry, misanthropic *Epitaph for George Dillon* of Mr. John Osborne—had made an appearance, and only one worthy musical, again a visitor: *La Plume de Ma Tante,* the conglomerate expression, superbly disabused of logic, of M. Robert Dhery and his Company. To be sure, Miss Lynn Fontanne and Mr. Alfred Lunt still held the boards in Herr Friedrich Duerrenmatt's black morality, *The Visit,* an event which offered the piquancy of watching the Lunts attempt—none too happily—a more ambitious substance, but beyond this, only the thin gruel of another *mittel-Europa* exercise in universal guilt. And four theatrical personalities of fearful magnitude—Mr. Eric Portman, the Misses Helen Hayes, Betty Field and Kim Stanley—had gathered early in October under Mr. Harold Clurman's guidance, to project the last of Eugene O'Neill's great studies in the necessary deceit of illusion. *A Touch of the Poet* enjoyed that esteem we accord ultimately to all objects of the national piety, but it can hardly be said to have enjoyed dramatic realisation. A prevailing greyness of tone and a dissonance of style—Miss Hayes at her most viciously exhibitionistic; Mr. Portman irretrievably Yorkshire—left only

the ardent Miss Stanley, with her unique conviction and ego-
tism, to carry the play into anything like its proper ironic bite.

Even of lesser pleasures there were few. Miss Claudette
Colbert, in clothes by Castillo, and Miss Arlene Francis, in
clothes by Scaasi, supported frivolities more with the aid of
their designers than their dramatists. The lavish *Goldilocks* of
Mr. and Mrs. Walter Kerr, a musical satire of the early silent
films, had promised much, but its attempt to cross brashness
with a kind of ersatz romanticism established a pattern of schizo-
phrenic disenchantment from which few of the year's subsequent musical exertions were to be released. And of 'trends'—
for nothing is so provocative to the theatre hound—only a
fanciful, irrelevant preoccupation with the Oriental *ambiance*
was evident. Miss France Nuyen created an image of insolent
allure as the tart with the heart in Mr. Joshua Logan's opulently
lurid *The World of Suzie Wong,* while the Messrs. Rodgers and
Hammerstein, in *Flower Drum Song,* turned their somewhat
weary amiabilities to a facile sketch in music of domestic manners among the San Francisco Chinese—an enterprise Mr. Kenneth Tynan nattily ticked off as 'the world of woozy song'.

With the quiet, Christmas appearance of Sir John Gielgud,
all took on a heightened lustre. One might have expected the
forthcoming critical praise, but nothing had prepared New York
for so unprecedented a storm of famished and grateful public
response—tribute not only to art achieved, but to the example
of the artist in his laborious quest after an ever-richer quality of
being. *The Ages of Man* became, ironically, at once a lifetime's
memory, and the scarcest ticket in town. It broke, too, the
winter frost, for within six weeks, and on successive evenings,
Broadway received its two most distinguished plays of the
season: the veteran Mr. Tennessee Williams's *Sweet Bird of
Youth,* and *A Raisin in the Sun* by the novice Miss Lorraine

Hansberry. Neither could have been less like the other; both could not have been more affecting. With prodigious color and energy of language, Mr. Williams imagined another of his contemporary fables of violation and decay, but in this instance, he imposed on his accustomed lyric grief a pattern of resolution and pagan fatalism which brought the work close to tragic austerity. Mr. Elia Kazan's feverish sensibility again washed the stage with brilliance, and as the two victims of 'the enemy, Time', Miss Geraldine Page—full of a vicious splendor and magnitude—and Mr. Paul Newman extended *Sweet Bird of Youth* into a macabre poetics.

Miss Lorraine Hansberry's drama of lower-middle class Negro life, and of the harsh impingement of reality on aspiration, offered no comparable distinction of style or singularity of mood. What *A Raisin in the Sun* rather commanded was dramatic contagion and a profound emotional immediacy. Nothing honored Miss Hansberry more than her ability to invest the popular image of Negro life with a new density, and to project a world in which the race situation is a tragic motif like any other, not didactic. Faultlessly played by Mr. Sidney Poitier, Miss Claudia McNeil and others, in a style of seamless realism, *A Raisin in the Sun* excelled as an infallible study of the weathers of the heart, and a worthy recipient of the New York Critics' Circle award as Best Play of the Year.

Sliding away from these peaks were the many pleasures and ambitions, rather more mundane, which give savor to a particular season: the sobriety with which *The Disenchanted* sought to determine why there are no second acts in American literary lives (Mr. Jason Robards Jr. won the 'Tony' award for his playing of the proto-Fitzgerald figure, though Miss Rosemary Harris gave her performance a deeper period actuality); Mr. S. N. Behrman's ambiguously nostalgic view, in *The Cold Wind and*

*the Warm,* of the American dream; the luxurious, though somewhat contrived, texture of *Rashomon,* and its provocative search
after truth; Mrs. Gertrude Berg's solid Jewish reality amid the
agreeable fabrication of *A Majority of One;* the panache and
civilised gusto with which Mr. Cyril Ritchard and Miss Cornelia
Otis Skinner gave stylistic finish to the rather pale posh manners
of *The Pleasure of His Company.*

And there were the 'big machines': Mr. William Faulkner's
*Requiem for a Nun,* which failed signally to match its European
esteem, and resolved a complex tangle of moral theology by
invocation of the most meretricious belief. But most of all—
praised, prized (Pulitzer and 'Tony' awards), publicised and
puzzled over; everything, it would seem, but enjoyed—there was
Mr. Archibald MacLeish's *J.B.* Opening to the total blackout
of a newspaper strike, it gathered momentum on the broadcast
accolade of Mr. Brooks Atkinson, critic of *The New York Times,*
as 'one of the memorable works of the twentieth century'. To
less partisan observers, it seemed considerably less : touching,
perhaps, in the poet's conscious sincerity, and ambitious as an
attempt to restate Job's tragic dilemma in contemporary terms,
but otherwise an especially melancholy instance of rhetorical
American abstraction. Mr. MacLeish's languid verse pointed
no advance in the problem of dramatic language, and the ultimate 'theology' of *J.B.* exhibited little more than the character
of a vapid ethicism and a cheating secular mystique. Mr. Kazan's
production brought a touch of eloquence to the whole, but not
enough to displace the air of insistent pretension.

Only the peremptory arrival of Miss Ethel Merman in *Gypsy,*
at the end of May, salvaged the musical estate from a complete
lassitude. Earlier, Mr. Abe Burrows offered a cartoon of *Pride
and Prejudice* in *First Impressions*—though Miss Hermione
Gingold made a sprightly Mrs. Bennet—and *Destry* added to

that classic frontier fable only raucuous spirits and the hard-driving choreography of Mr. Michael Kidd. Miss Gwen Verdon was a vivid incandescence among the rather damp Edwardian fireworks of *Redhead,* but it fell to Miss Merman, with her brass and slangy vitality, to project—in this somewhat soiled account of the lower depths of vaudeville—an image of what musical comedy might still be capable.

In the mushroom fields of Off-Broadway, freshly sprouting with new playhouses, players and producers, there was an amiable stir of activity. Chekhov's early *grisaille* of provincial decay, *Ivanov,* was rendered with most subtle modulations, and Ionesco's nonsense pieces, *Jack* and *The Bald Soprano,* achieved a superb frenzy of comic disintegration. An experimental ensemble, The Living Theater, made a notable if bizarre impact with Dr. William Carlos Williams's amorous poetic fantasia, *Many Loves.* At Circle in the Square, our most established and rewarding Off-Broadway playhouse, Mr. Jose Quintero presented a luminous revival of Mr. Thornton Wilder's reverie of mortality, *Our Town;* earlier in the year, he had less success with *The Quare Fellow,* Mr. Brendan Behan's exercise in gallows humor, which failed to reverberate in America as it had in Europe.

In a classical vein, the third of the international Stratfords—Stratford, Connecticut—continued its policy of offering Shakespeare without tears, as it were: youthful productions untainted by any great stylistic anxiety, and hence most successful when least is demanded. A diverting *Midsummer Night's Dream* was the largest pleasure of the 1958 summer. Elsewhere, nothing was more heartening than the firm intellectual and dramatic identity which the Phoenix Theatre arrived at after four years of vacillation. Under the guidance of a permanent director, Mr. Stuart Vaughan, and with the services of a constant en-

Toivo Pawlo, Gunnel Lindblom and Max von Sydow

**BERGMAN'S
'URFAUST'**
(Municipal Theatre, Malmö)

Bernard Dhévan and Micheline Boudet in *Les Femmes Savantes*

## COMÉDIE
## FRANÇAISE

Micheline Boudet
and Jacques Charon
in *Le Dindon*

Robert Hirsch in
*Les Fourberies de Scapin*

**'59' THEATRE COMPANY**
(Lyric Opera House, London)

Michael Gough
and Mai Zetterling
in Strindberg's *The Creditors*

Patrick McGoohan in Ibsen's *Brand*

*Sharp*

semble, it mounted three productions—a numinous *Family Reunion*, and engaging *Beaux' Stratagem,* and Mr. Graham Greene's *The Power and the Glory* powerfully illuminated by Mr. Fritz Weaver as the whiskey priest—of unimpeachable elegance and distinction.

# BROADWAY, NEW YORK

## Jerry Tallmer

THEATRE began on Broadway in the fall of this season with a play by a thirty-year-old Englishman, and it ended in the early spring with a play by a twenty-eight-year-old American Negress. Nothing else is actually worth mentioning in the same breath, and nothing else even justifies calling it a season. But John Osborne's *Epitaph for George Dillon* (co-authored, no one knows to what degree, with Anthony Creighton) and Lorraine Hansberry's *A Raisin in the Sun* were enough to give any season its justification, and they alone have done much to enable 1958-9 to take its place with stature and dignity among all its fellows.

This was the third play we had seen of Mr. Osborne's, and while it burnt with a slower fuse than the others, and therefore received only mildly enthusiastic reviews in the key metropolitan newspapers, it burnt a great deal more surely and steadily. It also set a historical precedent on Broadway: it had two quite separate runs there in the same season—an opening and a failure in November, then a re-opening in January under new producers with greater faith in the work. The original importer was David Merrick, the same gentleman who had brought us *Look Back in Anger* and *The Entertainer,* and been well re-warded for the effort. Mr. Merrick is a phenomenon on Broadway—an amateur (a lawyer by trade) who with deepest scorn has outsmarted all the old pros. His technique is to ignore the reviewers entirely and blast his shows through with massive publicity, newspaper and billboard advertising, and advance sales to theatre parties. And it has worked; he is the Man Who Cannot Fail (*Suzie Wong* and *La Plume de Ma Tante* are this year reaping him a fortune). But *George Dillon* did fail— perhaps the advertising budget was beginning to sag—and Mr. Merrick shut it down after a few short weeks without a fare thee well. I regret to say that the whole envious profession danced with joy, and I much more keenly regret to say that the second run of *Dillon* was also, technically, a failure; in the end it was booted out of its theatre to make way for the tripe of *Look After Lulu* (the sets for the second run, to do Mr. Merrick justice, were the same as those of the first, a donation from him without charge).

How to account for the failure? I think the best answer lies in a remarkable new book here by William Gibson, who last year gave Broadway one of its biggest successes, *Two for the Seesaw.* Mr. Gibson's book, *The Seesaw Log,* is a searchingly honest account, more or less in the form of a diary, of what happened to his play (and himself) as it went from his head and hand into the maw of the machine that is commercial theatre in America. The quotation I need is from the next to the last page of the book: you must do your best to imagine all that comes before. The italics are mine.

'And when in its subsequent productions I found it still impossible for valid box-office reasons to push through the casting I really wanted, my opinion acquired a fixative: one might say many enthusiastic and truthful things about the rewards of the professional theatre, such as the money, and the comradeship, and the money, and the self-espials, and the money, but to me they all lay in the arms of the truth that the theatre, in this country, in this decade, was primarily *a place not in which to be serious, but in which to be likeable;* and it behooved each of us in it to do careful book-keeping on his soul, lest it grow, like the dyer's hand, subdued to what it works in.'

Now you can call poor old George Dillon many things, but who—aside from the ladies in that play, and anyone else who is haplessly interested in actors, writers, artists—who could ever call him likeable? You may say Archie Rice isn't likeable, but Archie Rice was Sir Laurence Olivier at the absolute height of his brilliance, and that alone would have done the trick (it certainly did for me—an unforgettable experience). You may say Jimmy Porter is anything *but* likeable, but Jimmy Porter, three years ago, was Something New, and something new goes very far in America. *George Dillon* had no known stars (Miss Herlie is only now getting known here) and it had every ear-mark of just being the prescription as before—all those sick young men mucking around in life and making it a hell for the women. Who needs it? I go to the theatre to be entertained. I have enough troubles of my own, and why should I pay to be reminded of them? (Yet you will pay, my friend, and eagerly, if the Mr. Merricks have only bulldozed enough of your compatriots into paying first.)

In any event, *Epitaph for George Dillon* was Broadway's first play this year about living, breathing, important human beings, as *A Raisin in the Sun* was its last. I would assume that in an article to be published as part of a book in Britain as well as in the U.S., there is no need to write a critique of 'Dillon'. There would seem to be needed merely to say that in both its runs it was played with aching sincerity and verisimilitude by a British cast that had the guts and grace to hang around here for months between the two productions, living off nothing much more than hopes and promises. Mr. Robert Stephens gave us

the finest portrait of the artist I can ever remember seeing—
the artist as he really is and must always be, eternally, at war
with, eternally dependent on, gushing-hearted middle-class
security—and Miss Herlie counterpointed him each step of the
way with a rich warm portrayal of the first three-dimensional
woman (the left-wing aunt) Mr. Osborne has so far created.
The second-act dialogue between these two, where each calls
the other's hand, held a hardened New York audience breath-
less—only the 'sophisticates' of theatre were there—every evening throughout both runs. For those who *do* think that the
George Dillons of this world are as necessary as they are trouble-
some, the experience provided what practically none of the
theatre of our time ever provides : that wonderful therapeutic
thing called *catharsis*. That was the first and last taste we were
to have of it until Miss Hansberry's *A Raisin in the Sun* burst
in our midst like a bombshell.

*A Raisin in the Sun* is a play about the Younger family of
Southside Chicago—a modern, urban, lower-middle-class family
of sixth-generation American Negroes. It is a play about their
dreams, catastrophes, and realisations as human beings first,
Negroes second. It is a play quite obviously written out of
flesh, blood, and bone by a young Negro woman who comes
to us out of nowhere—out of Greenwich Village, to be exact,
by way of Chicago—to say *'Enough!'* to 250 years of dramatic
and other anachronisms about her people. And what she tells
us is : *We are not A People. We are people. The sooner you
learn this, the better off for all of us.*

But I make the play sound both too hostile and too unoriginal.
It is the opposite of either. It is a full-blown, full-blooded
family drama along the lines of *Awake and Sing,* old-fashioned
in that and the Chekhovian sense but completely new in the
nature of its personnel—new for them, is what I really mean.

Or perhaps no one but an American, white or black, can understand what I really mean. In a way it's as if we suddenly woke up, one fine morning, and found a play about Martians, by a Martian, tossed in our laps—a play very much in the standard form of most of our plays (the 'our' is now white), only far more dramatic and believable than most. And as if this play demonstrated to us, with the force of shock—but through its own hidden voltage, not through preaching—that Martians have to spend a lot more time and energy worrying about the rent and the job and the kids' educations rather than their green skins and long antennae; not that they don't have to worry about those as well, especially when (daily) driven to it. And as if this play, finally, were set before us on Broadway, that arena of a billion illusions, with a cast that sprang hot and true in its entirety, and with absolute verity in its calculus of intermeshing motivations, straight from the author's head to the playing boards. And why not?—for they, as she, have lived it, and so has the gifted young director, Lloyd Richards, who helped each of them toward peak performance. Their names— I am convinced their names will go down in theatre and perhaps American history. Here they are:

Claudia McNeil, a former night-club singer, as Lena Younger, the great matriarchal head of the household.

Sidney Poitier as her 35-year-old son, Walter Lee Younger, who wants to find something more in life than chauffeuring.

Ruby Dee as Walter's wife Ruth.

Glynn Turman as their small son Travis.

Diana Sands as Walter's sister Beneatha, a late-adolescent and rebelliously modern-minded pre-med student at the University of Chicago (Miss Hansberry's self-portrait of an earlier Miss Hansberry).

Louis Gosset as one of Beneatha's much-harried suitors, scion of a well-to-do Negro family and considerable of a 'white-shoe boy', as the phrase went in my days in college.

Ivan Dixon as Joseph Asagai, a second and more compelling suitor, the twentieth-century representative of an ancient and noble African blood-line, temporarily in America as a student.

John Fiedler as the nervous, 'well-meaning' little white man who is sent by a Neighborhood Improvement Association to try to buy back from the Youngers a house on which the mother, Miss McNeil, has put a down-payment, out of the insurance money left by her dead husband.

Lonne Elder III as one of Walter Lee's fellow suckers in a shady business scheme (for the dramatic fulcrum of the play is the clash of wills over how to spend the insurance money—on the house, on Walter Lee's mirage of personal aspirations, on the completion of Beneatha's medical courses).

Ed Hall, Douglas Turner as moving men (for in the end the family does move, into that house, despite tragic costs and losses for all of them).

It would take another article as long as this one just to try (and fail) to describe what each of these actors or actresses do in *A Raisin in the Sun*. What can words recapture of Miss McNeil's primordial coupling of mother-earth warmth and leonine tyranny, her uneducated old-fashioned wisdom as set against her deep-dyed wilful manipulativeness? What words can convey to you either Mr. Poitier's incredible freedom as an actor or his sheer beauty as a human male in action? What words can convey the last-ditch grey-agony stamina of Ruby Dee as his wife, the adoring counter-cockiness of young Mr. Turner as his son, the adorable twenty-year-old infuriations of Miss Sands as his sister Beneatha? There are none. Perhaps the show, and this cast, will some day get abroad, but that will be a long time from now, for it has quickly built by word of mouth —the opening reviews were no more than guardedly cordial— into one of the few *real* 'smash hits' of many recent seasons. (Astoundingly enough—and wonderful to be able to report— it has won the New York Drama Critics' Circle award as best

play of the year, and over the seven opposed votes of the seven
most influential of these gentleman! The second team—weekly
magazine and trade-paper reviewers, Kenneth Tynan of the
New Yorker among them—went out and carried the ball for
Miss Hansberry.)

There is, however, to be a movie, and the playwright has said
that she will insist in the contract on being allowed to ride herd
on it all the way. I think that if the movie even half lives up
to the staged drama, it can do more to save the Western World
from You Know What than all the uranium in creation. I think
that, at the very minimum, *A Raisin in the Sun* is the single
most revolutionary American play—quietly revolutionary—to
come along in any of the years of my maturity, which began just
about where Clifford Odets started leaving off. (It took an
Englishman, Mr. Tynan, to draw the Odets parallel immediately
upon seeing *A Raisin in the Sun.*) This is not to downrate
Tennessee Williams or (not one of my own gods) Arthur Miller.
I am talking about a revolution in the *material* of playwriting,
and of human understanding, not in the warp and woof of
playwriting. I am talking about the kind of understanding that
is added to our lives by hearing the old mother say in *A Raisin
in the Sun,* when her daughter is expecting a first visit from
Joseph Asagai, 'I don't think I never met no Africans before';
or the even greater kind of understanding that comes to us—
to whichever of us, white or black—from hearing that same
mother say to her dissident children that she just doesn't know,
in her day and her parents' day it was a lot different and a lot
more simple, you just tried to get out and get North with a
whole skin and as much dignity as you could manage to hang
on to, while now everybody seems to have put all that behind
them and gone crazy over things that no one ever even thought
about in those times, things she doesn't even know the words

for, except one of them is always money and position and what goes with it. In terms various to each of us, these are profoundly American preoccupations—*Where did I come from and where am I going?* is rather unarguably *the* American preoccupation —and *A Raisin in the Sun* is as profoundly American as any play that I can think of. That is its revolution: it is an American play, with, as it happens, Negroes—as *Our Town,* which I shall have cause to mention presently, is an American play, or a universal play, with, as it happens, New Englanders.

I said something above about texture, warp and woof. Let me emphasise that I find nothing to complain about in Miss Hansberry's remarkable looming. She appears to have known exactly what she intended to do, chosen her ground, her speaking voice, her characters, her 'type of play', and to have done it. Her type of play is naturalistic, but going back beyond current Broadway naturalism, or realism, to the original pre-hothouse soil. Says Harold Rosenberg in *The Tradition of the New,* a book which is coming off the presses as I write: 'The trouble with Broadway Realism, as with the Realism in painting, is not its intellectuality, but the fact that both its ideas and its reality have lost their character. Too much vermouth.' Well, not in this play, and much to the profit of the play as drama. Give me a good second-act curtain, every producer is supposed to declare, and I'll give you a hit. Miss Hansberry's second-act curtain, with the manhood all spilled out of Poitier as, having dissipated most of the insurance money, he clutches at the knees of his mother, is purest 'sock'. But Miss Hansberry knows better than to dissipate her own capital. Inch by inch during the third act, beat by beat, in a sort of slow agony of healing, she comes back to regain the field as, at the yet more shattering climax, Poitier will regain his manhood and speak for his family against the threats, degradations, enticements, illusions of a world which

can only be lived in by living up to it—not under it or over it,
wherever you come from, whatever your color. This is the
idea and the reality of *A Raisin in the Sun,* and this idea and
this reality have *not* lost their character, for they are the proud,
hard-won personal possessions of a thinking young woman of
28 in the America that is part of that world and our time. And
the people in her play likewise have character, are characters,
are people, living people, because they too are her personal
possessions as distinct from the personal projections that in-
habit nearly all the rest of contemporary American drama.
The only other Broadway play this year with people in it was
*George Dillon* (I am arbitrarily putting Friederich Duerenmatt's
*The Visit* back into the previous season, where, since it opened
in the spring—and not to my mind in an acceptable adaptation
or production—I should think it properly belongs, even if the
Drama Circle, which goes by a calendar of its own, voted it in
over *George Dillon* as the best foreign play of *this* season).
But enough of *Dillon* or *Raisin* or anything else on Broadway.
What about Off?

*          *          *

Ordinarily three or four times more interesting than its big-
money competition, the Off-Broadway scene this year went as
flat as yesterday's Pepsi-Cola. In fact most of the best of it
*was* yesterday's Pepsi-Cola, rebottled, recharged, re-merchan-
dised, in the Little Economy Size container ($10,000 to $20,000
per production).

And when I say yesterday I mean *yesterday,* not the day before yesterday or the day before that. I mean the revival of
shows which are hardly yet dead in their Broadway graves—
like *The Innocents,* by William Archibald, which comes to mind
only because it happens to have opened last night, and it is my
job to go to openings. *The Innocents*—Mr. Archibald's adapta-

tion of *The Turn of the Screw*—is a Broadway failure of no more than perhaps eight years ago; I don't have anything at hand in which to look it up, but it doesn't matter. An honorable failure, you would have to say—Beatrice Straight played the governess—but that doesn't really matter either. Now it opens in a house with one-tenth the Broadway seating capacity, if that, and with another sincere young actress (Peggy Feury) as the governess. But there is one big unanswered, unanswerable question: Why? Because you must not forget the $10,000 to $20,000. Is Mr. Archibald's adaptation from Henry James of an excitingly experimental nature? No. Is it then of very high conventional dramatic impact? No. Is it indeed even fish, flesh, or fine red herring, theatrically speaking? No? Then why undertake this modestly vast expense and even greater expenditure of effort and heartbreak to . . . but I think I need not go on, especially since *The Innocents* is well above this year's Off-Broadway average.

Much farther above the average were the revivals of two plays by Arthur Laurents, *The Time of the Cuckoo* and *A Clearing in the Woods*. But to continue for a moment on the same theme, the word 'revival' really must be put in quotes. It hasn't been five years, I should guess—editor please check me—since Shirley Booth opened on Broadway in *Cuckoo*, it hasn't been three, at the outside, since the Broadway production of *Clearing* with Kim Stanley.

The truth is that Mr. Laurents was deeply dissatisfied with both these Broadway productions and that, at the ripe old age of forty, he actively welcomed the first possible opportunity for an Arthur Laurents Off-Broadway cycle. Sitting in last year on a small one-week showcase production of *Cuckoo*, he admired the tone imparted to it by a young director named Jack Ragotzy; it was Mr. Ragotzy to whom he entrusted the staging,

now, of the cycle of 'revivals', and Mr. Ragotzy served him well,
for he put forth both *Cuckoo* and *Clearing* in better, more
sincere versions than the Broadway originals. Where many
thousands of dollars and countless ergs of work had formerly
gone into the elaboration and perfection of such things as
scenery—Mr. Laurents has publicly voiced his morbid hatred
of almost *all* scenery—the energy was this time wholly concentrated on the lines and situations of the plays as written. A
young television actress named Kathleen Maguire contributed
an exquisite lead performance to *Cuckoo*—the best performance
I saw anywhere Off-Broadway this season—and another young
actress named Nancy Wickwire, somewhat more familiar to
local theatre-goers, gave clarity and a kind of solid underfooting
to the much-tangled emotions of the heroine of *A Clearing in
the Woods,* which is a play about a woman who at the age of
thirty encounters a number of her earlier selves (characters in
the play) as she searches desperately through her past for some
answer to her suicidal depressions and bewilderments.

So that was where it began; and when it was seen that these
Laurents plays would enjoy good runs and perhaps even emerge
as Off-Broadway successes—an Off-Broadway success is a show
which does at least as good as coming not too far from breaking
even—it was suddenly and generally realised that Off-Broadway had inherited a New Function, the resuscitation and improvement of *recent* Broadway failures. Thus we were soon
thereafter to be confronted with Gene Frankel's hard-hitting
Off-Broadway improvement of the relatively recent On-Broad-
way despoilation of Mr. Arthur Miller's single-minded adaptation of Mr. Henrik Ibsen's old Scandinavian creation of . . .
where am I? It was *An Enemy of the People,* and it is well
enough done, and still running healthily, and it will very likely
run on for a couple or more years to come. But it is not, as

it happens, Ibsen, or not at any rate all that's in that great, free-swinging, tough-minded drama by Henrik Ibsen, and what is considerably more to the point, it isn't of 'the idea' of Off-Broadway. No more were the Laurents. But no more was most of Off-Broadway this season.

I take the idea of Off-Broadway to be an inexpensive forum for the try-out of new forms in writing and staging, for running risks that simply cannot be hazarded in the big-time commercial theatre (see *Two for the Seesaw*). Such a risk was the production, late last spring, of *Ulysses in Nighttown,* an adaptation from sections of the novel by James Joyce. I did not find it to my own liking, but I greatly had to admire its purposes. Such a risk was the production, also last spring, of two plays by Eugene Ionesco, *Jack* and *The Bald Soprano.* Both these efforts, though I am sure they lost money, ran on through the summer into the fall; if *The Visit* is part of this season, then they are part of this season. Such a risk was the production of Jean Genet's *Deathwatch,* which failed—deservedly, I had to feel, for reasons too complicated to go into here—and, in a quite contrary sense, so was the American première in a 200-seat house Off-Broadway of an early Chekhov play called *Ivanov.* This had meticulous staging, beautiful acting, excellent reviews, and a reasonably long run—yet it lost money. I would call it one of the year's leading successes. And there has been Ionesco, Genet, Chekhov, Ibsen, Brecht, Beckett, Joyce, Ghelderode, etc., etc., done here in all previous seasons of the present Off-Broadway boom, often by tinier groups than now exist, under much more difficult, more daring circumstances. All that is changing now, drying up; at least it did this past year, with a few isolated exceptions or partial exceptions. They were:

*Ivanov.*

*Deathwatch,* Jean Genet's earliest play, a three-character prison drama, passionate, circular, and frustrating.

*The Quare Fellow,* by Brendan Behan, another prison drama and one which in the reading seems to me clearly to be of that order which we call greatness. It received a too-loud, too-cumbersome production by the unit headed by José Quintero at the Circle in the Square—the best-known group and most prominent director of the whole Off-Broadway movement—but at least it received a production. That was a risk worth applauding.

*The Hamlet of Stepney Green,* by Bernard Kops, again an import from Britain and a very nice one, updating and reworking the Hamlet story into a comic-poetic parable of the London ghetto. The author's transpositions of the great Elizabethan lines into worldly-wise Yiddish seemed to me outrageously funny, and his 'serious' themes—angry young son, flighty Jewish mam, understanding father, (and father-ghost)—also seemed handled with a wisdom and sympathy far beyond the usual for so young a playwright. The play was hacked-up and mugged-up a bit by the young producers who brought it here in the fall, but not badly enough to prevent it from blooming on their hands into a quite substantial little winner which at last shut its doors in April.

*The Geranium Hat,* by Bernard Evslin, the first new American play I have had occasion to mention in this section. It is put on the list after *Stepney Green* because it too is a fantasy, somewhat similar in its *gemütlichkeit* if not its form. The plot defies condensation, but it centers around a romantic young puppeteer, an austere but beautiful lady chemist, a villainous old puppet-master, and a 'shrinking' elixir discovered by accident in the heroine's laboratory. In the second act the hero and heroine are reduced to puppet size themselves, when the villain gets his hands on the magic fluid. The cat gets after them during a Romeo-and-Juliet scene, but all comes well in the end, the cat and the puppet-master are routed, right prevails, and life's affirmative values are upheld. Ingenious sets and much tricksy business with props went far to extract the best values from a script which for the most part kept spoiling itself by pushing its genuine originality into the zone of over-cleverness. But *The Geranium Hat* certainly belongs among the season's risks. Its run is now petering out, after a fairish start about six weeks ago.

*Fashion,* by Anna Cora Mowatt, an American play though not exactly a new one, since it dates from 1845, in which season it is supposed to have become our first native hit. Deems Taylor added music to it for a revival on Broadway in 1924; now it was revived here again, Off-Broadway, with the music kept in, by a David Fulford and a William Dempsey, two young producers who for some years past have been running a highly successful way-Off-Broadway theatre in the little town of Fulton, Ohio. They chose well for their first invasion of New York, bringing us this charming comedy about nouveau-riche urban idiocies—still quite valid, of course—in an absolutely perfect production. Mr. Fulford's direction, based on concepts drawn from old steel cuts in *Harper's Weekly* and *Godey's Lady's Book,* was easily the best and most unified of the season, and the sets, costumes, songs, choreography were all of a piece. It got nice reviews, meagre audiences, and ended up losing a good bit of money. I include it here as experimental theatre on inverse grounds.

*The Power and the Glory,* as adapted by Denis Cannan and Pierre Bost from the novel by Graham Greene, would I suppose have to be placed somewhere on this list of risks, if only because it represented a departure in style for the Phoenix

Theatre, an institution which might be described as the culture-conscious rich uncle of Off-Broadway. (The Phoenix, over three times the size of any other Off-Broadway house, is not really rich, but it has a sort of chi-chi backlog of guilt-stricken wealthy subscribers who each year rally to pull it up out of its depthless pool of red ink.) In the past the Phoenix has chiefly relied on the classics, or modern classics, as directed by such as Tyrone Guthrie; it also has close links with the American Shakespeare Festival of Stratford, Connecticut, a group sharing many of the same sterilities, as well as the Canadian Stratfordites. Productions from these organisations often come down later to pad out the Phoenix schedule. This year the Phoenix management finally saw the light and hired Stuart Vaughan, a young man who had compiled a brilliant record of free Shakespeare stagings in Central Park—over 100,000 New Yorkers had flocked to them each of the past two or three summers—as its permanent director. Mr. Vaughan struggled against odds during most of his first season at the Phoenix to vitalise its choices of plays and actors. *The Power and the Glory* was his high-water mark. It was fervently hailed by most of the reviewers and won itself an extended run, but I did not happen to think it overly dramatic or truly communicable of the rhythms and meanings of the wonderful novel on which it was based. Fritz Weaver, as the priest, headed a young cast—graduates, for the most part, of Mr. Vaughan's Central Park productions—which at moments achieved real theatricality and at other moments bogged down into mere violent expressionism. Mr. Weaver's own performance was intense, perfervid, self-exacting. The questions remains whether it was not too much so.

*The Golem,* as adapted into English by Ruth Rehrer Wolff from the modern Yiddish classic by H. Leivick. A group with one-fiftieth the funds or know-how of the Phoenix undertook

Gerald O'Loughlin, William Smithers and Bruce Dern
in O'Casey's *Shadow of a Gunman* (Bijou)

## BROADWAY

Rod Steiger and Claire Bloom in *Rashomon* (Music Box)

Lloyd Gough
and Diana Wynyard
in *Cue for Passion*
(Henry Miller)

**BROADWAY
SEASON**

Arlene Francis
and Joseph Cotten
in *Once More, with Feeling*
(National)

In rehearsal:
Pat Suzuki,
Gene Kelly (director)
and Miyoshi Umeki

'FLOWER DRUM SONG'
(St. James, New York)

Miyoshi Umeki

Jo Sullivan in the musical version of John Steinbeck's *Of Mice and Men*
(Provincetown Playhouse, New York)

## AMERICAN MUSICALS

A scene from *Goldilocks* (Lunt-Fontanne, New York)

the recreation of this dark legend in a second-floor loft on the same avenue as the larger theatre, a few blocks south. Much was wrong with the production, but it was an evening which made a terrifying analogy with the present world of man-made monsters (atomic), and I left feeling that I had been *engaged* by theatre, as a gear engages, which at the Phoenix I had not been.

*Many Loves,* by William Carlos Williams, in its world première at the Living Theatre, a reconditioned playhouse in what was until lately Hecht's Department Store, on the northeast corner of Sixth Avenue and 14th Street—the street of bargains. I have left this particular bargain until last because for me it was the best and only real Off-Broadway theatre of the 1958-9 season. It also joins *Epitaph for George Dillon* and *A Raisin in the Sun* in that category of Only New Plays—new to America —worth mentioning. The funny part about it is that it isn't a new play, actually. It was written I think in 1944, and it took the courage of those who have started the Living Theatre to come along fourteen years later and give it its world première. Their names are Julian Beck and Judith Malina, a young director and his actress wife, each serving in those capacities for the present production.

*Many Loves* is a Pirandellesque play within a play—or three playlets, rather, wrapped inside an outer sheathing. Both the 'outer' and 'inner' plays are concerned with various forms of love: carnal, lesbian, homosexual, romantic. The 'outer' play deals with a theatre company which is rehearsing the three 'inner' plays. The director of the company, who has fallen in love with his lead actress, is trying to break off a certain half-defined intimate relationship with a rich homosexual 'angel' whom he would yet like to retain as a source of income and moral support. The homosexual fights back, viciously, probingly, wittily.

The actress fights back against the homosexual. Meanwhile, the show, or at least the rehearsals, must go on.

In the first playlet, a working-class Polish-American woman is ditched by her soldier lover, who has made her pregnant, and then, wandering aimlessly home toward the husband she detests, bumps into a thin bookish neighborhood boy who has been hanging around waiting for her. They start a rambling conversation, in the course of which the woman discovers that this boy, at whom she's never before looked twice, has always burningly worshipped her. That's about all there is to it. The woman is both angered and flattered, and they part with nothing resolved, everything in the air. But murky as it is, it is fresh air—this oxygen breathed forth by cagy old Dr. Williams— fresh with the invigorating keenness of clear-eyed unencumbered amorality. No judgments are passed. Truth is told. The bare reporting stands revealed as poetry.

In the second playlet, a gone-to-seed rural family is visited by a rental agent and his client, a New York lesbian who may wish to buy their farm. The lesbian is immediately attracted to the daughter of the family, a girl who is at bitter odds with her father and most of the rest of the world. A doddering grandfather dies in his sleep on a porch chair, with the Sunday funny-papers still draped over his face, while the sale of the farm is being discussed. The lesbian embraces the girl and says don't worry, she'll take care of her, and the play ends. Dr. Williams says in a program note that he received the inspiration for it from a tableau he caught out of the corner of his eye, for just one second, while driving through the New Jersey countryside on a Sunday afternoon.

The third playlet is briefer yet, merely a desultory conversation between a neurotic suburban housewife and the much-experienced old doctor (Dr. Williams, one is forced to imagine) who comes to attend her ailing child. They talk nostalgically of lost glories, first hers, then his; they touch each other in verbal romance; they come together in an absurd and disparate kiss just as the woman's child walks mother-hungry and sobbing into the room.

We then return to the wrap-around drama of director, actress, homosexual, other actors and stagehands, and general back-stage chaos. There is a showdown between the three principals, the director rejects his rich friend, and the tempo suddenly veers into outright farce with the homosexual hysterically forcing through a wedding before our eyes. The evening ends as in an Ionesco madhouse, and I am not sure that the entire 'outer' play isn't too artificial and superfluous, almost as if Dr. Williams felt he had to protect his first venture into play-writing with an intellectual apologia. But nothing in the evening is the least bit dull, the direction by Mr. Beck is quick and ingenious, the acting by a young company is enthusiastic and middling good, and the total product—well, the total product is what I have always believed theatre is supposed to be all about. I am happy to say that *Many Loves* at the Living Theatre may be entered in the books as one of those unique phenomena, an avant-garde box-office hit. Mr. Beck and Miss Malina—who, like the Phoenix, have their share, if a smaller share, of chi-chi backers—and I am glad they have them—are as close as anyone now in America toward the realisation of that permanent-repertory experimental company for which so many of us dream. More power to them, and more the gain for all the rest of us.

This takes me out of the category of the experimental. I should mention a few other productions. José Quintero turned his hand, following *The Quare Fellow,* to Thornton Wilder's *Our Town,* to my mind the best American play yet written.

He gave it one of his most sensitive stagings, comparable with
those first efforts through which his reputation was established
—*Summer and Smoke, The Girl on the Via Flaminia*—and it
has gone over like wildfire. It will probably run on at the
Circle in the Square through much of next season, giving thousands of latter-generation Americans a chance to find out about
life, love, and death in Grovers Corners, New Hampshire—
and the world. This too is a gain for all of us.

There was an Off-Broadway musical made of John Steinbeck's *Of Mice and Men,* a loving piece of work, beautifully
directed and acted. Unfortunately, it opened during the en-
forced silence of the midwinter newspaper-deliverers' strike,
and it never managed to recuperate. A loss for all of us.

There were a handful of brand-new American plays in the
not so brand-new styles of Tennessee Williams, William Inge,
and Co.

There was a little flurry of Restoration productions, or mock-
Restoration productions. The best of these was *She Shall Have
Music,* a gay and tuneful parody of Wycherly's *Country Wife.*
It was forced by booking conflicts out of one theatre into
another, where financial difficulties overcame it and finally
closed it.

There was a new play by Maxwell Anderson, *The Golden
Six,* which dealt with the lives of a few of the Caesars. I found
it in part fascinating, in part labored in the writing, and altogether atrocious in the staging. It was an expensive disaster.

There was T. S. Eliot's *Family Reunion* at the Phoenix, another expensive disaster.

There was ... but I think I shall not go on. The rest were
revivals, or trial balloons, or simple errata. If I have overlooked anything really important, I can only plead guilty. Or
perhaps it was the importance which overlooked me. I could

not however quite yet end this without citing one other work which stood for me, along with *Raisin*, *Dillon*, and *Many Loves*, as one of the four great illuminations of the season. This would be the ballet of *The Seven Deadly Sins* at the New York City Center, which is neither Off-Broadway nor On and of course isn't even theatre, technically speaking. By any other means of speaking it was nothing but theatre, naked and thrilling, with music by Weill, lyrics by Brecht (in the Auden-Kallman translation), choreography by Balanchine, vocals by Lotte Lenya, dancing by Allegra Kent and the company, and heart-stoppingly effective German Expressionist costumes, sets, lighting by Rouben Ter-Arutunian. When I say heart-stopping I mean that at the climax, when Miss Kent dove to her suicide through a blazing wall of Reynolds Wrap, my heart seemed to stop. That is one way I shall define Theatre.

# OFF-BROADWAY

## Noel Behn

SEVERAL weeks ago I completed the budget for a revival of Sean O'Casey's *The Plough and the Stars* which I plan to produce Off-Broadway next season. Budgeting is standard procedure for producers Off-Broadway and in the last six years I've had more than my share of experience at it. This budget, however, is slightly unusual. It's for a play I've produced once before Off-Broadway. In fact, it's the first play I ever produced anywhere. I did the play in 1953, when the present Off-Broadway movement was in its infancy. Not only was it my first show, but it was a successful show which ran more than six months (that was a success in those days) and did quite well financially. If it had failed, I probably would have given up theater for the security of a more practical occupation like tightrope walking or deep-sea diving. However, it succeeded.

A first production evokes the same kind of memories, I imagine, as a first kiss or a first ride on a roller coaster. Each year I would look back on that first production and compare it with contemporary presentations. Each year I would meet with the cast members and director of that first show and bathe briefly in the nostalgia of past glories. Each year I would become surer that it was one of the best damned plays I ever produced. It was no surprise to my present associates when I announced last month that I was going to do the O'Casey classic again, with the original actors. I drew up the new budget and reverently checked it against the budget of the first production. My romanticising ended, probably forever. The 1953 production cost was $500.00. The identical production in 1959 will cost $12,500.00.

There was no reason for me to have been surprised at the rise in production cost. I have been active Off-Broadway every week of every year since that first production in 1953, and during this time I have been in almost constant touch with each and every rise in cost. It was only after I went over the budgets in an item for item comparison that I realised what should have been evident from the first: the entire structure of Off-Broadway has changed. To exemplify this change I will compare sections of the 1953 and 1959 budgets to point up their differences. But first let me digress a moment, to explain what Off-Broadway itself is.

Technically, the name 'Off-Broadway' is a geographic reference to all theaters and theatrical activity in New York City outside of the Broadway area (defining Broadway as the section of the city between Sixth and Ninth Avenues, from 42nd to 57th Streets). Even though the majority of Off-Broadway theaters are found in Greenwich Village and near lower Second Avenue, the name generally refers to the 'little theater' movement in the city.

Physically, the Off-Broadway theaters are limited both in playing area and seating capacity. Very few houses are able to accommodate more than three hundred patrons, and the majority hold under two hundred. The theaters themselves are remodeled or improvised from such places as lofts, stables, nightclubs or, in some instances, movie houses. Not one of the Off-Broadway houses in existence today was originally built for theatrical purposes.

Another distinguishing feature of Off-Broadway is that its

ticket prices are substantially lower than Broadway rates. With small seating capacities and low ticket prices Off-Broadway theaters have a very limited money-making capacity. For just this reason several of the unions which are represented Off-Broadway, such as Actor's Equity Association, have formulated special concession contracts whereby their members can work Off-Broadway for salaries well under the minimum Broadway requirements.

With these factors in mind let us now examine the 1953 and 1959 budgets drawn up for *The Plough and The Stars* at the Cherry Lane Theatre, a 189 seat house in Greenwich Village. These figures represent pre-production expenses (costs up till opening night). They do not include operating expenses once the show is open.

### Physical Production

| | 1953 | 1959 |
|---|---|---|
| Scenery | $ 50.00 | $ 750.00 |
| Costumes | 25.00 | 250.00 |
| Props | 20.00 | 100.00 |
| Electrical | 10.00 | 100.00 |
| Audio | 10.00 | 250.00 |
| | 115.00 | 1450.00 |

Scenery: This category refers to the physical sets you see on stage—walls, windows, alleys, etc. Technically, scenery is anything that creates the illusion of location and is non-movable.

In 1953 we had no real set designer. One of my partners, who was a fairly good carpenter, roughed out the plans and, with the aid of a seventeen-year-old handyman named Leo and two actors, the set was built. The materials for building the set, such as wood and canvas, were collected in various manners.

The majority of the wood, for example, came from the junk pile of a church that was being torn down in the neighborhood. Additional wood came from a local junkman who felt friendly toward the theater and dropped choice pieces off from time to time. The third source of wood was tapped by what Leo called his 'donation policy'. I never really questioned him on this point, but it seemed that the acceptance of these donations, especially from construction projects, took place rather late at night. Nails were also acquired by 'donation'. Paint and canvas were a problem and eventually we had to buy them. Our tools were a borrowed saw, two screwdrivers and some used sandpaper. The sandpaper was an heirloom from a previous assignment of Leo's. Later we bought a new hammer and more sandpaper. The two doors needed for the set were taken off the men's room and a dressing room. The only available space we had for building the set was on the stage. Since the director needed the stage and half of our building crew for rehearsals most of the day, construction work usually began at one a.m. and lasted until nine the next morning. After much pounding, gluing, painting, and arguing about who had the use of the stage, the set was finished. It didn't smell too good, due to some of the old lumber, but to us it was beautiful and it cost only $50.00.

The 1959 set will be designed by a talented scenic designer and will be built by experienced stage carpenters in a shop or space rented for use as a shop. The lumber will be new, and the canvas and paint of top quality. The doors will fit and the hinges won't squeak. The carpenters and painters will be paid by the hour, quite possibly at union rates, with taxes and benefits withheld from their salaries. The scenery will be trucked to the theater by professional movers at exactly the hour specified. Not ten minutes of work will be lost by carpenters, painters or movers because they have to take a shift in the box office or because they are needed on stage for rehearsal. I am sure that the set will have no odor in the least. No one man working on the set will receive less than $50.00 for his services — in other words, each man working on the set will receive at least as much as the total 1953 set cost.

Properties and Costumes: Props (properties) are movable objects on stage such as dishes, books, or guns. These are things which the actors can use to further the action of the play. Costumes are self-explanatory.

In 1953 Leo was designated 'prop man' and assigned, with three of the actors, to the collecting of the various properties. The majority of these items were borrowed either from local merchants for program credits or from individuals. Some few items were bought at the Salvation Army. The rest were obtained through Leo's donation plan. Each day the director would make out his prop list and hand it to Leo who would perform the necessary expedition.

The 1953 costume problem was left up to each individual actor, who was required to get his own wardrobe no matter how difficult this might prove. One of the actresses who could sew tried to adjust the various outfits as best she could.

In 1959 we will pay a prop finder from the designer's staff. He will attempt to get loans from local merchants but, because of the number of plays operating in the neighborhood, will probably end up renting from a theatrical prop store or having the carpenters build or remodel what he needs. The designer will design the costumes and a costume woman will be hired either to find costumes that can be rented inexpensively or to make them herself.

Electrical and Audio: The electrical category refers to that lighting equipment which is necessary beyond what the house supplies, as well as bulbs and colored gels for different light tones. Audio refers to the sound system required for the music and sound effects.

In 1953 we simply used whatever lighting equipment the house had. If we did not have the proper color gels for the lights we used whatever was available. The director, Leo, and some of the actors, set and focused the lights and improvised such things as wire splicing and connecting of lines to the central control board as best they could. For the first three months of the run we had almost no electric bill at all because the director, in trying to connect some wires in the electric meter, inadvertantly switched the connections to our next door neighbor's meter. After three months of confusion our neighbor finally solved the mystery.

The audio system in 1953 was a borrowed phonograph with an extra speaker attached.

In 1959 the electrical system will be put in by a union electrician, who will make sure every instrument and every connection functions properly and safely. He will focus all the instruments to the designer's specification. The electrician will also install a new or rented audio system with amplifiers, control boards, sound mixers, and anything else that will be needed. Special records will be made for the requisite sound effects.

Comparison of the 1953 and 1959 *Physical Production* costs illustrates the major change in the operation of the production as well as the difference in expenses. The 1953 operation was based on an 'acting company' with a nucleus of actors and one or two other people handling as many jobs as possible. No one was paid and if the show made money, it was divided among the entire company. The basic change of the last six years is the specialisation of the producing company. In group activity, which is now rather rare, the producer and director make up the nucleus of the production unit. In most cases to-day it is simply the producer who initiates the production. Since there are no longer groups of actor-handymen who will work for nothing, the producer must hire people to compose his company in all its aspects.

The actor, who was the main labor force for odd jobs in the theater six years ago, is wholly an actor today. He is hired to rehearse and to act. The rest of the jobs are filled by paid employees, and most producers prefer experienced personnel in these positions. They have found that the better the people they get for specific jobs, let's say box office or set construction, the better their results will be. So they try to find the 'right man for the job' and this usually costs more money than settling for 'anyone'.

Another factor to keep in mind is the rising demand for quality Off-Broadway by both critics and public. The acting, directing and settings have by necessity become more and more expert. In 1953 there were very few standards of any kind Off-Broadway because there were very few shows, very few reviews of those shows and a very limited audience for them. With the great growth in the number of productions, and the serious attention of the public as well as the drama critics, who can now make or break a show with their reviews, the demand for quality by the producer is greater than ever. He must pay for this quality.

In 1953 a company of fifteen actors and three other people put on the entire production without one cent of salary paid to anyone. In 1959, for the same production, the payroll will list :

| | |
|---|---|
| 15 Actors | Prop Man |
| 2 Understudies | Seamstress |
| Stage Manager | Company Manager |
| Assistant Stage Manager | Press Agent |
| Designer | Box Office Man |
| Director | Secretary |
| Electrician | Porter |
| Carpenter | |

Their total salaries will come to $3,500.00.

Another area which has added to the cost is the theater itself. The upswing of interest in Off-Broadway produced such natural improvements in the theaters as better seating, better stage facilities, and air conditioning. As audiences grew the various city agencies, such as the Fire and Building Departments, took a closer look at the theaters to insure the safety of the public. Whole electrical systems had to be replaced, exits had to be added, proper fire equipment had to be installed and certain structural changes had to be made. A completely new wiring system was installed in the Cherry Lane, for example, as well as a forty ton air-conditioning system. This was reflected in a higher rent.

After rent raises, landlords were confronted with 'booking problems'. The demand for theaters grew, costs rose, critical standards stiffened, and more plays than ever before failed. Too many landlords found themselves with bankrupt tenants who couldn't pay their rent. The theater owners instituted an advance rent bond from producers, taking four to six weeks rent in advance. Not only did the landlords find themselves holding the bag when producers went broke, but so did the unions who were also quick to institute bonds as guarantees for their members. So in an area in which not one cent was laid out in 1953, the following will have to be paid in 1959:

*Bonds*

| Actor's Equity | $ 1360.00 |
|----------------|-----------|
| Press Agent    | 125.00    |
| Theater        | 1500.00   |
|                | $ 2985.00 |

The *General Expenses* category has also skyrocketed. With the larger costs producers now need expert help in legal and accounting matters, and they need space, material, and personnel to administrate their productions. The landlords also require that the producers take out insurance policies to protect the theaters and the theaters' property. Telephone, mail expenses, payroll taxes and office supplies have jumped this item greatly:

*General Expenses*

| 1953     | 1959      |
|----------|-----------|
| $260.00  | $1200.00  |

With all these items counted we find that what cost $310.00 in 1953 amounts to $9,050.00 in 1959. The producer now finds that he must lay out a good deal of money. Naturally he is looking for every possible way to secure the success of his operation and safeguard his production. In most cases his ultimate fate will depend on the reviews of his show. The one method by which he might possibly overcome bad reviews is advertising. He reasons that if he can build a big enough interest in his show before it opens he may sell enough tickets to offset critical disaster. Producers fanatically cling to this assumption, though it is very seldom proved valid. Nevertheless, pre-opening advertising has become a major expense. It takes a lot of space over a period of several weeks to acquaint the public with a show, especially in the face of dozens of competing shows in New York. In 1953 there were only three other Off-Broadway shows running. In 1959 there will be about forty.

The 1953 advertising budget was $190.00, the 1959 budget will be $2,500.00.

The addition of advertising costs brings the pre-opening budget to approximately $11,500.00. The $500.00 which covered all costs for the 1953 production was easily raised—we used our own money. Today, however, there are very few groups or producers that have $11,500.00 of their own money to invest in a play. Today's plays are financed by 'angels'. These are people outside of the producing unit who invest money in plays. Raising this kind of money requires more than a phone call. Lists of prospective investors must be compiled, they must be contacted both by mailings and by telephone and then those that show interest must be personally contacted by the producer. Facts, figures and contracts must be presented to them before you can get their money. Fund raising becomes a campaign in itself and must also be put into the budget. The 1959 budget will carry a last item entitled *Organisational and Reserve* and it will amount to $1,000.00. If we are lucky enough to raise the money quickly and inexpensively we may only spend $200.00 on the campaign, leaving $800.00 for a reserve fund. If we are unlucky it could cost $800.00 to raise the money, leaving only $200.00 in reserve.

With another thousand dollars added the total budget for the 1959 production comes to $12,500.00. Initially, the six year difference in production costs of the same play is staggering. But I hope to have illustrated here the basic change in Off-Broadway which has produced the increase. The 'acting groups' of 1953 have given way to the producers and producing units of 1959. The artistic aims of the two groups may be the same but their points of view are miles apart. The producers of 1959 are much more practical than their predecessors, primarily because they have to be with so much money at stake. The 1959 producer, more often than not, thinks in terms of making money; his play must be a hit. The acting groups of 1953 generally were interested in doing a play and being seen in it, all else be damned.

Whether or not the 1959 point of view is good or bad for Off-Broadway is hard to tell. It is true that the commercial approach of today's Off-Broadway theater, with an eye on the 'smash hit,' out for rave reviews at any cost, have made it a miniature Broadway. It is also true that this commercial point of view has eliminated many plays from production on the grounds that they may be too 'risky' for financial success. Despite the negative aspects of the 'new' or 'commercial' Off-Broadway, it is growing and thriving as never before.

Though exact statistics are not available, it has been estimated that approximately one hundred plays have been produced each year for the last three years. From the artistic and critical side such shows as *The Iceman Cometh, The Threepenny Opera, Purple Dust, The Crucible, The Quare Fellow, Ivanov, An Enemy of the People, Garden District, Career, Endgame, The Chairs* and *The Lesson, Our Town, Heloise, Ulysses in Nighttown,* and *End as a Man* certainly speak for themselves.

There seems to be every indication that costs will continue to rise Off-Broadway. Possibly in 1969 I will look back in disbelief at the relative inexpensiveness of a 1959 production. Although it is my own opinion that production costs have gone about as high as they should go I, and others like me, will probably go right on producing until it is absolutely impossible to do so—and I have no doubt that the Leos will continue on from there.

Gwen Ffrangçon-Davies and Alan Bates in the London production
of *Long Day's Journey Into Night* (Globe)

## LONDON HIGHLIGHTS

(top and left) Peter Shaffer's
*Five Finger Exercise* (Comedy)

Adrianne Allen, Juliet Mills, Michael
Bryant and Brian Bedford

Adrianne Allen and Michael Bryant

(above) Alan Bates, Ian Bannen, Gwen
Ffrangçon-Davies and Anthony Quayle
in *Long Day's Journey into Night* (Globe)

*McBean*

Donald Wolfit and
Flora Robson in
Ibsen's *Ghosts*
(Princes, London)

## LONDON

Sybil Thorndike
and Lewis Casson
in a scene from
*Eighty in the Shade*
(Globe, London)

Houston Rogers

Eileen Peel, Anna Massey,
Paul Rogers, William Squire,
Alec McCowen and
Richard Gale
in Eliot's *The Elder States-
man* (Cambridge)

## 'WEST SIDE STORY'

right: Chita Rivera and Marlys Watters

below: The Rumble

McBean

# PARIS

## Jacques Lemarchand

It is no longer possible, as it once was, to speak of 'the beginning of the season' or of 'the end of the season'. Changes in long-established habits, which I shall briefly discuss later, have so made it that theatrical activity in France—for those, at least, who follow it closely—is now continuous. There is always Paris of course. But, as the result of a gradual process of evolution, which I personally find most welcome, Paris is no longer the only place in France where the theatre lives and flourishes. It would give a false and imperfect idea of the French theatre if one were to limit oneself to a description of what happens in the capital between the months of September and July. When, in Paris, the August provincial visitors and the foreign tourists are confronted by so many closed theatres, the drama goes on elsewhere—almost everywhere, in fact. During the last ten years, the festivals of dramatic art have increased enormously in numbers. A development which was at first dismissed by the cynics as 'a fashion' has now come to be recognised as the response to a need. If, as I begin this article, I stress the importance of these festivals—which have of late become too numerous to permit an accurate account of them to be undertaken—it is because annual surveys of the drama have a tendency to neglect their importance, and to underestimate their effectiveness in renewing the theatre-interest of a public other than that of the capital. Another sign of this renewal of interest which it would be foolish to underestimate, is that the activity of the National Theatre Centres—they are five in number, spread throughout the French provinces—is still increasing and now beginning to bear fruit. The solution to the crisis in the provincial theatre offered by touring companies was most unsatisfactory. The public came to see plays which had exhausted their success in Paris and, of course, to see the stars who acted in them. The situation of the Centres Dramatiques is quite different. They produce their own plays and perform them with an independent and well-balanced company. They are led by directors who, living in the region and understanding local tastes and aspirations, are better able to satisfy them than is the average touring manager.

However, Paris still continues to present—in the theatre alone—two hundred new productions annually. This figure will perhaps surprise the layman. Although it tries them more than a little, it does not surprise those who, either by choice or by obligation, attempt to report more or less accurately theatrical activity in the capital. There are at the moment fifty-three theatres in Paris. This is not the place to discuss whether or not they are too numerous. We have to accept their presence as a fact. There are, among these fifty-three, several which are known as 'little theatres'. These are far from being the least interesting from the point of view of their activity. Two or three of these *petits théâtres* die every year and two or three new ones appear to take up the burden. It was in these 'little theatres' that were first performed the works of those authors who are slowly but surely coming to the forefront of the French theatre. Again, many theatres, both large and small, have begun the commendable habit of presenting on their closing day either a little-known classical work or a new play, to sound the reactions of the press and the public. This, of course, increases the number of productions but in a most useful way—by offering both to new authors and to actors who have not yet established themselves the chance of a direct contact with the public and with professional critics.

To all this activity, which normally attracts the attention of the theatregoer, have been added in recent years the seasons of the Theatre of the Nations which, from March to July every year, presents a series of operatic, dramatic and choreographic productions chosen from among the best of twelve or fifteen countries. And it is by considering the 1958 season at the Theatre of the Nations that I should like to begin this review of twelve months in the theatre. (I shall therefore not consider the activities of the Theatre of the Nations in the domain of the opera, music and the ballet). Among the troupes which the Director of the Theatre of the Nations, Monsieur A-M Julien, presented at the Sarah-Bernhardt Theatre, three seemed to me to merit particular attention for the deeply personal element they contained which represents, for the French theatre, a possible source of enrichment. The National Theatre of Greece, with Euripedes's *Iphigenia in Aulis* and *Medea,* Sophocles's *Œdipus Tyrannus* and *The Ecclesiazusae* of Aristophanes, presented three periods of the classical Greek theatre in a very different manner from that imposed by tradition upon French performances. Less pompous and more familiar, this style seemed to lend a different sort of grandeur to the tragedy. Here the presence of the City was as easily felt as that of the Gods or Destiny. The choice of *The Ecclesiazusae* was, however, a less happy one. Its static comedy could hardly fail to disconcert a public of which only a very small minority understood Greek.

The Old Vic brought its *Henry VIII* and *Hamlet* from London in which Sir John Gielgud, John Neville and Dame Edith Evans gave the French public an extremely interesting glimpse of the

*English* way of acting Shakespeare. It is certain that many of
our actors 'intellectualise' their characters too much. They push
them towards a monotonous lyricism which leads into a sort of
rhetoric. The players from the Old Vic, on the other hand,
interpret them more in terms of the action; they humanise them
(in the best sense of the term) allowing the Man to be constantly
visible beneath the surface of the Hero.

Finally, the Moscow Art Theatre presented their extra-
ordinary Chekhov productions, *The Cherry Orchard, The Three
Sisters* and *Uncle Vanya,* staged and acted with such minuteness
and diligence, the direct descendants of Stanislavski's inspiration. Beautiful to behold, these performances represented for
us a journey into a past which we know only imperfectly. It is,
of course, possible that this will to reconstitute the past adds to
the sadness of the nostalgia which one breathes in the plays of
Chekhov.

The Parisian season, strictly speaking, of the Théâtre National Populaire which Jean Vilar still directs, is rather brief.
It lasts merely from November to May, the T.N.P. devoting
the rest of the year to touring abroad, to the Festival of Avignon
(the most famous and the one which sparked off the proliferation of festivals that I have already mentioned) and to visiting
the larger provincial towns. From these last twelve months,
three new productions are worthy of note—each one of them
for a different reason—as testimony to the value of the elastic-
ity provided by a large, well-disciplined company. The first (in
March 1958) was that of Alfred Jarry's *Ubu.* The purists did
not miss the opportunity of criticising Jean Vilar for condensing
into a single work at the cost of a few sacrifices, the three
plays that Jarry wrote around this monstrous character. Personally, I do not share their discontent. Some day, no doubt,
we shall be obliged to consider textual accuracy with Jarry's

plays. But here, thanks to the T.N.P., Ubu, who had been nothing but a name in the public's mind, became flesh and blood and, with the aid of those remarkable artists Georges Wilson and Rosy Varte, Père and Mère Ubu stood revealed in all their absurdity—an absurdity rendered particularly actual by the political events in France at this time—for thousands upon thousands of spectators. The T.N.P. also turned to Musset with *Les Caprices de Marianne,* produced by Jean Vilar, and *On ne badine pas avec l'amour,* produced by the film director René Clair. René Clair's *On ne badine pas,* a triumph for Gérard Philipe and Suzanne Flon, was constructed and cut to a new rhythm, quite agreeably different from the traditional *lenteurs. Les Caprices* with Gérard Philipe and Geneviève Page—an actress whom Musset has brought into the front rank —was played at a skilfully-conducted pace, the poetry of which was emphasised with a light and intelligent grace by the musical accompaniment of Maurice Jarre.

It was only in November that the Compagnie Jean-Louis Barrault-Madeleine Renaud was able to return to Paris. They came back to the 'Théâtre du Palais-Royal'—quite close to the Comédie-Française—which, for many years, has been the home of Jean de Letraz's light and frivolous comedies. In this theatre the Bed was the traditional centrepiece of the stage. M. Barrault inaugurated his management by presenting a revival of Offenbach, Meilhac and Halevy's *La Vie Parisienne,* which was first produced on this very same stage a hundred years ago. It was an amusing way of emphasising the changes which this theatre was to see when, several weeks later, he added Paul Claudel's *Le Soulier de Satin* to the programme. These two plays have been running ever since. *La Vie Parisienne* has drawn—and continues to draw—*le tout Paris* to the Palais--Royal and it is a fact that Jean-Louis Barrault's company have made a masterpiece of vivacity and humour out of it. The new version of *Le Soulier de Satin* which the producer-adaptor has been obliged to shorten has become somewhat obscure for the non-initiate compared with the version produced in 1943 at the Comédie-Française.

Here, I feel, is the place to speak of the activity of the Comédie-Française during the last twelve months. This I should do with pleasure if anything of importance had emerged—unfortunately, this is not the case. It is said that receipts have been good which is, at least, something to be pleased about. But not a single important first performance has taken place, not one success either classical or modern, has marked the year's activity of this troupe which, although excellent in its potential, is rendered extremely unstable by continuous resignations and reappointments. This tricentenary institution is in process of reorganisation and we shall be better able to estimate its efficacy in a year or two. But what is two years in the history of Molière's company?

In Paris, there are a number of authors whom the public watches carefully every season. This is always done in the most friendly fashion but the public is prepared to come down on them like a load of bricks at the slightest error on their part. The most illustrious victim of popular judgment this year, indeed the only one, has been—to the general surprise—Henry de Montherlant with his *Don Juan* which he presented at the Théâtre de l'Athenée. *Don Juan* had the undoubted advantage of the presence of Pierre Brasseur. A great author, a great subject and a good actor—it was all to no avail and the play came off within three weeks. No doubt it was too cunning, too full of those secret traps which so delight the author but which are out of place in the real, living theatre. In treating the subject of vulgarity, the author had himself fallen into the

trap. Tending to depreciate both the hero of the play and his con-
quests, he had in fact debased his subject. Pretending to follow
step by step the famous theme treated so ably by Molière and
others, he produced a laughable parody of Don Juan whose
sixty years had replaced his principal virtue of enthusiasm by
something approaching a mania. The element of derision is
certainly intentional here but the public showed itself unrespon-
sive to it.

*L'Hurluberlu, ou le Conservateur amoureux* is Jean Anouilh's
first play since *Pauvre Bitos* (1956). After amusing himself,
with *Ornifle* (1955), in rewriting Molière's *Don Juan,* he has,
in the same way, continued *Le Misanthrope* in his new work.
It is a bitter play in which Alceste becomes an old retired general
who is irritated and scandalised by today's manners. One of the
general's speeches gives us a clue, not only to this play, but also
to a whole section—the most sombre part—of Anouilh's works.
'No', says the general, 'there is no hate in me, there is only
sorrow' ('je n'ai pas de haine, j'ai de la peine'). In fact, it is not
difficult to see, beneath the cruelty and the negative aspects of
Anouilh's writing for the theatre, the claims of wounded love,
the search—constantly frustrated—for a sentiment, for someone
who has retained a trace of his original innocence. This search
had, in his last three plays, taken on the aspect of a hunt, one
might almost have said a man-hunt. In *L'Hurluberlu,* while
neatly avoiding the danger of archness, this search is undertaken
for a lost paradise which, although perhaps imaginary, makes
life bearable in an otherwise atrocious world.

Albert Camus has also come back to the theatre this year, by
way of an adaptation. He has at long last realised a plan he has
been cherishing—so he tells us—for twenty years, to present
Dostoievski's *The Possessed* in the theatre. As the author of the
adaptation and also as producer, he has shown proof of a skill

which, without in my opinion justifying the transfer to the
theatre of a book so rich in thematic material, has nevertheless
made of Dostoievski's work the most lively and absorbing
evening's entertainment in the theatre this season.

To the works of Eugène Ionesco, which first appeared in
France eight years ago, amid indifference and sarcasm, has been
added a new play of primary importance, *Tueur sans gages*
which, by the force of its density and invention, has attracted
attention. Much has been said, in this connection, about a
renewal of Ionesco's writing. I see nothing of this in the new
play. The theme, he has often treated in his earlier works. It
is that of universal indifference towards a universal evil and
of the necessary condemnation of the hero who, attempting to
deliver the community from the evil, becomes, by so doing,
isolated and powerless. The means he uses to illustrate this
theme he has often used before: to increase the pathos of a
thought by derision of the vocabulary and to translate an essen-
tially tragic situation into terms of comedy—even of comic
sketches. If I add that this same year, while the tiny Théâtre
de la Huchette continues to perform *La Leçon* and *La Canta-
trice Chauve* every evening (this programme is now in its third
year), the Studio des Champs-Elysées has mounted an excellent
revival of *Victimes du devoir,* which dates from 1953, in Jacques
Mauclair's original *mise-en-scène,* it will serve to emphasise
the importance that the theatre of Ionesco (which is now, after
that of Anouilh, the most widely performed abroad) is beginning to assume in the country of its origin.

If we consider now the 'boulevard'—(this is not a geographical, so much as an aesthetic, term: it denotes plays that are
'well-made' and that attract by their use of traditional and
easily-analysed processes)—the successes of Marcel Achard and
Félicien Marceau must be mentioned. The former, whose *Patate*

continues, after three years, to fill the Théâtre Saint-Georges, has given us *La Bagatelle,* an extremely facile, traditional and sentimental play about the occupation of a country by the armed forces of a foreign power, which has proved to be a great success. Félicien Marceau is the author of *L'Oeuf* which ran for two years at the Atelier. He has now written *La Bonne Soupe,* 'the story of a woman's life', a woman whose morals seem to be limited to her fear of lacking money. The quality of the play's construction, the ingenuity of André Barsacq's production and the excellence of the principal actresses, Jeanne Moreau and Marie Bell, who both play the same character at different ages, all make their contribution to the great success of this play.

Considered among the lesser-known French authors but one upon whose talent I place great value, Jacques Audiberti has been badly treated by the most eminent of the dramatic critics this season with an injustice which I view with as much indignation as astonishment. The author of *Le Mal court, Pucelle, Quoat, Quoat* and several other plays which can be considered among the most original works of the post-war-period, had his latest piece, *La Hoberaute,* produced at the Vieux Colombier. It is a wonderfully poetic play, with such an originality and quality of language that I went to see it four times as one returns to a concert hall to discover new riches in a well-known symphony. This brilliant work, whose action takes place in the 8th Century and in which anachronisms are to be found cheek-by-jowl with delicate humour, where Man's eternal passions are brought into play, has as its theme the abrupt transition from the religion of Nature, the inspiration of the Druids, to a religion subjugated to political necessity and armed force. It is not a 'historical play': Audiberti himself admits that he knows little about the Druid religion but ... the confrontation of the fairies' world with the world of the warriors is treated with moving and tender generosity. Needless to say, the author's place is with the fairies.

Two other interesting works remain to be mentioned in the realm of the little theatres: two works to which the most inappropriate label of 'avant-garde' has been attached. They are both completely finished plays. Their only novelty lies in the simplicity of their form—a characteristic which rarely finds favour with the French public. The first is the work of Marguerite Duras, the author of *Barrage contre le Pacifique*. Her play, *Le Square*, is nothing but the conversation of an old man and a nurse who is looking after a little girl in a park. It is a brief conversation, in the simple and hesitant manner of two people who are little used to the vocabulary of *la vie intérieure* and who are trying to express themselves to each other in the spontaneity of their friendship. They share a secret—the secret of their loneliness. Theirs is not that metaphysical Solitude which is written with a capital letter, but the loneliness of the humble of which no-one speaks. The other play, *Tchin-Tchin*, by François Billetdoux, which is still being performed with some success at the Théâtre de Poche, is also a two-character play. It portrays the fall into the evils of drink—alcoholism here is merely symbolic, eroticism could just as well have taken its place—of a man and a woman whose only common bond is the memory of the other man and the other woman that they have abandoned. A series of short scenes with little action is used to convey the stages of their decline, which for them takes on something of the nature of an ascension. It is very intelligently written with an almost obsessive delicacy and the acting, by the author himself and an almost unknown artist, Katherina Renn, is of the first order.

Foreign plays, which French writers, through their Society of Authors, give the impression of fearing, have been warmly wel-

comed this year by the theatre directors who have found in them
their most satisfactory financial successes. Arthur Miller's *A
View from the Bridge,* adapted by Marcel Aymé, ran for nearly
a year at the Théâtre Antoine. Raf Vallone, the Italian actor
who made his debut in the French theatre in this play, no doubt
contributed to its success as did the brilliant production of Peter
Brook. The successful career of a play like *Lucy Crown* by
Irwin Shaw could only by explained by the prestige of Edwige
Feuillère and, in the same way, it is undoubtedly the skill of
those two excellent artists Jean Marais and Annie Girardot who
hold the stage alone the whole evening, which draws the public
to the Ambassadeurs to see *Two For the Seesaw* by William
Gibson. The American theatre or, at least, that part of it which
is presented to us by the experts of show business, has a summary aspect, an element of 'prefabrication' which lends a similar
taste to all the plays. Their only distinctions from each other
seem to depend above all on the flavour or the 'spice' added
either by great actors or great producers. The play *Twelve
Angry Men,* however, which was adapted by André Obey from
Reginald Rose's television programme, seems more original.
The actor and producer Michel Vitold has staged this in Paris
with extreme virtuousity.

The English theatre's only representative this season—if one
excepts the detective or murder plays which are often highly
successful—has been the adaptation of John Osborne's play
*Look Back in Anger* which Constance Coline has curiously
translated as *La Paix du Dimanche.* This play at first surprised
and later entranced the French public. It is said that the author
was pleased with the way in which the play was presented in
Paris. We were eventually able to recognise ourselves in the
rather unco-ordinated *délire* of John Osborne's hero, even in
his language which was both brutal and poetic. One of my

colleagues wrote that the play was 'the story of an unsuccessful attempt to escape'. But is an escape attempt really unsuccessful when the prisoner—the prisoner of himself, of all that surrounds him—succeeds as completely as does John Osborne's Jimmy in releasing in a flood of speech, in confessing so much anger and so much sorrow? And when, above all, he succeeds in making others listen to him? The play, which was produced in a faultless rhythm by Raymond Gérome, was very ably served by its cast and, in particular, by Judith Magre and Pierre Vaneck —two extremely promising artists.

Two Italian plays were of interest this season—both for different reasons. The first is by Diego Fabbri. Entitled *Procès à Jesus,* it is a modern review of the trial of Christ. *Procès à Jesus* is generous in inspiration but served by technical means of demagogic facility which I found very disturbing. The author has envisaged his scenes in the auditorium with actors interspersed among the public playing the parts of either converted or doubting Christians and, for me, these scenes rang as false as the worst possible theatre. The play had a certain success despite all this but this can, in my opinion, be dismissed as having little relevance to the theatre. Ugo Betti's play *Eboulement au Quai Nord* (Frana allo Scalo Nord), which was much more interesting, was also concerned with a trial but, in this case, a purely human one. It dwelt on one of the aspects—the broadest—of the problem of responsibility, in a personal and highly original manner. Taking as his starting point the question of personal responsibility for an industrial accident, the author enlarged his subject by successive stages to involve, finally, the whole of humanity through the complex web of interactions and resonnances in which men's actions and thoughts embroil them. This was not simply the 'Trial of Jesus' but 'The Trial of God'. These Italian plays were both produced by Marcelle Tassencourt, the wife of the critic and author, Thierry Maulnier.

From Russia, all we have seen this year has been Mayakowski's *La Punaise* (The Bed Bug), adapted and produced by
André Barsacq. This was the fulfilment of a long-cherished
plan by the director of the Atelier and its success did not repay
his hopes. Appreciation of the high degree of inventiveness of
the production was unanimous but the humour of Mayakowski's
work, which is undoubtedly foreign to French minds, clearly
escaped the spectators. What we had been told was an audaci-
ous satire on the Soviet regime, appeared to us as extremely
innocuous and lacking both strength and virulence.

And now, as I write these lines, the curtain is rising on a new
season at the Theatre of the Nations ... another year in the
theatre begins!

# AUSTRALIA

## H. Stafford Northcote

THE most critical of observers would hesitate to go all the way with the eminent Australian who averred—in anger and in private—that his fellow countrymen were 'nothing but a bunch of flaming crooks in Sydney: snobs in Melbourne: and hypocrites in Adelaide'.

But, sweepingly unkind though his expressed sentiment may be, it has the oblique virtue of giving voice to the marked differences—in atmosphere and attitudes—which prevail between the three capital cities, confirming the oft-felt suspicion that, wherever similarities do exist, the resemblance must be entirely coincidental.

Theatrically speaking, at any rate, tastes diverge as sharply as those of Manchester and London: Boston and New York. Distances between the State capitals are considerable: so are the changes in climate: and the historical circumstance of each city's birth and growth has produced a distinctive style or manner which persists to this day.

A further factor is emerging—as Richard Beynon's play *The Shifting Heart* has, so poignantly, illustrated. Australia's immigration policy has now brought her population to over the ten million mark and, whether or not the very active resentment of the local-born inhabitant to the newcomer arises from a fear that the much-vaunted 'Australian individuality' will thus be endangered, the melting pot is an undeniably established fact.

The influx of migrants from Poland, Greece, Italy, Holland, the Ukraine, Balkans, Baltic States and the United Kingdom, has created community stresses which can only be resolved if the 'Dinkum Aussie' is willing to learn tolerance, to live and work harmoniously with 'New Australians'—or else both parties will end up by hating each other. Despite the magnificent work of the Good Neighbour Council, there is a very definite prejudice against migrants which makes itself felt and, in far too many instances, has led to hostility and thence to tragedy. Too many 'Dagoes, Balts, Krauts, Pommies' have come to Australia with love in their hearts and hope in their eyes, have remained to learn the heartbreak of loneliness, the despair of the non-accepted and (if they could afford the return fare) have left, loathing the sight and sound of the very country in which they had intended to build a new life, a new home. Meanwhile, however, ethnic and sociological factors are having a profound —and it is to be hoped salutary—effect on the development of public taste and behaviour patterns.

Sydney, on the whole, does not at present respond with any particular warmth to contemporary drama. Melbourne, in the main, cold-shoulders the Classics. Adelaide, speaking generally, prefers a commercial entertainment which promises to tickle the fancy rather than a serious drama which might exercise the mind (and for which one has to turn to the amateur theatre), dotes on old-time vaudeville, approves of Shakespeare, and— with its undemanding acceptance of balletic performance—displays rather more enthusiasm than discernment in its reaction thereto.

Yet, within these three cities (for extension of this brief appraisal to include Canberra, the Federal Capital, and the three other State capitals, Perth, Hobart and Brisbane, would reduce its scope from the general to the superficial), theatrical advancement during the period under review has been such as to persuade the most entrenched Jeremiah that there may be cause for hope, controlled elation and some cautious festivity.

*In Sydney,* work has already begun on the new opera house. Designed by the Danish architect, Joern Utzon, for an enviable site at Benelong Point by the world's most beautiful harbour, the building will be an unorthodox series of interlocking shells, suggesting the billowing sails of yachts.

The judges, probably to counteract any adverse reaction which their daring choice might have provoked, did not fail to point out: 'The white sail-like formation relates as naturally to the harbour as the sails of yachts'. They could have spared themselves anxiety: despite an estimated cost of £A 5 million, public opinion registered very definite approval from the idea's inception.

The building will comprise two halls, the larger of which will seat 3,000 to 3,500 for opera, symphony concerts, and ballet; and a smaller hall for drama, intimate opera, chamber music, recitals and lectures.

*In Melbourne,* the Sydney Myer Memorial Bowl was opened by Prime Minister Menzies in the presence of Sir Dallas Brooks, Governor of Victoria, the inaugural ceremony including a concert by the combined Victorian and Sydney Symphony Orchestras. The Bowl cost £A200,000, was designed by the Melbourne architect Barry Patten, and comprises a canopy—like the cross-section of a huge tent—formed with rectangles made of half-inch plywood compressed between sheets of aluminium, bolted to a web of steel cables and supported by fibreglass-coated masts.

2,000 may be seated immediately before the fan-shaped stage under the canopy, and a further 20,000 can be accommodated on the lawns of the amphitheatre area. The Bowl may be adapted to the more intimate needs of drama.

IONESCO'S 'TUEUR SANS GAGES' (Récamier, Paris)

*Pic*

Katherina Renn and François Billetdoux in *Tchin-Tchin*
(Théâtre de Poche)

## PARIS PRODUCTIONS

Bernard Blier, Edwige Feuillère and Paul Guers
in *Lucy Crown*

*Bernand*

A scene from Claudel's *Le Soulier de Satin* with Jean-Louis Barrault   *Pic*

**PALAIS-ROYAL, PARIS**

Pierre Bertin, Madeleine Renaud and Jean Desailly in *La Vie Parisienne*

PARIS

Françoise Spira and Daniel Ivernel
in *La Hoberaute* (Vieux-Colombier)

The final scene from Mayakowski's *The Bed-Bug* (Atelier)

*Pic*

*In Adelaide,* a new general purposes hall has been added to the University. The Union Hall—avoidance of the term 'theatre' was a small price to pay for Government subsidy—has a seating capacity of 499, is comfortable and tasteful, generously equipped (the staging facilities include a 'remote control' lighting system). To use the forbidden word, it is a theatre of which any city might well be proud—and one for which any University might well grovel in gratitude.

The city's main park also possesses a fine open-air Sound Shell, the gift of South Australia's morning newspaper which recently celebrated its centenary. This Shell has already proved an ideal focal point for symphony concerts, art exhibitions, national dance displays and performances by migrant groups.

So much for bricks and mortar, glass, steel and concrete . . .

## New School of Drama

February 1959, saw the opening of the first full-time school of acting in the Southern Hemisphere. The National Institute of Dramatic Art will provide a two-year course of three terms each, and has been established under the auspices of the New South Wales University, the Elizabethan Theatre Trust and the Australian Broadcasting Commission.

The Trust and University will be responsible for the financial costs, and the course provides a practical approach to the professional theatre, besides special training in radio and television work and techniques (for which the A.B.C. will provide use of studio facilities).

Students, limited in number to 30 and who must be over the age of 17, must hold the Leaving Certificate (or equivalent) of any State in the Commonwealth. In their first year, they will be instructed in the technique of acting, in mime, dancing and fencing for the stage, and voice production. They will also be given an introductory course in stage management and mechanics, and they will be required to attend University courses in the history of the theatre and in English language and literature. First-year students will take part in 'workshop productions' each term, but will not be called upon to give public performances.

In their second year, students will be given an advanced course in acting while continuing with other studies begun in their first year. They will also take part in plays produced by the staff and presented to University and general audiences. The plays chosen for performance by students will be of theatrical distinction, whether classical or modern, and students will also have an opportunity to work in various styles of staging.

## Trust's first Permanent Repertory Company

Another exciting step forward was the establishment on March 11th, 1959, of the first permanent professional repertory company in Australia, when the newly formed Trust Players began a season of five plays in Sydney, with an all-Australian nucleus of eight actors.

So far, Australian playwriting suggests an Antipodean affinity to that of Sean O'Casey, and it is apposite that the Elizabethan Theatre Trust's intention is to model the newly-formed repertory company's policy on the lines of the Abbey Theatre, Dublin—with four-to-five week seasons of new productions (Classic, contemporary and Australian).

It is intended to extend this system of established repertory groups to other States—plans for the Melbourne Union are well advanced—recruiting most of the actors, on the 'ladder' system, from the Institute of Dramatic Art who, after experience with the country touring groups, will graduate to the senior companies.

Thus it is hoped to stem the flow of talent which annually goes abroad to get basic training and experience, and to provide incentives and opportunities for indigenous playwrights.

The Trust Players' first season includes Shakespeare's *Julius Caesar,* Shaw's *Man and Superman,* another play yet to be announced, and two new plays by Australian writers—*Slaughter of St. Teresa's Day* by Peter Kenna of Melbourne and *The Bastard Country* by J. A. Cockburn, at present living abroad.

*Slaughter of St. Teresa's Day* was first prizewinner in the General Motors-Holden competition for Australian plays, and it opened to critical acclaim (but then, so did the short-lived *Ned Kelly* during the Olympic Games season).

The play's locale is Paddington, a district of Sydney whose sleaziness rivals its London namesake, and concerns the convent-educated daughter of a middle-aged trollop. Arriving home to announce her intention of becoming a nun, she finds her mother preparing her annual celebration for those cronies who do not, at the time, happen to be in gaol or on the streets. The party leads to a knife-and-shooting affray, arising from the amorous advances of a philanderer just out of gaol. From this dilemma, mother's guilty conscience and daughter's revulsion produce a dramatic conflict which helps to clarify and solve the problems of a young couple whose marriage is drifting dangerously near the rocks.

In common with earlier versions of *The Shifting Heart* and *Summer of the Seventeenth Doll,* this comedy-drama is very much overwritten, and its situations are often too ludicrous to be convincing. (The author may well protest that his characters ARE ludicrous in real life: that does not necessarily make them acceptable in the theatre). But, as with the plays already mentioned, it is ALIVE, it has something to say, its message is no less effective for being delivered between laughter and tears, and it has the virtue of being Australian without the concomitant aggressiveness. So far, however, no one has succeeded in prospecting for an idiom beyond the 'O'Casey aspect' of Australia.

Peter Scriven, under Trust sponsorship, has taken his pioneering of puppet plays one step further. The enchanting *Tintookies* has been followed by a tour of *Little Fella Bindi*—the childlike delights of the former giving way to a more adult appeal in the latter: a story of an aboriginal boy and the indigenous livestock of the Outback.

Musically, the Trust's efforts have met with ill-fortune. Perhaps it would be kinder to ignore the musical *Lola Montez* but, despite the artistic success of the last opera season (*Peter Grimes, die Walküre, Carmen, Barber of Seville* under the baton of Dr. Karl Rankl and with Joan Hammond and Sylvia Fischer), the enormous costs of mounting and touring opera in Australia led to heavy losses and future plans have been shelved for the time being.

The Trust has gained a son and lost a daughter. Ron Hadrick has returned from Stratford to join the Trust Players: Zoe Caldwell, one of the Trust's and Melbourne Union's most interesting players, has signed a contract to appear at Stratford this season.

### Enterprise and the Theatrical Arts

Australia teems with talent: yet it is a country where, to be active in—or enthusiastic about—the Arts, is to invite the suspicion of being slightly odd, if not completely decadent. It would, therefore, not be out of place to pay tribute to the generous support the Arts receive from commercial and industrial enterprises—not forgetting the considerable amount of practical assistance given by the Press, in news, advance publicity, active sponsorship, guarantees against loss, and in hard cash. Paradoxically, the social reportage on any artistic venture has an opposite effect to that intended, and can be downright harmful. Photographs of those at an art exhibition become more important than the work displayed: the drivel about who wore what at a first night overshadows the offering presented on stage. The man in the street—thinking such things are only for the so-called social set (whom he regards with good natured contempt, anyway)—stays away in droves.

Mention has already been made of the General Motors-Holden quest for an Australian play, which has resulted in the Trust presentation of Peter Kenna's prizewinning *Slaughter of St. Teresa's Day.*

Television, comparatively new to Australia, was expected to give 'live theatre'—already battered to its knees by the counter-attractions and competitive price of cinema and sport—the knockout blow. If anything, it has proved a healthy stimulus.

The close co-operation of the Australian Broadcasting Commission, both in the medium of radio and television, has already been noted and will be referred to again. Many Trust actors are radio personalities.

In association with commercial A.T.N. and G.T.V., the Shell Company of Australia sponsored a £A3,000 T.V. play quest: the £A1,250 first prize of which was won by Robin Corfield of Heidelburg, Melbourne. *Day called Black* is a drama involving three timber cutters and four other people caught in the fires of Victoria's dreadful 'Black Friday', 13 January, 1939.

*Bed by the Window,* a hospital murder, won the second prize of £A750 for Paul Chadlow of Toorak, Victoria; Roy Napier of Artarmon, Sydney, won the third prize of £A400 with *They were Big: They were Blue.* A number of smaller prizes for 'adaptations' called forth the comment from one of the judges, John McCallum, that the standard was 'disappointingly low.'

In October 1958, the Little Theatre Guild of Melbourne, in conjunction with the commercial theatre enterprise of J. C. Williamson, announced an Australian play quest with prizes of £A500, £A300 and £A200. The Australian Broadcasting Commission has offered to present the winning play on radio and television.

Taking into account the small population, the Arts receive more support from private enterprise in Australia than in any other country in the world, save the United States of America. It is a pity, therefore, that a school of thought exists which considers that these competitions serve no useful purpose, particularly as the professional writers will not submit their work for appraisal on competitive terms. As matters stand in Australia at present, one wonders whether an attitude of 'everything or nothing' is the wisest one to adopt.

Whilst there may be validity and power in the argument that prizes do not provide the solution to problems facing the Australian playwright—the real solution being, as all recognise, the establishment of a national theatre presenting indigenous drama—it would be a pity if industrial concerns were to lose interest, and abandon their attempts to encourage the Arts, because of a lack of reciprocal interest on the part of the artists themselves.

In rounding up this review of support for the theatrical arts, a passing reference might well be made to the forthcoming Adelaide Arts Festival, planned for March 1960 (and thus beyond the range of this report, save to say the sponsors include the Elizabethan Theatre Trust, the Australian Broadcasting Commission, the Musica Viva Society and the Press: and that Ian B. H. Hunter, former artistic director of the Edinburgh Festival is, at the time of writing, already on his way to Adelaide to advise on organisation and direction of the Festival). Also, a one-act play festival has formed part of the Adelaide Eisteddfod in recent years which, under the sponsorship of the morning newspaper, has encouraged entrants and produced impressive work from all over South Australia.

## Drama and Education

The active participation in—and study of—drama enjoys the very active support of Educational authorities throughout Australia. Every University has its student group and many have graduate groups as well.

W.E.A. and the Department of Adult Education organise tours, lectures, discussion groups and performances. The Teachers' Training Colleges pay particular attention to the study of drama and its presentation; performances of the Old Vic and Stratford companies, and the Trust's classical presentations, are made available to schoolchildren and students at specially reduced prices; and whenever the Australian Broadcasting Commission presents a play of Shakespeare or of one of the recognised Classics, posters are circulated to all schools.

The inter-University drama festival has been established for some time; nearly all the senior schools have impressive facilities for the presentation of plays, and their drama groups achieve creditable results—the quality of the playing in the Adelaide Boys' High School *Macbeth* was such as to blur this writer's vision for a few moments, while *Toad of Toad Hall* by St. Peter's College for Boys was extraordinarily good. Drama has also become an accepted part of the curriculum in schools for retarded or partially incapacitated children.

Australian Children's Theatre tours Australia in large motor caravans, giving as many as three performances in one day in the various halls selected as a centre for each particular area. The enterprise is unique in Australia—two persons for each of the two groups (drama and ballet). Children's Theatre was founded and is still operated by the Misses Joan and Betty Rayner who, in the simplest of settings and with bewilderingly rapid changes of costume, voice and gesture, act a series of episodes from the folklore of many lands, following this with a slightly shortened version of a famous play.

## Ballet

The theatre's balletic section (which tours on a separate itinerary) works on the same principle, and it says much for the power of theatrical illusion—and the artistry of Algeranova and Algeranoff—that two dancers can hold the rapt attention not only of children but also of adults with a repertoire of international dances followed—believe it or not—by one of the famous ballets *Giselle, Swan Lake* or *Cinderella*.

Borovansky, whose last season with Elaine Fifield as prima ballerina was far from being an artistic success, disbanded his company and visited Europe. On his return, he commissioned a new ballet from David Lichine, with Australian migrant theme and a setting appropriate to its title—*King's Cross*—which is Sydney's cosmopolitan quarter.

Robert Pomie, former *protegé* of Serge Lifar, left the Borovansky Ballet and formed his own company *Le Français*. Beth Dean, choreographer and anthropologist, was invited to stage her ballet *Corroboree* (music by John Antill) at the Chicago International Fair, forming an Australian Ballet group of 20 to do so.

The Royal Ballet was unfortunate in visiting Australia almost immediately after the New York Ballet and, in the Eastern States, comparisons were odious. In Adelaide (which the American company did not visit and which is native to Robert Helpmann), its appearance was the signal for wild enthusiasm. Earlier, Adelaide had shouted 'Ole' to Luisillo and his Spanish Dancers who, after dancing through a sweltering Sydney season as if humidity did not exist, paid a return visit to the South Australian capital a little too soon to repeat its former triumph.

Cecil Bates, formerly with Ballet Rambert, continued to present interestingly choreographed original work, and restaged some of the Rambert repertoire for amateur dancers: Maxwell Collis makes up for any limitation in inspiration by taking a company of dancers around the country towns—no mean undertaking—and, in establishing her school, Madame Babicheva (late of Riga and Leningrad) provided a living link with the great Russian dance tradition and has already had one pupil accepted by Sadler's Wells.

### Commercial Theatre

The period under review started sadly with the death of David N. Martin, Managing Director of the Tivoli Circuit, who had been responsible for bringing a number of international artists to tour Australia.

*For Amusement Only,* feared by everyone to be 'too English' for Sydney taste, has proved a wild success. Peter Myers and Ronald Cass, its writer-composers, have been intrigued by *They're a Weird Mob,* a slangy portrayal of the Australian way of life, and are adapting it for the musical stage, for J. C. Williamson. This literary 'hoax' (purporting to by written by an Italian migrant, one Nino Culotta) was actually the work of Patrick O'Grady, and was adapted as a most amusing radio serial by the Australian Broadcasting Commission. The ability of Australians to laugh at themselves (hitherto a rare event) is a healthy sign of advancing nationhood.

Robin Bailey—whose 'Lew-chentio' in The Old Vic's *Taming of the Shrew* this writer described as a blend of Rex Harrison and a barrow boy—was selected for *My Fair Lady*, the première of which J. C. Williamson presented in Melbourne (which Sydney finds it hard to forgive!). His performance as Professor Higgins was well received, but public reaction to the show as a whole bordered on the disappointing—probably due to the anticlimactic effect of reality after so many months of hearsay.

Moira Lister, following the successful lead of Emlyn Williams in his solo recitals as Dickens and Dylan Thomas, toured in a one-person dramatic recital of seven playlets, under the heading *People in Love*, drawing capacity houses for Garnet Carrol, Aztec Services and the Department of Adult Education. Carrol was also responsible for staging *Auntie Mame* with Shirl Conway in the title role: John McCallum, who has taken a managerial post with the J. C. Williamson organisation, repeated his London performance in *Roar Like a Dove*—with Googie Withers.

In a country the size of Australia, costs of travelling are prohibitive, and many attractions do not play anywhere but Sydney or Melbourne—*Kismet*, *Damn Yankees*, *The Sleeping Prince* are cases in point, and it is doubtful whether *My Fair Lady* will travel beyond the Eastern States. For some unknown reason, the Trust did not stage *Twelfth Night* or *Peter Grimes* in Adelaide.

Often, when shows are sent on the full Australian tour, standards of presentation suffer—*South Pacific* and *The Boy Friend* were absolute travesties of the original; Margaret Rutherford's performance in *Time Remembered* was a great disappointment, and there were one or two farces which should not have been staged in the first place, and certainly not sent on tour.

Honourable exceptions to this unhappy state of affairs include the Roger Livesey-Ursula Jeans versions of *The Reluctant Debutante* and *The Great Sebastians*; Dame Sybil Thorndike,

Sir Lewis Casson, Patricia Kennedy and Gordon Chater in *The Chalk Garden*; and a delightfully gay *Salad Days*. Though very well presented, *The Pajama Game* met with a mixed reception, probably because it was not a 'dressy' show; and there was a most disconcerting amalgam of East and West in a show from Japan entitled *Cherry Blossom,* which was an export better reserved for the home market, or a case of 'Is your journey Really Necessary?'.

## Struggle and Success

If ever anyone has earned an O.B.E. the hard way, it is Doris Fitton who has kept Sydney's Independent Theatre buoyant for 29 years in the face of a series of disasters by comparison with which Job's were a child's treat. Sheer will-power, guts, a refusal to accept defeat—and solid slavery in which her non-theatrical husband and two sons found themselves playing their part—kept the Independent not only alive but a force in the land: advancing its standards and status from non-professional, semi-professional and onwards.

Practically every noteworthy play in the world's dramatic repertoire has been presented: controversy still rages over her Australian tour with *Mourning Becomes Electra*. (In Adelaide, Miss Fitton had to threaten to lower the curtain on one performance: on a later occasion she carried this threat into effect). But, whether or not her policy was in advance of its time, there is hardly an Australian actor of any worth who has not gained valuable experience with the Independent—which now has its own school for adults and juniors—and Australian playwrights have had cause for gratitude.

(Pausing for one brief moment for what James Agate called the illegitimate theatre, the latest Phillip Street revue—one of a series of Sydney slings and arrows, unique in Australia—is *Bats*).

## Amateur Theatre in Adelaide

It can be appreciated that, in a country the size of Australia, amateur theatre plays as prominent a role as it does in the United States of America.

Adelaide, capital city of South Australia, some 400 miles East of Melbourne, and about a thousand from Sydney—with Perth a further 1,600 to the West—has a population a little over the half-million mark. It has long been regarded as the theatrical Cinderella city. This is not to suggest that the rival capitals in the Eastern States in any way resemble the Ugly Sisters—save that they enjoy greater privileges. Sydney has its professional theatres: the Independent: and the Phillip Street revues. Melbourne has a goodly crop of professional theatres: the Union: and the Little Theatre Movement. Adelaide has two theatres —the Tivoli which, when it is not closed, is used for all-in wrestling; and the Theatre Royal, the most beautiful playhouse in the Southern Hemisphere, bought by a department store which plans expansion. The new Union Hall, where the Trust has already staged *The Shifting Heart,* could not be considered as a commercial proposition, even if University statutes permitted—which, of course, they cannot.

This far from satisfactory situation cannot last indefinitely for, as in the pantomime, Cinderella's future is very rosy indeed. Her Fairy Godmother and the Prince—in the form of uranium and oil—have not yet had their cue to come onstage, but they hover in the wings and when, as eventually must happen, the Trust can be persuaded to play Dandini and fit the Glass Slipper in the form of an established repertory group, Cinderella will discover she has had the Other Slipper for quite a long time— in the form of her amateur theatre.

Considering the difficulties under which it works, the record of the amateur theatre in Adelaide is a matter for some reasonable pride—though by no means an excuse for complacency. As with most amateur movements, the good is oft interred. Lack of discipline, lack of humility, lack of rehearsal, lack of attention to detail, a tendency toward exhibitionism, pretentious-ness and mutual admiration can be as deadly as the public indifference amid which the amateurs have carried on their activities.

Were it not for the amateur groups, Adelaide would experi-ence very little good theatre at all and—if only for that reason —their efforts have been worth taking seriously.

The Adelaide Repertory Theatre is the oldest, has the largest membership and is financially the best established. Unfortu-nately, it is not the best, for its artistic policy is wedded to that of the English drawing-room comedy or West End success. This can be all the more infuriating when, as occasionally it does, it presents first-class work in *The Diary of Anne Frank*, *The Lark*, *The Gioconda Smile*, *Under the Sycamore Tree*, *The Lady's not for Burning* and *Music at Night*.

With a policy of good plays, but presented in a 'hit or miss' fashion, the Adelaide Theatre Group can chalk up *Waiting for Godot*, *A Winter's Tale*, *No Sign of the Dove*, *Heartbreak House*, *Crime and Punishment* among its successes: both parts of *Faust* as a worthy failure: and *Uncle Vanya* and *Billy Budd* among those better forgotten. It totters from crisis, is finan-cially a Mr. Micawber, but is affectionately assisted to survive by its exasperated but amused friends.

Theatres Associated tend to veer from the superb to the near-dreadful but, on a tiny stage and in Miss Jean Marshall's pro-duction of *Death of a Salesman*, Adelaide was given an example of how to triumph over apparently insurmountable difficulties. Interesting work also occurred, now and again, in *Dark of the Moon*, *And So to Bed* and *The Inspector General*.

The Adelaide New Theatre's policy appears to be a blend of the aggressively Australian and the militantly Left, both of which can be wearisome in the theatre. A marked exception to this was the uninhibited fun of *Under the Coolibah Tree*, a sort of *Show Boat Down Under*.

The emergence of a new group—Independent Repertory—has been one of the most exciting events in Adelaide amateur theatre. Beginning disastrously with *Fallen Angels*, the company's exuberance sobered and it has since gone from strength to strength with *Power without Glory*, *Bus Stop*, *Cat on a Hot Tin Roof*, *The Country Wife*, a most original off-beat revue *Twisted Faces*, a fall from grace in *The Burnt Flower Bed* and, at the time of writing, plans are well advanced for *The Three-penny Opera*.

The University of Adelaide has two groups, the student A.U.D.S. and the graduate University Theatre Guild—both of which combined to present *Androcles and the Lion* in the newly-opened Union Hall mentioned earlier.

The climate of Adelaide being what it is, the University has staged open air productions in the Cloisters—with variable degrees of artistic success—*A Midsummer Night's Dream*, *Blood Wedding*, *Romeo and Juliet* and *Christmas in the Market Place*. An embarrassingly bad production of *Maria Stuart* commanded sympathy for the leading lady, Miss Joy Watson, whose performance soared above the evening's ineptitudes.

To say farewell to the much maligned University Hut, which had little comfort but much atmosphere and which had witnessed sterling effort in *Hedda Gabler*, *Cradle Song*, *Our Town*, *Murder in the Cathedral*, *Alcestis* and *Third Person*, the Guild presented *The Queen and the Rebels*, the poignancy of the occasion heightened by the intensely moving Argia of Miss Iris Hart. In the new Union Hall, the Guild has scored a notable success in *Under Milk Wood,* and the University French Club made a gallant attempt—in Anouilh's native tongue—at *La Sauvage.*

The actors tend to roam from group to group as and when suitable roles become available and, considering the demands on their time in their everyday activities, achieve some fairly remarkable results on occasions.

Apart from the already-mentioned Miss Hart (who is good in almost every role she interprets), Miss Margery Irving is excellent in Molière and Restoration Comedy, but should leave Coward plays severely alone. Miss Vivienne Oldfield's moral disintegration in *The Gioconda Smile* was a subtle performance which blended fascination and repulsion in equal measure. Miss Carmel Millhouse, who can appeal as Helen of Troy and appal as Lady Macbeth; Miss Mary McMahon, very able in brittle American roles; and Miss Joan McDonald, who will always be remembered in *Music at Night.*

Mr. Raymond Wheeler is a most conscientious actor who, when he has a part he can make suit him (as in *Godot* or the Dauphin in *The Lark*) is memorable, and even when he can't still manages to capture the imagination. Mr. Jeffry Dugan, when he stops playing up to his coterie in the audience, is capable of some first-rate performances; and Mr. Francis Flannagan, when he can be persuaded to attend rehearsal or bother to learn his lines, can be wildly, wickedly funny. Many of these actors appear regularly in A.B.C. radio plays and programmes.

Success has brought its casualties to the Adelaide amateur theatre—Miss Darlene Johnson has been lost to the Trust: Miss Mary Robin to educational Television in Sydney: and Miss Audine Leith to the Melbourne Union.

What the Adelaide amateur theatre lacks, however, is ex-

perienced producers of intelligence and integrity. Miss Jean
Marshall's superb handling of *Death of a Salesman* has already
been mentioned, and the University Theatre Guild will never
be able to accord sufficient gratitude for Miss Thelma Baulder-
stone's impressive, painstaking, self-effacing work. Mr. and
Mrs. Roy Grubb's handling of *The Lark* haunts the memory;
but only two men—both former professional actors—can be
regarded as first rate producers with any degree of consistency.
Both have uncanny control over unruly amateurs, can coax
extraordinarily fine performances, and can impose a sense of
discipline and teamwork.

Mr. John Edmund, formerly with J. C. Williamson and the
Melbourne Arrow Theatre, has formed his own school and
Theatre Workshop, for which he produced *Dark Lady of the
Sonnets, Village Wooing* and, on a claustrophobic stage, achieved
miracles with a crowd in *The Shewing up of Blanco Posnet*.
For Independent Repertory his successes have included *Bus Stop,
Power without Glory, Cat on a Hot Tin Roof*—having learnt
much from his baptism of fire with the same group, *Fallen
Angels*, where he allowed his players to run away from his
control. *Under Milk Wood*, which he recently produced for the
University Theatre Guild, has brought him great credit.

Mr. Alexander Hay is probably the most powerful actor in
Adelaide, with a mannered style which is difficult to modulate
to the limitations of lesser actors, and which finds its effect
only when displayed among players of equal merit. As a producer, *King Lear* and *Heartbreak House* were outstanding
successes; at the present time he is preparing *The Threepenny
Opera;* while his two-person presentation of *Macbeth,* and the
*Marriage of St. Francis* were strangely compelling.

This latter play was presented in the tiny underground Torch
Theatre of Miss Patricia Hackett, whose work for intimate

'TWO FOR THE SEESAW'—
LONDON AND PARIS

Gerry Jedd
and Peter Finch
(Haymarket, London)

Bernand

*McBean*

Anne Girardot
and Jean Marais
(Ambassadeurs, Paris)

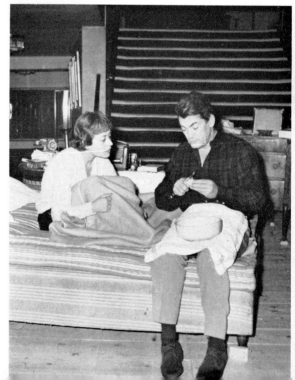

Therese Giehse, Christa Keller and Friedrich Domin
in *Nathan der Weise* (Kammerspiele, Munich)

**GERMANY**

Agnes Fink
and Anne Kersten
in *Die Herzogin von
Langeais*
(Residenz, Munich)

*Betz*

Werner Schulz-Wittan,
Manfred Gorges and
Erich Mirek
in *Die Lohndrücker*
(Maxim-Gorki, Berlin)

*Simon*

*Richter*

The entrance to Die Schmiere

Interior: the patrons in the front row have to put their feet on the edge of the stage...

*Reinbacher*

Bergström

World première in Stockholm of O'Neill's *Hughie* with Bengt Eklund as 'Eric Smith'

*Nydtskov*

DENMARK

Erik Mørk and Mogens Wieth in Kjeld Abell's dramatised version of *The Lady of the Camelias* (New, Copenhagen)

theatre Adelaide has not yet had the grace to appreciate. Miss Hackett has staged the type of play which might not be considered good box-office, even for amateur theatre, but which has given amateurs invaluable experience. In this Australian equivalent of the Kammertheater, no prompt is permitted, and the players are almost at one with the audience of 45, in plays such as *Lord of the Three Worlds*, *The Beautiful One*, *Medea*, *The Ways of Women*, *Thieves' Carnival* and *The Old Ladies*.

Finally there are the writers. The Adelaide amateur theatre has had the enterprise and the courage to stage original work by local writers: *Governor Bligh* by Dr. Brian Medlin, *Papinian* by Dr. John Bray and *The Administrator* by the late Professor Charles Jury (whose death was a sad blow for amateur theatre). These three plays were in verse, all were interesting and each needed pruning. The last-named was the most successful (and the most witty) but all tended to lack dramatic impact.

*Believe It or Not* was an acceptable comedy-fantasy in gentle vein by Mr. Alex Symons; *Trial by Error* sketched Miss Betty Smallacombe's idea of the return of an erring son to his family; Mr. Hedley Cullen, probably inspired by Noel Langley, amusingly adapted Shakespeare's *Rape of Lucrece* into *Catch me a Cuckoo*; and *Interrupted Rehearsal* was Mr. Alexander Hay's adaption of *Six Characters in Search of an Author*.

Thus, the work of the amateur theatre in Adelaide has assumed an importance which puts the professional theatre to shame. Paying it the compliment of taking its efforts seriously can, for the critic, often be frustrating—for amateurs are reluctant to accept anything but adulation and the public often misinterprets the critic's aims and intentions.

In a vigorous, growing country like Australia, however, it is a hazard which the critic gladly accepts as a challenge, for he need never find himself bored—if he is prepared to stick to his guns and justify his critical ethos.

There comes, even in the worst performance or presentation, that vagrant moment of truth which makes up for all the dreariness of awaiting its arrival. It is something the critic always looks for and considers himself well rewarded when it occurs—and there is always the hope that it may prove a stepping stone for better things in the future for, to echo the opinion of this Annual's distinguished editor, when the amateur theatre puts its mind to it, there is nothing it cannot do.

# ENGLISH PROVINCES

## Frank Hauser

WHEN people talk about the state of British drama, they mean 'What's On in London'. Young playgoers fulminate against the narrow-minded timidity of commercial managements, older ones point proudly to the West End Honours List. Progressives mean to support the Royal Court, though too often they leave it too late. Reactionaries thank God for Terence Rattigan. Everybody blames the Lord Chamberlain.

But the health of a theatre has nothing to do with all this. Theatre, like politics, is significant only as far as it is taken seriously: considered as games, both are contemptible. That is why the cry of 'Entertainment!' is so misleading. It is certainly the function of commercial managements to make money; it is equally the function of anyone who cares for theatre to persuade, dazzle or shame them into making money the hard way, that is with plays and productions on a higher level than the public is supposed to require. People who 'Go to the theatre to be entertained' surely won't be if that is all they go for. When *Look Back in Anger* burst triumphantly on the West End (i.e. when the obstinate championing of two highbrow critics turned a tedious wordy failure into a solid, commercial success) what surprised everyone was that an author was using the stage in order to say something worth listening to. The theatre had become educational again, not in terms of Living Newspaper, but in dramatic terms—obstinacy, conflict, a voice which meant what it said. The object of the play was not to entertain but to shock, to dismay, to instruct, to get something off the author's chest. Entertainment, like happiness, is a by-product.

It is striking that virtually all the good young directors since the war have made their reputations (and a fair amount of cash for the managements) in 'uncommercial' plays: Peter Brook in *Huis Clos*, Peter Hall with *Godot*, Peter Wood with *The Iceman Cometh*. All these were presented by the same tiny highbrow theatre, the Arts. Ten years ago there were four more such places where these plays could have been tried out; now the Arts alone survives, though the Royal Court and occasionally the Lyric Hammersmith provide support. Where can the young producer back his fancy? Where can the new or unknown dramatist get a hearing, without which he can only wither or evolve into eccentricity?

In the past few years an answer has come from what would have seemed to be the most unlikely source: the theatre outside London, the Reps. Repertory in England has always been an odd institution. 'My years in rep.'—it conjures up a wry picture of landladies and local reporters and pompous councils and lack of rehearsal, most of it quite true. There were the shining exceptions, Birmingham, Bristol, where three or four weeks rehearsal were given to a largely classical programme; but repertory companies existed almost entirely on a diet of re-hashed West End successes, old and new.

My own experience was no different, until I came across a play called *The Queen and the Rebels* by Ugo Betti. This was while I was directing the Midland Theatre Company, an Arts Council troupe centred on Coventry, which toured nearby towns as well. It was not a promising ground for displaying an unknown foreign tragedy; but thanks largely to the presence of Irene Worth, who came down to play the lead, the play was not only moderately successful locally, but attracted favourable notices from the national press. This was the first time it had occurred to me that the production of important new plays was not the monopoly of London or a couple of favoured provincial theatres; anyone could play, and the penalties were not likely to be higher than if one revived *Dangerous Corner* for the twentieth time.

When I took over the Oxford Playhouse in 1956 this experience had hardened into a policy. It seemed possible that by concentrating on new plays you could do three things simultaneously :

(1)  Use the interest and goodwill of the national press to offset the audience's reluctance to see something they had never heard of.

(2)  Through the double promise of good new parts and wide critical coverage persuade first-class actors to come into the company.

(3)  Do only those plays that you urgently wanted to do, instead of the usual proportion of three bread-and-butter pieces to one 'prestige' play.

Financially, there was always the chance of a play transferring to London, with a steady royalty accruing to the parent theatre. (This has happened three times so far, and has enabled the Playhouse to keep alive in spite of considerable losses.)

At the same time that the Playhouse began its new life, important changes were happening elsewhere. In Liverpool Sam Wanamaker re-opened the New Shakespeare, with the intention of making it not only a home for new plays, but a meeting-place for all sorts of other activities—cinema shows, fashion parades, exhibitions of paintings—the kind of Arts Centre which so many people have talked about but none before had actually tried to put into practice. At Bristol John

Moody was finding that the new plays (Giraudoux, Arthur Miller, Angus Wilson) were more than holding their own against the classics. The classics, however, were well looked after at Birmingham: not the safe Shakespeares and Sheridans, but the *Henry VI* trilogy, the two *Iphigenia's* done as a double bill, and the three Elizabethan rarities which appear in this year's Edinburgh Festival programme. Lincoln, under John Hale, pulled themselves within two years from bankruptcy to a state where the English première of Arthur Miller's *An Enemy of the People* adaptation could play to packed houses. At Nottingham, Willis Hall's immensely successful *The Long and the Short and the Tall* had its first performance; and it is there that Chekhov's *Platonov* finally, and triumphantly, reached the English stage.

This was not all: a little at a time, the companies began to help each other. Here Oxford has given a clear lead. In the past three years the Playhouse has played host to Theatre Workshop (long before their West End phase), the Coventry Belgrade Company, the Nottingham Playhouse (whose *Peer Gynt* filled the theatre for a fortnight) and the Lincoln *An Enemy of the People.* It has been possible for any Oxford theatre-goer to get a very good idea of the strength and variety of the off-centre theatre, in addition to seeing their own company give twenty new plays by such authors as Giraudoux, Canetti, Anouilh, Robert Bolt, Ustinov, Bernard Kops, Roussin and de Filippo. And in every case, the new work being done was done because either I or the director of the other company urgently wanted it to be done. There are much easier ways of making a living than trying to find worthwhile new plays. The difficulty, the challenge is part of the value. When Oxford mounts *The Bacchae,* commissioning a translation from the producer, Minos Volanakis, or when Nottingham present an unknown

Chekhov comedy with four sets and a cast of twenty, there is little expectation of even covering costs. What there is instead is material for the producers and actors to improve their work, refresh their ideas, and assist in the statement of something they believe should be stated—the serious view of life implicit in Chekhov and Euripides, which should be no less immediate to a modern audience than Osborne or Beckett are.

Why has this happened outside London? My own theory is that the immense expense of mounting productions in the West End will always preclude any but a State-supported theatre from attempting this sort of programme. Of course all the theatres I have mentioned are heavily subsidised, most of them by the Arts Council; but because costs are so much lower in the provinces, theatres can often survive failures which would literally bankrupt their London counterparts. As a result, a new race of producer-managers is arising, who are encouraged to follow their own bent without being held up all the time by purely financial considerations; whose great ambition is not to spend their lives producing popular stars in popular plays; who are prepared to cope with the problems of casting and setting complex plays on a low budget, the dismay of much of the old-time audience, the difficulty of extracting new plays from under the various options which bury so many of them, and the sheer wearing grind of presenting a different play every few weeks, because the rewards are something they will not get elsewhere. Avant-garde or traditional, committed or bourgeois—the labels make no difference; these provincial repertory companies, traditionally the breeding-ground of future star actors, are now becoming the intellectual centre of British theatre. It is they who, together with their allies in the capital, are keeping the pressure up on the timid, the complacent and the despairing.

## The Resources of the Theatre:

## IN AMERICA

### John Beaufort

On the 5th of July 1935, the Congress of the United States granted 'a charter incorporating the American National Theatre and Academy, a non-profit corporation, without capital stock, to present theatrical productions of the highest type . . .' According to its preamble, ANTA was to be: 'A people's project, organised and conducted in their interest, free from commercialism, but with the firm intent of being as far as possible self-supporting. A national theatre should bring to the people throughout the country their heritage of the great drama of the past and the best of the present, which has been too frequently unavailable to them under existing conditions.'

On the 2nd of September, 1958, Congress established the National Cultural Center in Washington, D.C.; set aside a 9.4-acre site in the 'Foggy Bottom' section of Rock Creek Park (not far from the Lincoln Memorial) for a performing arts building; and established a board of fifteen trustees plus the Secretary of Health, Education and Welfare to administer it. On the 13th of March, 1959, the center's board held their first meeting. The trustees' major challenge was to raise by 1963, the Congressional deadline, the fifteen to twenty-five million dollars needed to construct the center envisaged by the act.

The founding of ANTA was not the first attempt to create a national theatre in the United States. At various times in the first half of the century, proponents of the idea tried unsuccessfully to bring it into being. The late Robert E. Sherwood's plan for a National People's Theatre and a 1949 congressional measure to subsidise the theatre arts with a modest $250,000 were among the efforts which came to naught. The depression years of the thirties temporarily produced something resembling a national theatre. But the Works Project Administration's Federal Theatre was primarily a form of unemployment relief. Like other similar New Deal agencies, it ceased to exist when the crisis was considered at an end.

The spasmodic, high-minded efforts to create a national theatre and the failure with which these efforts have been historically attended would appear to hold a less than dazzling prospect of success at this juncture. Yet the goal is perhaps within reach. 'Foggy Bottom' in the District of Columbia may yet become the national theatre's promised land. Some of the reasons for optimism can be quickly cited. To begin with, Robert W. Dowling, chairman of the board of directors of ANTA, is one of the Cultural Center's fifteen general trustees. Mr. Dowling, a New York real estate man whose City Investment Co. owns playhouses and who invests in plays, has been an ardent supporter of the present plan. Despite the 1963 deadline (which could, one assumes, be extended), the passage of the National Cultural Center legislation reflects a new surge of support for the arts among U.S. lawmakers. (The first act of Rep. Frank Thompson of New Jersey, on his first day in office was to sponsor the aforementioned bill.) President Eisenhower, in his 1955 State of the Union message expressed the opinion that the 'Federal Government should do more to give official recognition to the importance of the arts and other cultural activities.' Although Mr. Eisenhower has provided little personal leadership in the cause of the arts, bipartisan support has assured the continuance and even the extension of international cultural exchange programs. Reports in the American press of overseas tours by Marian Anderson, *Porgy and Bess,* Dizzy Gillespie, *The Skin of Our Teeth,* as well as other productions, groups, and individual artists have quite possibly helped stimulate Americans' interest in and appreciation of the talent in their midst.

While prospects of a Washington home for a national theatre have shown some signs of improvement, the state of the commercial stage remains critical. Broadway's thirty remaining playhouses—some of them expensively rehabilitated in recent seasons—continue to accomodate the odd and uneven array of hits and flops, an array consisting of musical comedies and assorted trivia interspersed with occasional serious works. Except for the Old Vic's periodic engagements, no Shakespearean play has been presented by a commercial manager for more than five years. The bard is left to the North American Stratfords (Ontario and Connecticut); to such annual Shakespeare festivals as those of Ashland, Ore., and San Diego, Calif.; and to the college and community theatre. The Shaw franchise is preserved principally by *My Fair Lady.* As far as America's theatrical capital is concerned, the standard and classic works of the unlimited international repertory have become the almost exclusive property of the Off-Broadway movement. Broadway will have none of them.

On the basis of the foregoing, it would be easy to draw up quick indictment of the Broadway managers. But it would also be unfair and misleading. To survive at all in the nervous, hit-or-flop economy of the current New York theatrical system requires a particular kind of daring and a resilience in the face of frequent failure. Trivia is a staple of commercial 'show business'—whether in the Times Square district, the Paris boulevard playhouses, or the West End. The point to be made is that certain Broadway producers come before the public each season with plays which, in an era of continuously rising costs, represent both courage and a dedication to the theatre as art. Productions of Beckett's *Waiting for Godot,* Anouilh's *The Lark* or *The Waltz of the Toreadors,* O'Neill's *A Touch of the Poet,* Faulkner's *Requiem for a Nun,* MacLeish's *J.B.,* Duerrenmatt's *The Visit,* Giraudoux' *Tiger at the Gates,* could scarcely be called sure-fire commercial propositions even when—as has usually been the case—bolstered by the presence of one or more stars.

The commercial theatre, both in New York and the nation at large, has suffered an almost continuous erosion ever since the motion picture learned to talk in 1929. Quality has been sustained to a remarkable degree, for the ailing theatre continues to attract the very best specialists in production, direction, design, in acting and in subsidiary craftsmanship. But the number of plays produced each year has continued declining whilst more and more playhouses have been demolished to make way for parking lots, office buildings, and similar improvements.

A survey conducted several years ago by Dr. O. Glenn Saxon of Yale University, disclosed that the total number of theatres available for professional productions in the United States dropped from 647 in 1921 to 234 in 1954. The decline has continued steadily. Of the more than sixty-five legitimate playhouses in New York in 1931 only thirty remained in 1959. Broadway stage productions numbered 195 in the 1931-2 season (the peak of the depression). The average for recent seasons has ranged from fifty to sixty. Finally, 'winter' or 'permanent' stock companies fell off from 413 in 1928 to less than thirty in 1959.

As goes New York so goes theatrical U.S.A. 'The road'—

that scattered and disorganised assortment of commercial theatres which serve the nation at large—has continued to deterio-
rate alarmingly. A 1959 survey by *Variety*, the leading trade
weekly of American show business, documented a cheerless
headline (' "LIVING" THEATRE—BUT ON WHAT?') with the
following bleak observations:

'Only seven out-of-New York legit theatres have done profitable business over the last five years. If the present trend
continues, less than a dozen theatres will be available in the
entire U.S. for touring shows within a few years. Moreover,
those few operating will be in only six cities, including the four
major eastern tryout spots. In that case, such centers as Detroit,
Cleveland, St. Louis, Baltimore, Pittsburgh, Cincinnati, and
even Los Angeles would be virtually closed to touring Broadway
productions.

'That's the obvious answer to people who, pointing to the
occasional mammoth grosses registered by powerhouse hits like
*My Fair Lady* and *Music Man,* argue that there's nothing wrong
with the road that a good show won't cure. Their point that
there's an ample public for entertaining shows, is unrealistic.
The crux of the matter is that there can't be any shows, good
or bad, unless there are theatres to house them.'

*Variety's* Drama Editor, Hobe Morrison, went on to report
that the only profitable 'road' theatres in recent years have been
the National, Washington (not a national theatre in the European sense); the Shubert, Boston; the Shubert, New Haven:
the Shubert and Erlanger, Chicago; the Curran, San Francisco;
and the Forrest, Philadelphia. The profitable status of these
theatres, standing for many years, is based on former real estate
valuations, not replacement at current, inflated costs. Since the
remainder of the nation's legitimate theatres have managed to
keep open 'only by booking occasional films and whatever

concerts, ballets, sports events, and other such miscellany as they can pick up, it's inevitable that their survival is just a matter of time'.

'In a capitalist system, you can't buck economics, so unless the supply of touring shows is substantially increased (or some form of subsidy is arranged) there may soon be only about half a dozen regular legit houses available for regular Broadway productions', observed *Variety*. 'The powerhouse grossers could book auditoriums, but there would simply be nowhere for straight plays and moderate-business musicals to play'.

The plight of 'the road' is naturally the subject of much head-shaking and also of periodic 'emergency conferences'. Yet the diminution or even disappearance of commercial playhouses outside New York would not reduce the United States to a theatrical desert. 'The road' has long since ceased to comprise the principal purveyor of stage entertainment to audiences outside New York. A handful of professional and semi-professional stock companies, an abundance of college and community amateur theatres, a seasonally emerging assortment of summer tent and 'hard-top' theatres, regional 'symphonic dramas', Shakespearean and other festivals have come into being across the years to serve the immemorial demand for living theatre. With the exception of the Shakespeare festivals and the 'symphonic dramas', written to commemorate regional history, the provincial producing enterprises rely on recent Broadway hits to win audiences. As a result, much community theatre fare is merely an imitation of Broadway commercialism, diluted by mediocre acting. An occasional manager, like the pioneering Margot Jones of Dallas, has risked all with a repertory exclusively of new plays and classics. This bold and successful program did not long survive Miss Jones's untimely death in 1955. A larger number of managements vary the conventional diet of Broadway hits with an occasional standard work or classic—a proportion which has been described with mild cynicism by a community theatre director as 'three for them and one for us'. For the most part, however, the so-called regional theatre, whether professional or amateur, relies heavily on the well publicised escapist fare provided by a Broadway which it so often decries.

Nothing is more characteristic of the theatre's astonishing resiliency than its capacity to belie the diagnoses of its would-be mourners. Just when it appears to be gasping for breath, the fabulous invalid leaps out of bed and dances a jig. Sometimes the giddy defiance of doctor's orders is spontaneous and inexplicable. More often, it results from a well-aimed injection —of talent, money, idealism, determination, or a combination of the four. Since the living theatre—by virtue of the very fact that it *is* alive—exists in a constant state of transition, generalisations about its total condition are more easily made than proved.

One way of portraying the total state of the American theatre today is to set down certain trends and beneficial developments. (The negative forces—competition from the mass media, inflation, dispersal of urban populations, and all the rest—have been detailed with sufficient frequency not to require further repetition in this short chapter.)

From one observation post, the most conspicuous positive developments of recent years in New York and the continent at large have been (1) the addition of new Shakespearean festivals, notably at Stratford, Ont., and Stratford, Conn., to those already in existence; (2) Off-Broadway's rise to a major position in the New York theatrical scheme of things; (3) the increasing role of the foundations in supporting the theatre arts and theatre construction; (4) the launching in New York of the

$75,000,000 Lincoln Center for the Performing Arts, scheduled to open in 1961; (5) the growing degree of *rapprochement* between commercial and non-commercial segments of the theatre, a development in which ANTA has played a significant role; (6) the high regard for professional standards encountered repeatedly among the more forward looking leaders of the academic theatre.

The sum of these developments helps create a climate favorable to the growth of all theatre. Whether this climate will ultimately produce a 'national theatre' and whether this 'national theatre' will actually make its home among the landscaped acres of Washington's 'Foggy Bottom' remains to be seen. A decentralised *nationwide* theatre is considered by many enthusiasts a more suitable solution for a country with a continental area of 3,022,387 square miles—a country, furthermore, whose capital is now nearly 5,000 miles from the citizens of its most distant state, Hawaii.

The aforementioned developments may be summarised briefly as follows :

## I. FESTIVE SHAKESPEARE

Shakespearean festivals are nothing new on the north American continent. They have been featured at World's Fairs, sponsored by educational institutions, and received support from the commercial theatre. Until recent years, the festivals at Ashland, Ore., San Diego, Calif., and Antioch College (Yellow Springs, Ohio) were among the more prominent. With the launching of the Stratford Shakespearean Festival of Ontario, in 1953, Tyrone Guthrie, Alec Guinness, Irene Worth and company gave the movement a forward thrust whose effects have continued to be felt ever since. In Canada alone, the Stratford Festival directly or indirectly resulted in the stimulus to professional stock companies; the formation of Canadian Players, a touring group which has trouped from the American South to the Arctic Circle; and the establishment of the Canada Arts Council, with federal funds at its disposal to subsidise worthy undertakings. (No such government subsidy has yet been achieved in the republic to the south). In 1956, the Stratford performances were given for the first time in a $1,500,000 permanent theatre, a playhouse in the shape of an 'O' provided with a platform stage which Tanya Moiseiwitsch and Mr. Guthrie adapted from Elizabethan models.

The theatre is one of the most beautiful in North America. Its existence helped stimulate interest in the American Shakespeare Festival and Academy in Stratford, Conn., which has been making steady gains after an abortive start in 1955. The two-year-old Vancouver International Festival likewise took its inspiration and some of its personnel from the Ontario Stratford.

Not only has Stratford, Ont., drawn hundreds of thousands of patrons to its annual summer performances; it has also provided opportunities for numerous young players whose work at Stratford has helped prepare them for subsequent successes in the cinema, on television, and on Broadway.

## II. The Off-Broadway Movement

'Off-Broadway' existed as an entity long before it gained currency as a phrase. The Washington Square Players of 1914 (from which grew the Theatre Guild) and Provincetown Players of 1916 (who first presented Eugene O'Neill's early plays) were the distinguished antecedents of the mid-century Off-Broadway movement. During the years between, there have almost always been a variety of intently earnest, often talented, usually impecunious groups dedicated to a concept of theatre far removed

## LONDON COMEDY

Barry Jones, Judith Stott, Nigel Patrick and Coral Browne in *The Pleasure of His Company* (Haymarket)

*McBean*

Hugh Williams and Joan Greenwood in *The Grass Is Greener* (St. Martin's)

In London, the
Mermaid Theatre at
Puddle Dock

*Sholomovich S.C.R.*

*Miles*

In Moscow, the new
Kremlin Theatre

Moscow production of *The Bed-Bug* with G. Menglet, L. Osipov,
B. Tronova and V. Lepko

**RUSSIAN THEATRE**

)leg Tabakov and N. Pastukhov in *In Quest of Joy* (Sovremennik Theatre Studio)

Anna Synodinou (kneeling) in *Iphigenia in Aulis*
(Greek National Theatre)

Pic

from Broadway first-nights, 'hot tickets', scalpers, and associated nonsense.

The simplest and perhaps most accurate explanation for the tremendous Off-Broadway boom the past decade is the demand, among actors and audiences alike, for something more than Broadway was providing. Hence the movement which makes its home in approximately thirty cellars, converted apartments, church basements, club rooms, rehabilitated cinemas, ex-night clubs, and other auditoriums including a few actual playhouses —a movement concentrated in Greenwich Village and extending uptown along the East Side of Manhattan. A count at one time numbered more than a hundred Off-Broadway groups. They play on Sundays (when Broadway theatres are dark) and continue active throughout the summer (when Broadway managers retreat to count their gains, brood upon their losses, and rally their forces for the ensuing season).

Off-Broadway has given their first New York performances to plays by Sartre, Ionesco, Genet, Duerrenmatt, and others. It has nourished itself and its audiences on classic and standard works—adaptations like *Ulysses in Nighttown,* little known works like Chekhov's *Ivanov,* O'Casey's *Purple Dust* and *Cock-a-Doodle Dandy.* It has rescued from the oblivion of Broadway failure or semi-failure Tennessee Williams's *Summer and Smoke,* Arthur Miller's *The Crucible,* O'Neill's *The Iceman Cometh* (credited in part with launching the recent O'Neill renaissance), and a number of other works which deserved a further hearing. It has helped familiarise the public with new writers, among them Leslie Stevens, Bernard Kops, James Forsythe, and William Carlos Williams (an eminent poet but little known as a playwright). Off-Broadway has given initial New York acting opportunities to such subsequently eminent young players as Kim Stanley, Jason Robards, Jr., Jacqueline Brooks,

Geraldine Page, Ben Gazzara, Albert Salmi, Anthony Franciosa, and George C. Scott, to name a few. New directors, designers, and impresarios have won vitally needed recognition in the little theatres on the edges—for Off-Broadway is covered by most of the first-string metropolitan drama critics. Finally, Off-Broadway has initiated into the pleasures of playgoing a generation of young people who find its bill of fare and its prices inviting. In this connection, honorable mention should be made of the New York City Center's annual popular-priced series, which offer ballet, opera, and musical comedy although drama has been dropped in recent years.

Harold Clurman, who criticises plays in addition to directing them, wrote in the *New York Times* about Off-Broadway:

'It has been estimated that approximately 500,000 people attend Off-Broadway productions yearly. If this number seems negligible, one should remember that, in terms of volume, the theatre public in general is negligible compared to the audience the movies still command. (In a cynical mood, we might say that the Broadway theatre is the Off-Broadway of the movies and TV.) But in the life of the arts, numbers are not a primary consideration. Every artistic venture, if it has any vitality at all, is a seed in which the possibilities of growth are present . . .

'I would go so far as to say that I strongly favor the subsidising of several theatres off Broadway by foundations—because Off-Broadway productions, even good ones, can rarely make enough profit to sustain themselves.' Indeed, one might add, Off-Broadway is a public service and an economic anomaly.

### III. SUBSIDY TO THE FORE

'Subsidy' is a word considered suspect by many Americans when applied to the theatre. The Cultural Center in Washington referred to at the beginning of this account is therefore significant. It marks a great forward stride and a gain in cultural maturity for Congress to provide government land for a building intended, among other purposes, for theatrical performances. But the money for the building—and the money for what will be played, sung, danced, and acted in it—will in all probability have to come from private sources. This reflects a characteristic American attitude which is slowly changing. Americans have in the past been willing to spend public moneys on hospitals, welfare, education, on libraries and even museums. They have built municipal auditoriums in which the performing arts could be performed (usually at the going rental price). But the idea of extending public subsidy to the arts themselves, let alone the artists, has found little or no response in the hearts or pocketbooks of a pragmatic people.

Gradually, and frequently without the public's appreciation of its significance, this situation has been changing. The tax moneys which support state and municipal schools of higher learning often include well equipped auditoriums suitable for both plays and musical performances. In a few cities—and the state of Virginia—theatrical performances receive subsidy. Private beneficence, in the form of individual gifts and foundation grants, has financed the construction and expansion of many a community theatre. With the growth of cultural centers, it seems likely that the theatre will receive an increased amount of aid. One of the major obstacles to be overcome is the traditional American disposition to elevate music and the fine arts whilst relegating all theatre to the inferior status of what *Variety* calls 'show biz'.

Yet there is a growing tendency to acknowledge the drama's right to a share in the millions of dollars of subsidy extended to the country's symphony orchestras, art museums, and other cultural institutions.

The most conspicuous tangible evidence of this new attitude will emerge from the drawing boards of a committee of leading architects when the $75,000,000 Lincoln Center for the Performing Arts rises on an 11-acre plot just north of Columbus Circle. On the 14th of May, 1959, President Eisenhower broke ground for Lincoln Center on the site of the 2,550-seat Philharmonic Hall, future home of the Philharmonic Orchestra and the first building to be erected. The spacious complex of auditoriums will also include a 3,800-seat opera house (for the Metropolitan Opera Association), a 1,200-seat repertory theatre, and several smaller halls. The project will benefit from an indirect federal subsidy of some $26,000,000 in urban renewal, slum clearance funds. Other needed moneys are being solicited from individuals and foundations. Inclusion of a legitimate playhouse recognizes drama's proper place in what the Center's chairman, John D. Rockefeller 3rd, has called 'a symbol of the United States' cultural maturity and a major step forward for New York City in the world of the performing arts.'

While the Lincoln Center project dwarfs anything of the kind being currently undertaken in the rest of the United States, it should not be assumed that such projects are confined to New York. In the latter part of 1959, the Dallas Theatre Center began operations in its new 450-seat theatre and workshops— an educational-experimental institution housed in a spheroid building for which the late Frank Lloyd Wright revised plans which he first drew near the turn of the century. The Dallas center is a graduate school for nearby Baylor University. Baylor's energetically visionary theatre director, Paul Baker, and his controversial experiments have drawn praise, criticism, and the enthusiastic participation of such professionals as Charles Laughton and Burgess Meredith.

The long arm of philanthropic subsidy has seldom, in the

past, embraced theatre professionals or producing organisations. Lately, a change has been taking place. Playwrights for instance, have been receiving help for ten years from the New Dramatists Committee, an organisation supported by gifts and foundation grants. Every year the committee selects a number of promising young playwrights for its program of workshop discussions, seminars with topflight professionals, attendance at rehearsals and performances, 'rehearsed readings' and (wherever possible) productions of their plays by college and community groups. When such a production takes place, the dramatist receives the travel and subsistence funds which permit him to join the producing group from first rehearsal to opening night. Former 'New Dramatists' include Robert Anderson, Joseph Kramm, William Inge, Joseph Hayes, and Paddy Chayefsky. Mr. Chayefsky gives the New Dramatists Committee complete credit for starting him on his playwriting career.

In recent years, the Ford Foundation, one of the most munificent distributors of corporately earned largesse, has initiated several programs of direct aid to the theatre. With the assistance of the New Dramatists Committee, the foundation selected eight plays by promising newcomers for subsidised production by eight theatres in various parts of the country outside New York. In another program, the foundation provided the Cleveland Play House, one of the country's most eminent community theatres, with a $130,000 grant to finance a three-year program which enabled the organisation to enter the professional ranks of theatres employing members of Actors' Equity Association (the actors' union). The three-year experiment concludes with a Play House tour of middle-western states. In yet another field, the Ford Foundation has made grants of $10,000 each to ten stage directors 'to help stimulate their creative development'. The foregoing subsidies were embraced in an $800,000 'grants-in-aid' program which included stipends for poets, novelists, musical artists, painters and sculptors.

## IV. THE PROFESSIONAL STAGE.

Since the rise of the 'little theatre' movement in the 1920's, play production has been roughly—sometimes sharply—divided between professional and amateurs. Broadway oriented professionals tended to disdain or at least to disregard the amateurs. Provincially oriented amateurs traditionally scorned the professionals. As the academic theatre grew in numbers and importance—by 1959, there were close to 400 colleges and universities offering drama degrees of some kind—the amateurs gained an ally. The teachers found themselves for the most part in sympathy with the prevalent anti-Broadwayism of the provinces. As the years passed, it grew increasingly evident that neither a dwindling commercial theatre nor a largely amateur community theatre (nor even the demands for teachers in the burgeoning groves of theatrical academia) could accommodate the increasing number of young people eager to make their careers in the living theatre. More and bigger departments, millions spent on the most modern, best equipped physical facilities were not alone the answer. They were in some cases an illusion.

Perceptive educational theatre people began increasingly to realise the need for new approaches. In 1958, Edward C. Cole of Yale University in his address as retiring president of the American Educational Theatre Association, challenged the assumption that the nation's approximately 13,000 regional (and mostly nonprofessional) producing groups had 'more than taken the place' of 'the road'. After reminding his listeners of all the elements that go to make up authentic professionalism in the theatre, Mr. Cole observed: 'We ... cannot by force of circumstances equal (the professional theatre) ... We should not attempt to take its place. We should rather work for its achievement throughout the country'.

Like others seriously concerned with the future of the theatre in America, Mr. Cole has been looking for ways to bridge the 'great chasm which now contains the dead hopes of so many promising young actors who have gone to New York, failed to get parts, and gone home with disillusion and disappointment'. This brighter future, in Mr. Cole's view, 'begins with more opportunities for aspiring young actors, directors, designers, and writers, opportunities to work steadily at their art, and to live by it. It depends on creating new professional theatre situations'. Yale's drama school director cited the summer theatres of thirty years ago, the more recent Equity Library Theatre, the ANTA Experimental Theatre, the Off-Broadway movement which has created a 'vital and profitable second theatre in New York'.

Uncertain himself whether he was 'dreaming' or 'prophesying', Mr. Cole speculated that: 'Sometime, somewhere, a group or groups of people, trained in theatre as well as we can train them, but strongly inspired in theatre by their own emotions, are going to pioneer a new path. They are going to find the way to take Off-Broadway *off Manhattan* . . .' With hard work, frugal living, a modicum of philanthropic support, these young people were envisaged by Mr. Cole as pioneers of a new theatre. 'By the quality of their productions, they are going to attract ever bigger audiences', he declared, 'until finally they will become a part of our American cultural pattern, the residential professional theatre'.

Perhaps the pattern has begun to emerge. Perhaps the element of professionalism apparent in the Shakespeare festivals, the foundation support of programs aimed to raise standards (not merely buildings), the vitality of Off-Broadway, the determined attempts (in the face of all difficulties) to maintain existing professional stock companies and start new ones, the stimulus to craftsmanship provided by the New Dramatists Committee, the efforts of ANTA and other organisations—perhaps all of these developments are part of an equation in which the professional state is the common denominator.

Early in 1959, the American National Theatre and Academy held a four-day assembly which some ANTA veterans considered the organisation's most important conference in its 24-year history. As defined by ANTA's executive director, Willard Swire, the purpose of the assembly was 'to further weld together participants in the three major categories of American theatre—community, educational, and professional. It is our hope that through the co-operation of the New York professional theatre we may provide panel discussions of such unique and special value that the assembly may become an annual event to which theatre people throughout the country eagerly look forward'. Whether or not this happy state was fully achieved, the more than 250 representatives of seventeen ANTA chapters from all principal regions of the United States were greeted with an agenda which blended practicality and hospitality. Participants in the series of panel discussions and meetings included Ralph Bellamy, president of Actors' Equity Association, Helen Hayes, Raymond Massey, Harold Clurman and ranking professionals in virtually every other field of theatrical production. Elia Kazan, with scenic designer Boris Aronson and lighting designer Tharon Musser, traced the history of Mr. Kazan's production of 'J.B.' from script to the stage of the ANTA Theatre. Whatever its ultimate significance, the effect of the assembly was to produce a new degree of *rapprochement* among the spokesmen for community, educational and professional theatre.

Out of this greater communion and mutual respect may come an important stimulus to the national theatre which has been an American dream for more than half a century. Public opinion has not reached the point at which the U.S. equivalent of a Comédie Française, a German state theatre, or a Moscow Art Theatre would be possible. But there are signs in many directions of a maturing process. Now that Congress has designated a site for a Cultural Center, the next step can be taken.

The case for a national theatre has been stated frequently, ardently, and eloquently down the years. In the words of one such earnest plea:

'With a National Theatre at the dramatic centre of the United States giving an ever-increasing round of great plays, occasionally perhaps sending its company to other cities and always holding up the banner of dramatic art and progress, there would be hopefulness where there is now uneasiness, not to say dismay. Is not all that a fruitful thing to consider?'

It is indeed—as fruitful today as when Joseph I. C. Clarke posed the question in 1897.

# IN FRANCE

## Jean-Pierre Lenoir

*'Je hais les coeurs pusillanimes qui, pour trop prévoir
les suites des choses, n'osent rien entreprendre.'*
Molière.

THIS is all very well for an actor. Even a playwright can make
it pay dividends although, in this domain, Molière skated on
rather thin ice on several famous occasions. But for an Administrator, it is a philosophy which cannot fail to bring his activities to a premature and somewhat painful conclusion.

The salary which the Administrator-General of the Comédie-
Française receives is a closely-guarded secret, but it is difficult
to imagine a sum so princely as to fully compensate the bundles
of damaged nerves and perjured reputations which scuttle out
of the venerable building in the Palais-Royal every six years (et
encore!), bury themselves in mountain fastnesses and try to
pretend it was all a horrible dream.

M. Pierre-Aimé Touchard, who not only survived a full term
of office in the *Maison de Molière* between 1947 and 1953 but
actually emerged with health and strength unimpaired, recently
concluded a list of the qualities of the ideal Administrator in
the following terms: 'He must be able to draw up a season's
programme to satisfy his Minister, the season-ticket holders, the
snobs, the people who pay for their seats, the students who get
them for almost nothing, the Sociétaires, the Pensionnaires, the
authors . . .'

For those who remain candidates for the post, let me add that this quotation is taken from Paragraph 12 of M. Touchard's list of desiderata. And even such a comprehensive catalogue as this contains one or two omissions which the most modest student of twentieth-century labour relations would point out in a trice.

M. Pierre Descaves, whose six-year term of office is drawing to a close even as I write these lines, took over from M. Touchard in 1953. It is not so much the odiousness as the impossibility of comparisons here which drives them from consideration. M. Descaves, whom many British readers saw during the March visit to the Palace Theatre this year, is a bland and genial man not given to jollity but not adverse to well-tempered wit. He would, I am sure, be the first to admit that during his six years at the *Théâtre Français*—as the purists and the bus-conductors continue to call it—he has had few difficulties with his Minister(s).

Yet, in more settled times, his progressive policy would certainly have buried him, as the head of what many Frenchmen persist in regarding as a museum, neck-deep in ministerial fire and brimstone.

For Pierre Descaves it is who has finally begun the formidable task of committing the repertoire of the Comédie-Française to film. Under the genial guidance of M. Jean Meyer, the first, and not by any means the easiest, step was taken when *Le Bourgeois Gentilhomme* was filmed at the end of last year and the long association between the actors of the Comédie and the cinema which began in 1908 with Le Bargy's famous *L'Assassinat du Duc de Guise,* made with an almost exclusively Comédie-Française cast, reached its logical conclusion.

It is also M. Descaves who has at last succeeded in bringing the controversial Jean Anouilh into the National Theatre of

France. It is true that *La Foire d'empoigne,* which I had hoped to see before this article was written, is not to be produced now before the autumn. The fact remains that it has passed that short but tenebrous passage between the Comité de Lecture and the Salle des Répétitions which has proved the despair of many aspiring authors. The rest is only a matter of patience and perspiration.

M. Descaves's plan to invite Mr. Peter Brook to produce a play from the Shakespearean repertory at the Comédie-Française is, unfortunately, not likely to mature if, as seems most probable as I write, a new Administrator is appointed before the 1959-1960 season begins.

Pierre-Aimé Touchard was Administrator of the Comédie during a particularly difficult period. When he assumed office in 1947, the great unheaval caused by the exodus of Jean-Louis Barrault had not yet quieted itself. Throughout his office he was to be plagued by the problem of the second theatre, the Salle Luxemburg or the Odéon as it is still called, which his company detested and did their best, by fair means or foul, to get rid of.

He also had innumerable personal difficulties to contend with among the *comédiens-français,* most of them traceable either directly or indirectly to his open and unashamed support of Jean Meyer and the 'new' approach to the classics which he represented. These troubles came to a head in the 1950-1951 season when he was driven to request the Ministry to consider the secession of the Salle Luxembourg. Calmed by such incontrovertible evidence of his sympathies (and not altogether indifferent to the fact that Barrault would inevitably be given the direction of the independent Odéon), the company then rapidly withdrew their demands, although whether this was for the ultimate good of the French theatre or not remains a matter of opinion.

This question of the *deuxieme salle* apart, M. Touchard had ample opportunities to prove during those six stormy years, that he possessed an inexhaustible supply of tact. Not the least demanding of the situations with which he had to deal was the duel to which an irate journalist challenged Jean Meyer in 1950. This incident he managed to settle without loss of blood or prestige on either side.

The Odéon must be one of the unluckiest theatres in France. In nearly two centuries of existence it has hardly ever ceased to be a thorn in the flesh of its directors.

The King's brother, Monsieur, who paid the two millions for its erection in 1782, saw it in use for a very short while before the Revolution spoiled his social plans. Even with a subsidy of 100,000 francs, it rarely managed to top 200 francs a perform-ance. In 1796 when it reopened and things were in dire straits, a fire reduced the building very opportunely to ashes.

During the nineteenth century, even such names as Frédérick Lemaître and Mademoiselle Georges could do nothing against what appeared to be a popular conspiracy and the success of Sarah Bernhardt in Copée's *Le Passant* came so unexpectedly in 1869 that the Director of the moment died, so we are assured, of a heart attack on the opening night!

Antoine seemed to have lifted the curse in the first years of this century, but since its absorption into the Comédie-Fran-çaise, it has been a constant source of problems. It is unpopular both with the public and with the actors—especially with those unfortunates who are required to give performances in both theatres on the same evening.

It seems likely at the moment of writing, that Jean-Louis Bar-rault will be offered the management of the Salle Luxembourg as an independent, but of course, state-subsidised, theatre. If this happens, it will mean a renewed lease of life for this sadly-neglected theatre and, since M. Barrault is known to favour a revival of the classics-with-a-small-c (he is particularly fond of the repertoire of the first forty years of the century) this will automatically entail a reappraisal of the Comédie-Française's policy.*

We may consequently expect to see more emphasis placed upon revivals of Molière, Racine and Corneille at the Salle Richelieu in the near future. And this supposition, in its turn, brings us to the problem of the company.

The average age of the present troupe of *comédiens-français* is probably lower than it has ever been before in the history of the theatre. This is, on the face of it, a happy state of affairs. But, although it is due principally to the gradual assumption of power by the younger element led by the ubiquitous Jean Meyer —the exponents *par excellence* of the cold shoulder and a gentle nudge technique—which has characterised the post-war period, there is more to it than this alone.

No doubt the present statute of the actors leaves a great deal to be desired. While the younger members of the company are quite happy to take advantage of the unique experience offered them by the vast repertoire of the Comédie, relying upon their summer film-making, broadcasting and television work and the odd provincial tour to bring their salaries up to subsistence level, the same is not true of their elders.

It has always been a policy of the Comédie-Française to do its best to encourage well-known artists from the commercial theatre to join the troupe, if only as temporary members, but the number of unhappy experiences of this sort is legion. The names of Jean Marais and the great Raimu (whose *Bourgeois*

---

* M. Barrault has in fact now been made director of the Odéon since the above article went to press.

*Gentilhomme* led directly to Jean-Louis Vaudoyer's resignation from the post of Administrator) spring readily to mind.

In the sphere of comedy, the situation is not serious. Robert Hirsch is a man of amazing versatility who, in his 'star' rôles, can fill the 'Salle Richelieu' even on Tuesday evenings. His talents, allied to those of Jacques Charon—the man with the most eloquent sneer in Europe—and Jean Meyer and sustained by the experience of such widely-experienced artists as Louis Seigneur, are capable of tackling most of the Molière repertoire.

For the great tragedies, however, it is another matter. I remember, with a most satisfying chill of the blood, Lise Delamare's wondrous Bajazet last season but, with the greatest of good will, my recollections, as far as the present members of the company are concerned, go no further within recent years.

The Conservatoire is always there, happily, and from its yearly contribution to the ranks at the Palais-Royal may yet come the salvation of tragedy, but more immediate hope probably lies in such actresses as Maria Casarès (at present with the T.N.P.), Catherine Sellers, Loleh Bellon and Jeanne Moreau, could they but be tempted into the fold.

The observation is, I suppose, not original but it often seems to me that the root of the problem of the Comédie-Française is not so much to present the repertory in an up-to-date manner as to bring the public's conception of it into line with modern developments.

Ever since Louis Jouvet's production of *L'Ecole des Femmes* in 1936, the influence of the producers of the Cartel has been making itself more and more apparent in the style of presentation at the Comédie-Française. In Jean Meyer, the pupil of Jouvet, it finds one of its most enthusiastic exponents. M. Meyer has shown on numerous occasions that he is capable of producing the plays of Molière and others in the most stimulating fashion, not as Jouvet produced them twenty years ago, but as he would perhaps have produced them, had he lived, today.

To accuse the Comédie-Française of a retrograde policy towards the classics is to confuse the fidelity of a lover with a widow's obsessions for her thyme-preserved trousseau.

Many people, both French and foreign, go to the Comédie-Française as others go to the Folies-Bergère or the Capucines, to see 'classical plays presented in a classical way'. The difficulties of changing this attitude, of persuading the public, not necessarily to accept, but at least to consider a new and fresher approach to the great literary heritage of France, should not be underestimated. They probably represent the hardest task which confronts any national theatre as long established as that of France.

In the French theatre today, there is a place for the *avant-garde,* a place for the commercial theatre, a place for the *boulevard des intellectuels*—yes, and a place for the Chatelet school of production—beside the Comédie-Française and complementary to it.

The *Maison de Molière* is one of the columns on which France's temple to Thespis is built and, as Mr. Belafonte assures us:

> 'House built on a rock foundation,
> It will stand, Oh yes!'

# IN BRITAIN

## Mary Clarke

Now that the Old Vic has completed its Five Year Plan (to produce all the plays of Shakespeare that are contained in the First Folio) and now that it has returned to its more usual policy of staging English and international classics as well as Shakespeare, it may be interesting to look ahead and consider the part the Vic will play in the theatrical life of the country when the National Theatre has been built.

In discussing any future relationship between the Old Vic and the National Theatre I think it is important to set down what the Old Vic has been and what it is hoped the National Theatre shall be.

The Old Vic for nearly fifty years has been doing—sometimes well and sometimes badly and always on far too little money—the sort of work which a national theatre should do. It is a theatrical institution which, for want of anything better, has come to be regarded as a sort of national theatre and this fictitious reputation (understandably fostered by Lilian Baylis) is now leading to endless misunderstandings.

The fact that we have the Old Vic—and the Stratford-on-Avon Memorial Theatre, and many 'commercial' managements willing and able to put on good productions of Shakespeare's plays—does not mean that we do not desperately need a properly endowed National Theatre, working on a long-term programme and not existing from hand to mouth, season to season.

At the same time, the building of the National Theatre will not necessarily absorb or make redundant the Old Vic, any more than it will spoil the attraction of Stratford as a shrine and memorial, or prevent independent managements from producing, if they wish, the same plays which are in the repertoire of the National Theatre.

The desirability of a National Theatre in London, at the heart of the Commonwealth, has been persuasively argued by many great men and women for over one hundred years. If it was desirable before, it is surely now a necessity, for in the British theatre today private patronage has virtually disappeared and the Arts Council has neither the power nor the money to guarantee any long-term theatre project.

Briefly, the official programme of the National Theatre Movement (as set out by Geoffrey Whitworth) is as follows:

1. To provide in the capital of the Empire a theatre where the people may have continual opportunities of seeing the best drama, past and present, produced with the utmost distinction and played by a permanent company of highest merit.

2. To maintain the efficiency and dignity of the art of acting by providing opportunities for its exercise in its highest classical departments.

3. To keep the plays of Shakespeare in its repertory.

4. To revive whatever is vital in British drama.

5. To prevent recent plays of merit from falling into oblivion.

6. To produce new plays and to further the development of modern drama.

7. To produce translations of representative works of foreign drama, ancient and modern.

8. To organise National Theatre tours throughout the country, and overseas.

9. To stimulate the art of the theatre through every possible and suitable means.

To this list might be added a tenth point: To provide an institution which will jealously maintain academic standards and from which young rebels may break away—as Jean-Louis Barrault and Edwige Feuillère broke away from the Comédie Française, as Roland Petit broke away from the Paris Opéra Ballet, as John Cranko, from time to time, breaks away from our own Royal Ballet.

These aims cannot be achieved by any theatre which is handicapped by shortage of time and shortage of money. For lack of time and money, most productions today are put on in a half-finished state. The commercial managements rely on a provincial tour which will take money at the box office while things are being tidied up prior to the London opening. Repertory companies, like the Old Vic and Stratford, work to an exhausting schedule. The producer can just about get the framework of a production completed during the three or four weeks of rehearsal time at his disposal. Refinements are made during the course of the season—which is one reason why houses tend to be better at the end of the run of each play.

Time, then, money and—eventually—tradition are the things that are needed if the best results are to be obtained from the many gifted young actors and actresses in this country. They, I think, are the people to be considered in the plans that are made for the National Theatre. It is no use signing up the Knights and the Dames for a gala opening unless something is being done to provide for their successors in the years ahead.

It is, therefore, the administrative machine which runs the National Theatre and its subsidiaries which must be put into workable order first. Time enough, afterwards, to look for and rehearse a company.

So far as the building of the National Theatre is concerned, the position is as follows: The National Theatre Committee, starting with a handsome donation from Sir Carl Meyer in 1909, has built up its assets until today they stand at something like £70,000 plus a site in the Cromwell Road which the L.C.C., with great generosity, has offered to exchange for one on the South Bank *when the Government agrees to a start being made on building*. In 1949 the House of Commons, on a unanimous vote, empowered the Treasury to pay one million pounds towards the cost of a National Theatre as soon as funds, labour and material became available. In 1951 the Queen laid a foundation stone on the South Bank and received bouquets from the grandchildren of Sir Carl Meyer.

As Lord Esher put it in a letter to *The Stage* in March 1959, 'Everything has been done that could be done. The best site in London is waiting empty. The theatre has been designed. The foundation stone has been laid. An Act of Parliament has been passed. No money need be collected. All that has to be done is to break through the last barrier and persuade the Treasury to implement its statutory obligation.'

The last barrier consists mainly of fears that building costs have risen so steeply since 1949 that the theatre will cost much more than the promised million pounds and, secondly, of fears that it will be inordinately expensive to maintain.

Let us now go back to the Old Vic. The Old Vic came into the National Theatre scheme in 1946 when an agreement was signed with the National Theatre Committee providing for amalgamation between the two bodies when the National Theatre building was erected. Since that time all Old Vic productions have been presented by 'The Joint Council of the National Theatre and the Old Vic'—and this, again, has led to misunderstandings and to a general belief that when the

National Theatre is erected the then Old Vic company will move in, and the theatre in the Waterloo Road will close down.

Another alternative, however, deserves consideration. Suppose that the National Theatre, instead of being a grandiloquent building with large and small auditoria, is a suitably handsome but economically designed building with one stage. (By economically designed I mean designed with a view to economic operation, that is, not a beautiful but thoroughly uneconomic building like the Royal Opera House.)

This building would house the plays which call for production on a large scale—which means a scale that allows for spaciousness and grandeur of conception just as much as Beerbohm Tree spectaculars. The Old Vic Theatre, retaining its identity, its traditions and its hold on the affection of Londoners could then be used for more intimate productions.

Sympathetic co-operation between the two houses would, naturally, be vital to the success of this scheme and the co-operation might go further. The Old Vic Trust at present takes full financial responsibility for its subsidiaries, the Bristol Old Vic and the Bristol Old Vic School. Here has been established the nucleus of a ladder system which might well be developed to include liaison with regional and provincial repertory companies. They could be invited to London to play at the Old Vic for specific seasons, while the resident Old Vic company played in their home theatres. Thus the National Theatre structure would reach out into the provinces and it would become truly national, not just metropolitan.

Imagine, for a moment, the administration of such a theatrical structure. Sitting in a office, outside of any of the theatres, might be an Administrator, appointed by the Treasury and the Joint Governing Body. His job would be to budget for the whole National Theatre structure and to be able to view it as a whole. He would have to know how to offset expensive productions in one place by remunerative overseas tours, television contracts, gramophone recordings, even film work, elsewhere. He would have to be able to get on with the directors of all the component parts, to guide them without antagonising them, and to create for them the utmost freedom of action within their own orbits.

The National Theatre itself would, presumably, be headed by an Artistic Director—not necessarily a producer and certainly not an actor but most definitely a practical man of the theatre. The Old Vic would have its own Artistic Director, and so would the Bristol Old Vic. The Bristol School (which, in this imagined plan would be training some of the stars of the future—and the word 'some' is important because the National Theatre must never become a closed shop) would have its own Principal. All these jobs would involve different kinds of talents and the first major 'casting problem' would be to get the right men in the right places at the right time.

None of these appointments need be—or should be—for life, but all of them must obviously be for a sufficiently long term for serious work to be accomplished. It would be rather like the Presidency of the United States, term of office being limited, perhaps, to five years.

One tends to think in periods of five years because the Old Vic's Five Year Plan is so recent and because it does provide, in a modest way, a pilot scheme for the way in which budgeting could be done. The Old Vic envisaged this scheme as a quinquennium but the Arts Council was unable to support it as such. Consequently the grant was whittled away year by year as the Vic showed increasing prosperity and the Arts Council eventually contributed far less than the sum first deemed necessary to ensure the proper working of the plan. (The yearly contribution was, in fact, cut from £44,500 in 1950-1 to £23,000 in 1958-9.)

The Plan, inevitably, suffered because the box office had to be watched with caution and the artistic risks—which are the life-blood of the theatre—had to be few. The lessons of the Five Year Plan were two: that quinquennial budgeting is possible and practical, and that a subsidised theatre can make its fullest contribution only if it is properly endowed, not for one year, or for two years, but in perpetuity.

The Old Vic has always maintained that the right use of public money is to maintain solvency and, on a larger endowment, the National Theatre could do the same. This 'larger endowment' is the nigger in the woodpile and ridiculously large sums have been mentioned. Yet a number of shrewd, experienced and throughly practical people are convinced that the amount of money needed each year is only three times as much as the Old Vic needs in a season. If this much cannot be raised, Britain is indeed a bankrupt nation.

# MORALITY

## Angus Wilson

The recent decision of the Lord Chamberlain to allow the serious presentation of homosexual themes upon the English stage has hardly been greeted with any marked feeling, either gratified or hostile. It is not really difficult to understand why: the decision, like so many official decisions in England, has come as an anti-climax. The much publicised public interest in the position of male homosexuals in this country, what may perhaps be called the journalistic exploitation (for good and for bad motives) of this interest is in one of its periodic troughs.

It may even be that the subject as a sensational one is finished. Opinion favourable to altering the criminal laws has tested and found that it has much influential and even numerical support. Opinion hostile to such change has proved that the opposition is not as yet strong enough to effect the Wolfenden reforms. The battle will no doubt be fought at a later date but one may doubt if the publicity will ever again be as great.

The administrative changes promised by the Government make it unlikely that there will be any more of the recent *causes célèbres* which more than anything else served to excite sensational interest in the matter. This does not alter the view of reformers like myself who regard the present law as unjust and absurd; nor, no doubt, the opinion of those who fear that a change in that law would have ungodly, or unhealthy results.

Nevertheless the public as a collective body is a little tired, even perhaps blasé, on the subject.

Private consciences are no less sensitive one way or the other, but the outward expressions they find are likely to be more truly individual, less conditioned by the sense that this is 'the issue of the day'. I am sure that this is a better mood in which to discuss a socially controversial topic, but it may well seem an irony that the Lord Chamberlain should give his licence just at the moment when the subject is becoming a trifle 'old hat'. One might even suppose that the authorities had waited for such a moment in the hope that censorship would no longer be needed when the topic had lost its news value. One might suppose, that is if one was not sure that governmental bodies seldom act from such subtle motives and nearly always arrive on the scene late in the day from sheer ignorance and sloth. Nevertheless for once I am inclined to think that the tardiness of authority may be all to the good. The Lord Chamberlain's office may suppose that they have bravely and democratically permitted the stage representation of a 'controversial theme' because the 'controversial theme' has by now largely been relegated to a small column on the back page. There will now be less possibility of plays that are merely written to shock or of ill-considered polemic, however high-minded, than there would have been two or three years ago when homosexuality was still the 'talk of the town.'

What sort of plays are we likely to get on this theme? And, perhaps a slightly different question, what may we hope for? I suppose there's a little 'shockingness' in the subject still to be exploited, but not much. And for social debates disguised in play form, we may be thankful that the climate of the English theatre is on the whole set against 'problem' plays.

Of one thing we may be fairly sure: the proportion of plays

worth presenting will be no greater than on any other subject once the small residue that could not pass the censor in the last ten or fifteen years has been exhausted. But will that residue be small, may there not be many excellent plays that have await- ed this moment of liberation, indeed the more because authors have been angered by censorship into writing against it? I doubt it. Hostility to censorship is an excellent social emotion, but not a very good incentive to artistic creation. If there are plays on homosexual themes awaiting production that were conceived in rebellion against censorship as the primary motive I shall be surprised if they are good ones. Also the incentive for any writer to get his work presented, to communicate, is so strong that it is likely that a number of plays on this theme have already been modified or disguised to circumvent the Lord Chamberlain's ukase.

Here, I believe, we have the first, if only negative, value of his new ruling. Most playgoers can remember excellent plays in these last years that were clearly conceived in homosexual terms and presented in heterosexual ones. There is little doubt, I think, that they were the poorer for the transformation. Little is improved except the author's dexterity by these sexual meta- morphoses.

Or again, how weary we all are of plays in which adult people have homosexual emotions, or wake to the discovery in adult years with shattering results. Why is all this tedious? Surely because it is so false. There are adolescents and even adult people in naïve milieux who suffer such pangs and their predi- cament is a tragic one. But the greater part of men over eighteen in England today are a good deal more informed than play censorship has allowed them to appear. They may be deeply concerned at the discovery of homosexual tendencies in them- selves or in those around them, but not with the kind of half innocent, tongue-tied horror that they show in most stage representations.

Then again we are so often given plays in which after all this labour of conscience we learn that the homosexual tendencies have been little more than some schoolgirl crush. This again was a ridiculous circumvention imposed by censorship. There are many homosexuals in this country whose consciences have denied them physical expression of their feelings. A very interesting play might be written about whether such abstinence strengthened or dessicated a man's life. But simply to present the phenomenon as interesting, surprising or horrifying in itself is to lag absurdly behind public sophistication.

To my mind both *Cat on a Hot Tin Roof* and that excellent play *Five Finger Exercise* suffer from an improbable naiveté, or at any rate, inability to speak upon the central theme of the play. I am sure the new licence to the stage will rid us of this gentility, this once necessary fiction. It is arguable that homosexuality is too limited a human emotion to be the subject of art, it is not arguable surely that if it is to be presented it should not be truthfully or in adult form.

Is the subject too narrow a one to make for art that communicates to more than a coterie? This seems on the surface a powerful argument. The number of homosexuals in society is minute. That doesn't affect the case for a change of law, but it may make the subject too tangential for communication on the stage. This view, I think, rests on a false premise. The factor of importance in artistic communication is the intensity of feeling of the author (given, of course, his power to shape this feeling), not the experience of the audience. I am not convinced, for example, that Proust's genius could not have made an even more telling effect of the claustrophobia and destruction of obsessive love and jealousy in the Albertine/

Marcel theme if convention had allowed Albertine her true sex.

But the number of plays or novels on homosexual themes written by geniuses like Proust will in any case be small. We are more concerned with what the new licence may provide us of good plays rather than rare masterpieces. Here the value of the theme is not its timeless, general application but its relation to contemporary conscience. The subject is no longer so sensational or shocking, but it is a litmus of truth or falsity in contemporary England as were the social attitude to adultery in 1900 or the admission that women could feel physical passion at the time of *Jane Eyre*. It is this that makes it an interesting theme for writers. The falsities are not, of course, all on one side. There are smart, false 'broadmindnesses' as there are hypocritical defences of conventional morality. In my belief it is in this that the playwright may get rich material for satire, comedy or pathos, not in the relations of homosexuals themselves. It is the tangential aspects of the subject that leap to my mind as funny or moving. For example a play about women's feelings towards homosexuality would surely be rewarding — all sorts of women, tolerant or intolerant. How deep can their tolerance go? Can it be really felt? Does it do outrage to their true feelings? Or is their intolerance affronted pride or genuine distressed love? The two best novels which have treated male homosexuality as part of their theme in recent years have been by women — Iris Murdoch and Mary Renault.

Or again a homosexual relationship can be treated as one of the many varying patterns of social comedy in the broadest sense as William Cooper did in *Scenes from Provincial Life*. Or again, if we are concerned with social satire—there are two absurdities not yet touched on. The one mocks homosexuals, the other their detractors. They are these; the excessive conventionality in politics and social snobbery by which homosexuals seek to compensate for their sexual rebellion, and the degree of abuse thrown to excuse their own lives. This last theme Miss Delaney only glanced at in *A Taste of Honey*. Finally if we are determined on melodrama and tragedy, a recent case has shown that society may still destroy the career of a useful, brilliant man à la Parnell for what seems by comparison a ridiculous peccadillo. But each and all of these themes are concerned with the homosexual in society, for it is there that the subject is the contemporary testing point of sincerities and manners. With such and not, one hopes, with either pseudo-shock tactics or tediously moralising (in either direction) text book cases, the theatre may gain from the new liberty.

# SOCIALIST REALISM

## Ossia Trilling

HISTORICALLY, the method of 'socialist realism' in the arts goes
back to the early days of the Bolshevik Revolution. Its author
was the first Soviet Commissar of Education, Anatole Luna-
charsky, who was himself something of a playwright. Luna-
charsky was a reasonably tolerant man. He supported both
wings of the early Soviet theatre, that represented by the traditional Moscow Art Theatre and the Stanislavsky system on
which it had fed and flourished since the turn of the century,
and that represented by its opponents, who numbered among
them such outstanding men of the theatre as Meyerhold and
Tairov, directors both, and the playwright Mayakovsky. After
the revolution he realised the need to keep in continual contact
with the 'bourgeois' west and hobnobbed with the likes of
Bertolt Brecht in Berlin; at the same time he held back the
extreme radicals who were all for sweeping away the past and
creating something alleged to be wholly new and proletarian.
Perhaps he realised that this was in any event a mirage, for, as
it proved, much of what passed for proletarian art was often
nothing more or less than 'petit bourgeois' art; art, that is, that
unconsciously reflected the way of life and the prejudices of its
lower-middle-class practitioners and their lower-middle-class
patrons. The conscious and unconscious pre-occupation with
'lower-middle-class morality' (if I may be allowed to misquote
Bernard Shaw) lies at the root of all the subsequent trials and

tribulations which overtook the arts first in Soviet Russia and then, after the last war, throughout the Communist east, until the coming of the Big Thaw. Even after the 20th Party Congress, when the excesses of the intervening years, which are frequently called the Stalinist years though it is quite wrong to put the blame wholly on Stalin's shoulders, were first exposed by his own countrymen and when their victims began to be rehabilitated, often only posthumously, the battle about 'socialist realism' still raged and continues to rage but common sense seems to be winning the day at last.

Mayakovsky's *Mystery-Bouffe,* the first Soviet play, first performed in Petrograd in 1918, on the first anniversary of the revolution, and revived, by Meyerhold, in Moscow three years later, was the diffuse, symbolical and expressionistic forerunner of a whole assembly-line of revolutionary and propaganda plays that followed. It is worth mentioning that a great deal of the ascetic symbolism of the day was dictated not so much by fundamentally preconceived aesthetic principles as by the mere accident of the shortage of materials with which the naturalistic settings and properties of the pre-revolutionary stage were made. Necessity, being the mother of invention, also brought forth the suggestive method of stage presentation, in which either a part did service for the whole or else, for example, a bare stage indicated a battle-field. This device was no new thing, of course, but, after years of naturalistic representation the meaning of the expression 'this wooden O' had been quite forgotten, if, indeed, it had ever been understood. As the quantity (and quality) of wood, canvas, nails and paint increased, so expressionism began to give way to representationalism once again. Opulence of décor and faithful photographic reproduction came back into the theatre. The habit of artistic selection and suggestion, called 'laconicism' by the Russian critics, was replaced by another need, that of satisfying the aesthetic hunger of the masses who had begun to fill the seats left empty by the displaced middle classes. State subsidies on a generous scale helped in the process and artistic directors had no trouble in footing the bills for the expensive realistic settings and costumes that began to be reproduced with scrupulous accuracy though with little imagination. The stage was set for the hegemony of socialist realism.

Whether it was Stalin who first set the ball (and the heads) rolling, or his henchman, Zhdanov, or some other party theorist with an axe to grind, is unimportant. The essence of the situation lay in the twofold fear of the unknown: the unknown quantity represented by subversive influences from the 'bourgeois west' and the unknown quantity represented by a power greater than oneself, by the simple inability of the uninformed to grasp the significance of what lay beyond their mental capacity. The authorities, being themselves ill-informed and suffering from the incurable malaise of the amateur, who suspects anything beyond his intellectual grasp, tried to impose the 'party line' from above, in mere self-protection. This fear of the intellectually unattainable and the suspicion that the layman often feels of the professional still underlie most of the party pronouncements on the arts in eastern Europe today. Less than two years ago, in a series of speeches calling for a closer alliance between 'literature and art and the life of the people' in the ... 'sharpening struggle between the rival socialist and bourgeois ideologies', Khrushchev voiced identical prejudices in defending the party line against the professional artists. The difference today is that the professional who either stands up to answer the criticism of the uninformed layman or else ignores it, and sticks to his own chosen path, instead of being hauled away, like Meyerhold, is awarded a Lenin Prize, like Tovstonogov.

Irene Browne and Denholm Elliott in Anouilh's
*Traveller Without Luggage*

John Warner, Douglas Wilmer and Elizabeth Sellars in *Madame de ...*

*McBean*

Beatrix Lehmann

'GARDEN DISTRICT'
(Arts, London)

Beryl Measor, David Cameron, Patricia Neal
and Gwen Nelson

*McBean*

Eugene Miles and
Mitzi Hoag in
*Heloise* (Gate)

*U.S.I.S.*

Rosemary Harris
and Jason Robards, Jr,
in *The Disenchanted*
(Coronet)

Maureen Stapleton
and Eli Wallach in
*The Cold Wind and the War*
(Morosco)

*U.S.I.S.*

Julie Newmar,
Claudette Colbert
and Charles Boyer in
*The Marriage Go Round*
(Plymouth)

In the heyday of the anti-formalist persecutions, Meyerhold
was ignominiously attacked and unceremoniously sent into exile
to Siberia, from which he was never to return. What did 'socialist
realism' mean to a man like Meyerhold, who had graduated as
an actor from the Moscow Art Theatre (where he had created
the role of Treplev in *The Seagull*) but had left in revolt against
Stanislavsky's principles to become the virtual creator of the
new Soviet theatre after the revolution? Let him answer himself. Charged with the mortal sin of 'formalism' at a conference
of directors and party propagandists in 1939 he blurted out, in
his tactless way: 'if what I see in our Moscow theatres today is
the best we can do, I'd rather be called a formalist. Call it
Antiformalism, or Realism, or Naturalism or any other ism, it
is pitiful and trashy. What you call 'socialist realism' has
nothing to do with art. The theatre is art and without art there
is no theatre. You can only tell one inept Moscow production
from another by the degree of their mediocrity. If that was
your intention you have done a dreadful deed. You have thrown
the baby away with the bathwater. In trying to destroy formalism, you have destroyed art'. Tairov, the first director of
Vishnevsky's revolutionary drama of the Soviet navy, *An Optimistic Tragedy,* was removed from the Kamerny Theatre.
Okhlopkov, Meyerhold's prize pupil and director of Pogodin's
*The Aristocrats* on an open figure-of-eight arena-stage and of
Gorki's *Mother* in the round, lost his ironically named Realistic
Theatre. Akimov, a leading designer, had to go. The list is
long and has its parallels in the other arts. Everything which
went beyond the understanding of the self-appointed laymen-
critics in the party was proscribed and condemned as formalist
or decadent. What was so painful during this period is the
confident arrogance with which the amateurish party hacks
pronounced artistic judgments. If only they had been more

faithful to the example set by their own master, Lenin, who had
the honesty to admit, in a discussion of Mayakovsky's expressionistic poems 'I am not an admirer of this poet, although I
recognise that I have no competence whatsoever in this sphere'.
If only more of his epigones had shown the same humility!

Today Meyerhold is fully rehabilitated, though the wave of
xenophobia dies hard, and the tories in the communist party are
reluctant to admit their errors. They attacked his young pupil
Ravenskikh for overlaying with symbolical overtones his production of Tolstoy's *The Powers of Darkness* at the conservative
Maly Theatre. But Ravenskikh quoted Brecht and his former
master in self-defence and won a prize for his direction. In
Leningrad, Tovstonogov has staged *An Optimistic Tragedy* with
all the spectacular skill of the original production, and not only
carried off a Lenin Prize for his efforts (which he repeated in
similar productions of the play in Prague and Budapest) but
earned the right to bring the Pushkin Theatre company with it
all the way from Leningrad to the Theatre of the Nations in
Paris. But the most striking phenomenon of all is the return
to the Soviet stage and to the stages of many east European
theatres of all the three satirical comedies of Mayakovsky, in
which the poet is preoccupied with the anti-socially harmful
survival of that very 'lower-middle-class morality' which the
party functionaries had failed to root out by ukase. *The Bath-
House,* which pokes fun at the party bureaucrats, *The Bed-Bug*
which takes the party puritans to task, and *Mystery-Bouffe,*
which flays the 'bourgeois mentality' mercilessly, are the current
hits of the Satiric Theatre in Moscow and are directed with the
same keen sense of the visually ridiculous as that for which
Meyerhold, the original director of the plays in the twenties,
was noted. Bureaucratic prejudice and the right of the individual
to withstand the party bigots who would interfere in his private

life are the opposing elements in Pogodin's penultimate play, *Petrarch's Sonnet,* at the Mayakovsky Theatre, where Okhlopkov is once again in control and where *Aristocrats* can again be seen in its original mould. Pogodin's critical unorthodoxy has not prevented his winning this year's Lenin Prize for the trilogy about Lenin, of which the third and last play, *The Third Pathétique,* has now been staged by the Moscow Art Theatre.

The Thaw has not only seen the rehabilitation of the old 'formalist' teachers and experimentalists and their disciples, but has brought the benefits of greater freedom of expression and choice of repertoire. Theatre directors are no longer responsible to centrally placed party blimps or subservient to their decrees. If there are exceptions to this, they prove the general rule. One would like to know, for instance, why the production (directed by a Russian guest-director) of *The Bath-House* at the East Berlin Volksbühne failed to survive a handful of performances. Perhaps the reasons were no more sinister, after all, than those which obliged André Barsacq to close down his production of the same play in Paris soon after it opened. Or it may be that the champions of 'socialist realism' in East Berlin political circles found themselves too identifiably portrayed on the stage of the theatre where Sartre's *Nekrassov* has entered its fourth year. Hans Anselm Perten, Intendant of the Rostock Volkstheater in East Germany, awarded a state distinction for his services to 'socialist realism', is responsible for productions of distinction that have no more to do with that mystical phrase than Wolfgang Langhoff's at the Deutsches Theater or Walter Felsenstein's at the Komische Oper in East Berlin. Langhoff has been attacked on more than one occasion by party critics but always counters with the irrefutable argument that 'critics must be qualified before they presume to enter the artistic arena'. Felsenstein, one of Germany's most gifted directors—his productions of Janáček's *The Sly Little Vixen* in 1957 and of *The Tales of Hoffmann* in 1959 astounded Paris audiences at the Theatre of the Nations by their consummate artistry no less than his own audiences at home—confessed to me that the term was meaningless, and that he had never obtained a definition of it even from those who were glib in its use. Jan Werich, director and supreme clown of the Satiric Theatre in Prague—which was to have come to Paris in 1959 but scratched at the last moment for reasons that may never be known—gave as good a definition as anyone is likely to give, in the role of court jester, which allows him to speak his mind openly in every comedy in which he appears. 'The impressionist paints what he sees' he tells his 'feed' in a discussion on modern art, 'the expressionist what he feels, and the socialist realist what he hears'.

Krystyna Skuszanka, director of the four-year-old People's Theatre in Nowa Huta, the new steel town adjoining Catholic Cracow, has shown by the success of her expressionistic productions of the classics and of modern works that the official cynical view of the intellectual level and taste of the average working-class theatre-goer is far wide of the mark and indeed the full houses throughout the socialist east testify to the errors into which the party pundits, with their old slogans, are still apt to fall. This pattern, repeated over and over again, is a clear victory for the professionally trained artist and writer everywhere. Once they have been able to consolidate their gains, they will know that the dictatorship of the amateur is forever doomed.

# POLITICS

## Irving Wardle

THE English theatre, so we are constantly being told, is coming out of an Ice Age. No doubt there is a good deal of naivety in all the confident jubilation about the impending crack-up: but plainly it will not do to describe the upheavals of the last few years simply as signs of stylistic transition. Consider the new playwrights. For every one well-behaved cadet like Mr. Peter Shaffer, there are ten raw recruits whose blunt aim is to kick down the doors of the commercial theatre and let in an icy blast from the street.

It is easy to exaggerate the influence of the new arrivals on the basis of the widespread publicity they have received since the cry for a 'Writer's Theatre' went up a few years ago. But their emergence is not an isolated phenomenon, for the campaign against that Boyg-like adversary 'the Establishment' has been at its fiercest in the theatre. The abandoned causes of the Barker-Vedrenne era have been freshly agitated; the younger critics have declared war on the 100% copper-bottomed commercial play; and 'transfer' is a mild word indeed to describe the direct hits that have been raining on the West End from the rebel outposts in Sloane Square and Stratford East.

Various estimates have been given of achievements so far: new plays are said to have broken down the West End class barrier, and to have set about obliterating the dramatic categories. But amid all the talk of realism and social comment the subject of political drama has been ignored.

On the face of it, this seems a curious omission. The most hopeful work of the last few years has come increasingly from the Left, and its exponents incline more to the forthright popularising ideals of Theatre Workshop than to any exclusive variety of drawing-room pink. Nevertheless the new English playwrights (with the possible exception of Doris Lessing) have given politics a wide berth, and the only politician to suffer attack at their hands is Sir Robert Walpole.

Many have been the onslaughts on the Licensing Act of 1737, but it cannot be held directly responsible for keeping public affairs off the stage. Introduced for political reasons, censorship now operates chiefly to prevent obscenity and blasphemy: political censorship is self-imposed by playwright and management. (In Brendan Behan's *The Hostage,* for example, the censor struck out over thirty religious references; there were no political deletions). Nor would this voluntary muzzling come to an end if the present regulations were relaxed, for the main obstacle to political drama is the audience, not the censor.

Audiences have two over-riding objections to it : they are afraid of partisan tactics; and they are afraid of being bored. The second objection is by far the more important. Occasionally there are flare-ups when local opinion is outraged—as it was in Liverpool, for instance, by Alfred Noyes's *Roger Casement,* or as it was in Scarborough when Theatre in the Round began omitting the National Anthem from their performances. But such events are few; and when Mr. George Devine remarked early in 1959 that of all subjects politics was the most dangerous for the stage, he was thinking of an empty theatre, not of one swarming with demonstrators. He even believes that the marginal political content of Willis Hall's *The Long and the Short and the Tall* worked against the popularity of that play.

Generalisations about audiences are at best imprecise, but it is plain that the Box Office rarely manages to reconcile entertainment with politics. Neither the growing allegiance between socialist nonconformity and the theatre (exemplified in such publications as the *Universities and Left Review* and *Encore*), nor the increasing number of young people who are supporting its return to intellectual esteem, have affected matters much. A serious and thoughtful piece, such as Doris Lessing's *Mr. Dollinger,* is cold-shouldered equally by those out for a night's enjoyment and those (as the term is) in quest of 'theatre'.

The Box Office has yet to be proved wrong. Whatever the political convictions of the younger dramatists, realism may be an entirely inadequate instrument for expressing them. Mrs. Lessing's play, for instance, impassioned and well-informed though it may be, is a four-wall piece if ever there was one. Thus, in setting out to portray the anomalies implicit in African colonial rule, she is driven to the laborious and unrewarding exercise of smothering her characters with mud. Representative figures have to be 'real people' as well—a formal requirement which confuses the broad political action with the trivial doings of a group of unpleasant people.

Mrs. Lessing is the only one of the younger English playwrights with any claim to a professional knowledge of politics. The others tend to be strongly swayed by particular issues, to have a deep mistrust of all governments, and, when they express political opinions, to do so with the blinkered aggressiveness that is the mark of the amateur. They do not make politics a central issue of drama.

Outside their circle, however, there have been a variety of attempts, during the past year, to digest a political subject in a form capable of attracting the public. Perhaps the unhappiest of these was Mr. Richard Thomas's *The Russian*, a slapdash piece of anti-Communist propaganda that appeared at the Lyric, Hammersmith in September 1958. This is precisely the kind of thing that makes political drama suspect, for it is a Western version of Soviet realism. Designed to show how a good man can be turned into the instrument of a corrupt society and destroyed when his humanity re-asserts itself, the play is conducted in a vein of intellectual tendentiousness, crude melodrama, and cruder comedy (at the expense of a farcically mannish secretary) which speedily discredits its didactic as well as its dramatic claims.

Another slight, but more enjoyable piece, was Mr. Michael Kelly's *Judgment in Sunlight*, presented by the Repertory Players in January 1959, a play addressed fair and square at the West End playgoer. This is worth mentioning because it extracts all its comedy from political situations, never relapsing into safer means of raising a laugh. The plot—a parable on the danger of combining ignorance with good intentions—concerns the efforts of a fearsomely public-spirited Englishwoman to get justice done in a remote British protectorate. Hearing that a native youth has been arrested on a charge of rape she flies to his aid, freely salivating at the prospect of exposing corruption in high places. But her every move makes matters worse; and it is no thanks to her that in the end the accused boy is freed, for her campaign has led her into becoming party to conspiracy, arson, kidnapping, and murder.

A sharp satire lies buried in these events, but Mr. Kelly chose not to unearth it. Instead he spared a thought for his audience and set about making the characters acceptable. The zealous reformer thus is presented almost on her own terms as a brisk sensible J. P.; while the natives, those responsible for correcting her blunders, are introduced as a stereotyped collection of wogs. Opposition between plot and character could not be more complete.

The only other English playwright to venture into the political field recently is Mr. Ted Willis whose powerful and awkward play, *Hot Summer Night,* collected a good deal of publicity on its way round the provinces and rapidly expired on reaching the New Theatre in November 1958. Nobody but Mr. Willis could have written this piece: it preserved the expected features of commercial drama, but it preserves them for entirely personal reasons. In the opening scenes Mr. Willis soberly prepares us for a workmanlike near-documentary on the operation of the colour bar in trade unions. All is brisk and generalised with plenty of frank cues for set speeches on distinct topics. But half-way through, the play undergoes a total change in character and grows into a marital drama of Strindbergian intensity. Although the colour bar is the pretext for this drama, other devices could have touched it off equally well; and once it is under way Mr. Willis abandons all pretence of writing on a public issue.

This withdrawal, once again, is largely a matter of dramatic form. It is hard to make a documentary sound other than dutiful; and, in the theatre at any rate, one is relieved when it is cast aside for something less chilly. But this is not so say that the subject itself is alien to the theatre. Mr. Willis proves how thoroughly at home it can be in his early play, *God Bless the Guv'nor* which was revived in a rough and ready fashion at the Unity Theatre in March 1959. This melodrama, sub-titled *The Twin Evils of Strong Drink and Trade Unionism,* enlists a theatrical style as a means of expressing a political point of view: the form, indeed, does most of the work. In writing straightforward Victorian melodrama from the point of view of the parental employer, Mr. Willis, without having to descend to detail, is able to make him appear as absurd a relic as the form itself.

This neat contrivance, however, offers no scope for future developments; and in any case Victoriana no longer appears as laughable to us as it did in the days when *God Bless the Guv'nor* was written.

Mr. Robert Ardrey's *Shadow of Heroes,* the most obviously political play to be seen in London during 1958, is also an *ad hoc* piece of work. It concerns the events leading up to the Hungarian Revolution—one of the very few political events since the war to seize the public imagination—and without an initially sympathetic audience it could never have been so austerely written. Even with that advantage it had only a six-week run at the Piccadilly Theatre.

*Shadow of Heroes* is in the tradition of the Living News-paper, a type of stage documentary originated at the New York Federal Theater Project in the thirties. The idea was not taken up in England (except by Theatre Workshop who experimented with it before the war and got into trouble for ridiculing Hitler and Mussolini). As Mr. Ardrey practises it, the aim is to present the facts (stating evidence for them) and to allow them to make their own impression without any impertinent intrusion of creative egoism. And the censor was so far convinced of his impartiality that he permitted the figures of Kadar and Mikoyan to be represented.

At its best the chronicle has a quietly massive dignity which subdues the actor to the task of exhibiting historical event. Mr. Ardrey is at pains to deflate any illusions caused by the unavoidable necessity of acting. His narrator undermines emotional response by stating the names of the performers, and by coolly informing the audience when a character is imaginary.

The staging is non-representational: boxes of various sizes are made to stand for whatever setting is needed.

Boxes, that is, and lighting. Here one begins to doubt Mr. Ardrey's firm restraint, for there is no more powerful invocation to emotion in the theatre than the darkened stage and the disembodied head caught in a spot-light. And however severely he has held himself in check for the spoken text, Mr. Ardrey has fairly let himself go on the stage directions. They are full of atmospherics—dark figures painfully breathing in the background, and deliberate tugs at the heartstrings such as:—'He is thin. This is a society of thin men.'

There is no disputing the accuracy of the play's documentation: but equally it distorts by omission. Kadar is sympathetically drawn (another example of the 'good man led astray' theme), and consequently his administrative life is ignored; Rajk is presented as a noble martyr, even though there is evidence that he was as well hated in Hungary as Rakosi.

These are matters of interpretation which might be defended (even though interpretation lies beyond the play's declared limits). Mr. Ardrey's sympathies also break through in ways less open to defence. There is the matter of Julia Rajk's son— a child not integral to the drama who is thrust forward with all the tricks of pathos at the author's command including a toy bear symbolising his lost father.

The play's inadequacy of understanding appears most glaringly in the scenes of dialectical discussion. In these one finds wily old Party professionals reduced to stolid blunt-witted disputation. 'I have never found anybody without a sense of humour who could understand dialectics', Brecht remarked. Perhaps it is too soon for any humour to spring from the Hungarian Revolution: but the lack of it in this play is one reason for the pervasively solemn and sentimental tone that marks it out, peculiarly, as an American product.

Solemn writing, no matter what the topic, is doomed in the theatre; and, so far as politics are concerned, it is unlikely that even good serious writing will make much headway. Both the remaining plays that impinge on politics are comedies, and by the time they got to the stage they had turned into romps.

Brendan Behan's *The Hostage* is a romp natural, and whatever politics it contains have been put there principally to display the Irish character. One feels that Behan's political beliefs were exhausted in active political life, and that, as a writer, he survives as the Dublin Dionysus, the great joker at whose thunder-clap laugh whole edifices of cant subside to dust. Although there is scarcely a thought in *The Hostage* that escapes instant contradiction, the play as a whole does amount to a parable on the folly of enthusiasm: and thus Behan's nihilistic comedy and the socially positive policy of Theatre Workshop are roughly aligned.

By all accounts George Tabori's *Brouhaha* was anything but a romp before it fell into the hands of the International Playwrights' Theatre. But even without being able to make the comparison, it was clear in production that the protectorate of Huwyat had undergone reforms before it was put on show at the Aldwych Theatre in August 1958. So much comic intelligence remained in some scenes that it was inconceivable that Tabori would have restricted the court-yard chorus to their random and barely connected utterances; and still less likely that he would have written in the final revolt of the Sultan's subjects merely as a pretext for letting off fire-crackers in the wings.

The play, so far as one could judge, was entirely political in conception; and its governing idea—the Sultan's scheme to fabricate native riots so as to qualify for foreign aid—was open to limitless comic invention. Intermittently, as in the bargaining scene with the Russian envoy, one's hopes were realised. But the management seemed swayed by the opinion that the play had a better chance of succeeding as the Peter Sellers Show than as a work in its own right.

*Brouhaha* belongs to the same rare class of comedies as *Romanoff and Juliet,* and these are the most likely candidates for making politics theatrically viable; they are immensely entertaining and, to put it crudely, they could do a great deal of good. It is a pity that the play was not put to the test; the risk was worth taking.

# SATIRE

## Rudolf Rolfs

In many of the larger towns of Germany today small theatres can be found which are in fact not theatres at all, but are classified under the general heading of literary and political *kabaretts*. They use a Germanicised version of the word *cabaret* to indicate that the entertainment they offer is not in the traditional night-club style, but is in fact as far removed from a cabaret proper as a risqué revue is from an opera.

The tradition of literary kabaretts has existed in Germany since about the turn of the century, when Ernst von Wolzogen heard of them in Paris, and on his return to Germany founded some small theatres of this kind, calling them *Brett'l* and later *Überbrett'l*, or variety show. The fashion for this kind of literary entertainment started after the first World War (even Max Reinhardt ran a kabarett, which he called *Sound and Smoke* (*Schall und Rauch*)) and the cultural climates of Munich and Berlin in particular were breeding-grounds for such witty, artistic and often most reputable satirical theatres. During Hitler's regime there was no outspoken political criticism, once the last satirical kabarett *The Four Reporters* (*Die vier Nachrichter*) had been banned.

After the end of the second World War innumerable political kabaretts sprang up as outlets for the problems, thoughts and conversation which had been stifled for so many years, and mostly took the form of non-professional, one-night stands.

In Berlin for instance at one time more than a hundred such theatres existed simultaneously. Even Gustav Gründgens produced shows in his own *Cleaning-mirror* (*Ulenspiegel*) and Günter Neumann founded the *Black Fair* (*Schwarzer Jahrmarkt*).

A few of the existing satirical theatres are already ten years old, among them *Das Kom(m)ödchen*[1] in Düsseldorf, which acts as court jester for the nearby Bonn Government, *Das Rendezvous* in Hamburg, *The Porcupines* (*Stachelschweine*) in Berlin, which principally deals with the situation peculiar to that city, and *Die Schmiere*[2] in Frankfurt, which calls itself 'the worst theatre in the world' and in its strong social criticism forms a delightful contrast to its commercial home-town.

Munich's lively atmosphere has bred several kabaretts—*The Small Fishes* (*Die kleinen Fische*) is a typical example—though they are often short-lived and quickly replaced by new ones. Most of these small theatrical ventures have taken root in cellars, where the necessary intimate atmosphere can be created and which—most important of all—are usually cheap to rent. Expense is an essential consideration since these undertakings, unlike most municipal theatres in Germany, are privately owned and receive no official subsidy.

*Die Schmiere* in Frankfurt, which is illustrated on these pages, has been housed for ten years in the same cellar, the approach to which lies through the courtyard of a Gothic patrician mansion. A steep staircase without a red carpet or marble walls leads into the cellar, and such an approach conditions the theatre-goer to a possible fare of unconventional, off-beat enter-

---

[1] *Das Kom(m)ödchen:* without the optional second *m* this means *little comedy,* but with it *little cupboard.*

[2] *Die Schmiere:* Grease, or oil, also in the sense of bribery; or, a touring theatrical company.

tainment. The primitive interior is a protest against the perfection of most modern cultural institutions, but although first impressions may be to the contrary, this is no poor man's theatre: the cars of patrons and actors alike stand nose to tail outside. This particular theatre seats about one hundred, which means that it contains a hundred different chairs, without upholstery or arms, yet it is sold out almost every day. The programme *Dornröschen im Mistbeet* (*The Sleeping Beauty in a Hotbed*) holds the attendance record, having already received more than 750 performances. The curtain is made of a piece of pasteboard, and the modest stage decor indicates that this is more a matter for listening than looking. The patrons in the front row have to put their feet on the edge of the stage and no footlights separate them from the actors. This proximity compels the audience's attention to the matter in hand, and since make-up can only be sparingly used the realism of the show is enhanced.

The audience in these satirical theatres is drawn principally from the more intelligent strata of society, and in *Die Schmiere* a representative cross-section gathers, including many young people, because the admission charge is very low. There is always a strong contingent of foreigners who, insofar as they can take in the words, get an impression of the current problems in our country, and through the audience's reactions learn many truths which no journey through Germany could teach them. The programmes are mostly given witty titles which prepare one subtly for the content. Here are a few from the repertory of *Die Schmiere* :

'For men and asses'
'Windbag with mustard'
'That must have been forbidden'
'Danger, ants!'

Beatrix Lehmann
and Michael Hordern
in *Macbeth*

*McBean*

Catherine Lacey and
Irene Worth in
Schiller's *Mary Stuart*

Dennis Chinnery,
Barrie Ingham and
Michael Hordern in
Pinero's *The Magistrate*

*McBean*

Pauline Jameson
and Derek Francis
in Molière's
*Tartuffe*

Zoe Caldwell and
Edith Evans in
*All's Well That Ends Well*
(Stratford)

*McBean*

Hugh Griffith and
Barbara Jefford in
Shelley's *The Cenci*
(Old Vic)

Miles Malleson as *Sganarelle* in the Old Vic production of Molière's play

'Children pay double'.
'In Camera'
'Why does a worm cough?'
'The ABC of hollow teeth'
'The sleeping beauty in a hotbed'
'The hour-hand is warped'
'Decoys must be ducked'
'. . . hangs on the wall'
'The devil in a rosy shirt'
'Grown-ups are also human'
'Families may make coffee here'
'Gutter tragedy'
'Mauve lady-bird in his beard'
'Dead rat in the lemonade-bottle'
'A penny per corpse'
'Hurrah, we are breathing!'

The programmes always consist of songs, political sketches and recitations. Up to now they have been entirely uncensored and often seem to an uninitiated spectator outrageously vindictive. Government organisations and public figures are openly ridiculed in sketches or songs. Here is an example:

Ballad (to be sung headless):

Attention! Don't be old-fashioned but move with the times
Without your head!
Authorised depots accept heads and
On surrendering your head you will receive
An air-balloon!
Feel whether it's still there firmly on your shoulders.
If it's not well supported, don't worry, just turn it in.
Such a head is just a nuisance; it's no good trying to hide it.
Whether pretty or ugly it spoils the harmonious

picture.

It will be much nicer without it, and you'll command just as much respect,

So flush it down the plumbing—we march with legs, not heads!

Each headless person is helping progress—helping the country to save on steel helmets!

You can spot the enemy by his head.

Breasts are all you need for medals (or stardom!)

Headless you will experience the joy of living; headless your face will at last be happy.

Citizen, take off your son's head and throw the cumbersome load away.

Replace it with a balloon if you don't like the look of the stump on top.

Modern decor for the home:

the dressed head on the television set.

On surrender of ten heads of opposition members you will receive a cross of merit.

Attention! Authorised depots accept heads!

Often little significant quips are thrown in on the side and seasoned patrons know that in some such casual aside may lie the key to a whole scene.

It will be interesting to see what becomes of these theatres in Germany. If any censorship of the spoken word is introduced, experience leads one to assume that they will die out. (At the moment, although there is no organisation linking them together, tolerance, antimilitarism and nuclear disarmament are preached by all). Time has already taken toll of many of them and is still doing so. The *Small Freedom (Kleine Freiheit)*, which began as a boldly satirical theatre, has resigned itself to revues with an intellectual slant, and the attempts of the cinema and television to attract actors threaten the very existence of literary kabaretts, which can only operate effectively with above-average talent. The consumption of good, original, provocative texts is enormous, but there is also a great temptation to be content with superficial hits. In no other genre is mediocrity so fatal, yet nowhere else does the audience tend to identify the subject matter so indissolubly with the performance. It is therefore hardly to be wondered at that in the country which has fostered politico-literary kabaretts one can count on the fingers of one hand the kabarettists who stage their own shows.

# MUSIC

## Kenneth Pearson

THE world is divided into two classes of people: those who
when they hear a snatch of music wish to dance, and those,
under a similar influence, who wish to sing; those who like cats,
and those who like dogs. This may be challenged by the tone-
deaf for whom there is no hope, but yet if the rhythm of the
piece is conveyed to them in however primitive a form, they will
rock bridges, march against nations, and still the twitching of a
foot at the risk of breaking an ankle. The inquirer will find a
solid consistency. Poets galore have not neglected the power of
music. Dryden asked, 'What passion cannot Music raise or
quell?' 'For there is music,' said Sir Thomas Browne, 'wherever
there is harmony, order and proportion.'

There is no finer example of music's compulsive attraction
than that to be found in *The Music Man,* a musical comedy of
New York, which makes no claim on the intellect, but instead
bathes its audiences in a therapeutic wash of honest theatrical
sentiment (a brief pause while the exquisites shudder), a rich
score, and a zest for virtue which may console, if not cure, the
most angst-ridden egghead. Among the many first-class numbers
which the composer recovered for this show from the discard
pile on his desk, Meredith Wilson has put on view a song called
*Seventy-Six Trombones,* which is played with such a blast of
brass that Jericho and not the audience seems to be its objective.
At any rate, it never fails to bring *this* house down. If, at a

matinee I attended, the orchestra had marched out of the stage door and down Broadway, I have no doubt that two thousand American matrons would have risen to their feet and pounded after it, so bewitched that in order to stay close to the band they would have queued all day for the Staten Island ferry. The Pied Piper of Hamelin was on to a good thing.

The reason is not obscure. Music appeals directly to the emotions. It demands, except in the more advanced styles, no especial concentration. It is a mystery which makes contact with the mystery in us. It can soothe and stimulate. It goes straight to the heart and catches the throat. It evokes an immediate response from senses otherwise dulled by the prosaic mechanics of living. It carries a greater electrical charge than any other medium of art so that its significance is appreciated by the widest audiences, and thus, applied to the theatre in a popular form, it will assist a play to entertain for five years or more. Under its influence an audience may suffer a release from its tension which it may not understand but which it will pay to enjoy. It strikes deep to our fundamental instincts.

'Mark the music.' It is no accident that this essay on the musical play begins where J. W. Lambert's article in *The London Magazine* ends. Mr. Lambert was concerned with the rhythm of speech, with pointing out that theatre in this stage of its history lacked just those qualities of music which the great playwrights have exhibited. He drew attention to the almost operatic characteristics of plays by John Osborne and others, with their monologues like 'exhilarating arias.' His argument, carried to its logical conclusion, albeit crudely, would lead the drama to that point where, in fact, these speeches were sung. As a critic, Mr. Lambert has arrived at a rational explanation for a phenomenon which the creative artist achieves instinctively.

Not so long ago I heard Oscar Hammerstein expound these very principles as he spoke of his aims and intentions in the writing of musical plays. There was, he said, a need to pace dialogue and plot in step with the music so that the actor arrives at a point where he can burst into song and his audience accept it as the most natural thing to do. Monologues were, he thought, a means of expression which could be sung, as were those passages where a character gave voice to his dreams. 'If I were to write *The Corn is Green* as a musical, I can hear the school teacher singing of her hopes for her pupil.' This cannot be done suddenly, he went on. The audience must be prepared emotionally for the outburst, led to it by the ear so that at that moment where dialogue turns into lyric the concentration remains unbroken. Hammerstein is in good company. Brecht thought so, too. His interior monologues in *The Exception and the Rule* appear in the form of ballads.

But I am discussing the musical at a date in its development where it looks as though it is about to embrace a great deal of social comment. It has taken forty years for the musical 'comedy' to be dignified by a change of title and to become instead the musical 'drama'. In its earliest manifestations (and long may they endure) musical comedy was a rough amalgam of songs and comic patter. No one was concerned to create an organism which had its life purely and simply on the stage; no one strove to give a musical play a circulation of its own, or to breathe into it a puff of genius without which it could lay no claim to art. It was there to divert and to entertain; to do no more.

Music has been associated with the drama ever since the heathen invoked his god to the sound of a wild pipe on a lonely hill, but, if I may dismiss the intervening few thousand years, it was not until 1892 that the first English show which could decently be called a musical comedy appeared in London. George Edwardes transferred *In Town* from the Prince of Wales to his own Gaiety, followed it with *The Shop Girl,* and thus launched that memorable series forever linked with his name. In those days London and New York swopped shows as though they were cigarette cards and have done so ever since even if at this juncture the balance of trade demands urgent attention. However, in the years before the first world war London borrowed the *Belle of New York* and exported *Floradora* and its versions of *The Merry Widow* and *The Chocolate Soldier.* In fact both theatrical centres were then heavily in debt to the Continent. While Victor Herbert provided palm court orchestras with tea and *schmalz,* and George Gershwin was a young man who played the piano at rehearsals, it was Jerome Kern who was interpolating some distinctive melodies into Viennese operettas.

New York was taking no chances. At the little Princess Theatre for which Guy Bolton and P. G. Wodehouse were about to write a number of successful musicals, their producer was asking, 'What's it a musical version of? I don't want anything original. I want something I've heard them laugh at.' (Not so reactionary as we shall see.) Even then the shadow of the future touched the shows here and there. After three miserable failures Bolton, Wodehouse and Kern advanced their reputations with *Oh, Lady, Lady.* The apprentice-butchers of Broadway were unanimous in their delight. Dorothy Parker, probably the most acid of the twenty critics, was especially satisfied. And she noted in passing, 'I like the way the action slides casually into the songs.'

By 1924 Gershwin was in London with Adèle and Fred Astaire and about to embark on the score of *Lady Be Good.* On the other side of the Atlantic Rodgers and Hart had pro-

gressed to the stage where they were writing for amateur shows
to be performed in schools and churches. They had even colla-
borated with Herbert Fields on a three-act comedy called *The
Melody Man,* whose authorship was credited to one Herbert
Richard Lorenz, a pseudonym which strained no one's imagination. In the September of that year Arthur Hammerstein in-
vested 85,400 dollars in *Rose Marie,* spent a nervous first night
at the back of the stalls, and breathed a sigh of relief as it stayed
at the Imperial for one year, four months and a week, then a
record-breaking run. The programme notes place: 'Book and
lyrics by Otto Harbach and Oscar Hammerstein II (Arthur's
nephew), music by Herbert Stothart and Rudolf Friml.'

The development of Rodgers and Hart as the writers of
musicals was of great importance to the growth of this type of
theatre. Almost from the beginning they assumed that the story
was as significant as the score. The plots of *A Connecticut
Yankee* and *Babes in Arms* contained more substance than the
usual boy-gets-girl adventure with a jolly final chorus. (*Babes
in Arms* included some of the best songs that Rodgers and Hart
ever composed: *Where or When, The Lady is a Tramp, My
Funny Valentine* and *I Wish I Were In Love Again*—we were
getting literate; note Hart's use of the subjunctive.) Moreover,
their scores began to carry numbers that advanced the action
so that they could not be sung out of context. This was a bold
stroke at a time when other composers and lyric-writers were
rhyming 'moon' with 'June', with one eye on Tin Pan Alley and
their royalties from the sales of sheet music. How many
crooners were going to entertain the customers with the songs
from *I'd Rather Be Right?* Who was going to take his girl out
dancing and woo her with *Labour Is The Thing, A Little Bit
Of Constitutional Fun,* and *A Homogeneous Cabinet?* John
Mason Brown was writing, 'Richard Rodgers' music seems to

be more serviceable than catchy.' It was not meant to be prophetic.

Deems Taylor, the American music critic, has noted another characteristic fundamental to the work of these two innovators. Including reprises, the musical comedy of the early part of this century carried on an average some eighteen numbers. Rodgers and Hart changed that. Apart from *Betsy*, one of their spectacular failures, the score of which included twenty-four melodies, and *Chee-Chee*, another misfire, which contained six, the two collaborators, who in all wrote the words and music for twenty-seven musical comedies, produced on an average thirteen numbers for each show. The significance of this factor is obvious. If the show was running for the normal time, it allowed an extra fifteen or twenty minutes for the plot to unfold through the additional dialogue. The development of the story became then a contribution with its own intrinsic merit instead of a series of cues for song.

Until the middle thirties dancing in a musical comedy had been one of those decorations designed to remove the glaze from tired eyes. It consisted for the most part of line of high-kicking chorus girls (or boys), or of fresh English maids trotting round the stage in diaphanous chiffon at one-and-eleven-three a yard. Diverting and not unstimulating? Yes. But as with many other aspects of the musical, stuck on like a luggage label. In 1936 Rodgers, Hart and George Abbott put together *On Your Toes* and shared their triumph with the choreographer, George Balanchine, and Ray Bolger who played the lead. It was the first musical in which a ballet had been conceived as an integral part of the plot. This was not quite unexpected for *On Your Toes* was in fact a satire on the ballet. However, the famous dance scene, *Slaughter On Tenth Avenue*, was to set a fashion without which no musical comedy of today would consider itself adequately dressed.

There is one further point worthy of comment concerning these two distinguished careers. In the first ten years of their work for the professional theatre they produced an average of three shows a year. From *Jumbo* (1935) onwards the tempo slowed down to a point where Rodgers and Hart were writing three musical comedies every *two* years. At the same time the run of the shows began to lengthen, from five to nine months. It is doubtful whether any profitable conclusion can be drawn from these sets of facts. No one can be certain that the two writers were taking more trouble with their work. There are many other factors which could account for the longer runs, but it is true that throughout the second period of their collaboration four of their five musicals were written or adapted by Rodgers and Hart themselves, and the fifth was the creation of the novelist, John O'Hara, whose book provided the core of *Pal Joey,* another milestone in the musical theatre, with its scabrous hero and atmosphere of realism which did much to discomfort many of the critics. Brooks Atkinson of the *New York Times* was appalled: 'If it is possible to make an entertaining musical comedy out of an odious story, *Pal Joey* is it ... a joyless book about a sulky assignation.' Many years later, on its revival, when the climate of public opinion had grown acclimatised to the closer contact the theatre was making with life, Atkinson changed his mind.

The book, in fact, from then on began to call the tune. It is as though, aware of their limitations—an inability to create character with any sort of third dimension—the authors of musical comedy have been content to rely upon already proven material, drawing from the gallery of fiction's portraits men and women who had a life of their own. ('I don't want anything original. I want something I've heard them laugh at').

When Rodgers and Hammerstein came together for the first time in 1942 to rescue the Theatre Guild, then on its knees from a succession of failures, it was to Lynn Rigg's play, *Green Grow The Lilacs,* that they turned for inspiration. The result was *Oklahoma.* And when, on the tragic death of Lorenz Hart, this new partnership sought a successor to its first significant triumph, they converted Molnar's *Liliom* into *Carousel.* I feel it is no accident that Rodgers and Hammerstein's least successful musicals, *Allegro* and *Me and Juliet,* have both grown out of original stories.

This more literate approach to musical comedy has brought in its train other benefits automatically contingent upon the recognition of this new force. If the dramatis persona up there on the stage had abandoned his tennis racket for a copy of *Pride and Prejudice,* it followed that no producer would be satisfied with less than the complete realisation of its potentialities. The legitimate actor was on his way in. It also followed that this newcomer would be unhappy with the sort of instructions that bade him 'do something up in the corner, darling'. The need for more compelling direction was urgent. Out of these factors has arisen a new school of 'musical' actors and directors; the one desperately keen to develop his powers to sing and dance, the other combining an intelligent approach to choreography with a desire to interpret his story in terms of the truth.

I do not think I am guilty of miscalculation when I say I believe that all these trends have come together for the first time in the London and New York productions of *West Side Story*; if not come together for the first time, they have at least arrived at an unprecedented state of perfection. The secret lies in the assembly of like minds—and of comparable gifts—urged forward by a dominating director, in this case Jerome Robbins, who, like a Wells Fargo coach driver, holds all the reins secure in his powerful grip. Directors such as he bring to the theatre, and to the musical drama in particular, a respect for their profession and, what is more important, for their audiences, which somehow, with a few notable exceptions, seems to escape the English. All too often I have heard their accomplishments disparaged with 'sheer professionalism', 'tricks', as if there was some peculiar merit in being a happy bunch of amateurs. I am aware that technical efficiency is only a means to an end, but how I wish some of it was employed through a greater number of our own musical productions. I have seen so many scene-shifters—and this *after* the first night—that I wonder Equity does not force them to join its union on the strength of so many personal appearances. If the English musical, through sheer weight of the American opposition, should die, it will not be through devotion to duty. Happily the signs augur well. *West Side Story* is not, as has been suggested, a new step in the development of the musical but the fruition of a number of elements long apparent individually. I hope we can learn.

*Two Americans look at Europe*

# AGAINST?

## George Savage

EXPLORING theatre in English and American universities is not unlike leaving a well-posted highway to drive down an unfamiliar lane. You are quite delighted at first. You have leisure to look about. Because a great deal of what you see is new, you feel something of the elation of the discoverer. You're never going to submit to the predictable freeways again. Abruptly you are brought back to the immediate by a deceptively deep rut. Although you then drive more cautiously, you still are not ready for the curve so sharp you feel you're turning back on yourself. After this, you will keep your eyes on the road. There's no hazard that alertness won't anticipate and reason won't solve. And this proves to be true except for the sign: ROAD UNDER CONSTRUCTION: PROCEED AT YOUR OWN RISK. By this time to turn back is an admission of failure. Still, you have been warned. Certainly it is the mark of a civilised man that he may admit he's been wrong. Yet, go ahead you do, even discounting the ultimate warning: CLOSED TO THROUGH TRAFFIC. By now you've reached a place in the road where you face the unknown or back up over a road that seemed clear when it unfolded before you but tortuous when it lies behind. Searching your mind for a properly ringing quotation, you plunge forward.

Comparing English and American professional theatre has become a profitable if repetitious activity for writers and journalists and a dangerous obsession for everyone else, particularly

Americans. Perhaps no American should visit an English theatre for the first time. Or, if he does, he should post a bond not to compare it with what is done in America. The bond should be substantial and assigned to the Arts Council because it will be broken within twenty-four hours and thereby provide a rich source of income for the arts.

Yet the idea of comparing American and English *university* theatre, because it had not yet been over-done, proved at first to be delightful. I proceeded leisurely down a little traveled road and what I saw gave me a comforting sense of discovery, particularly when my conclusions seemed at first non-controversial.

On both sides of the Atlantic student activity is strange, exciting, fearful, rewarding, and wonderful. Students act, direct, write plays, design, build sets, light shows, work sound, sing, dance, do revue sketches, compose songs, improvise mad, satiric signs, floats, displays, dress up wildly on and off stage, try out ideas of an outrageous and improbable nature. They criticise, denounce, storm and rage. The theatre has never fallen so low. The future, never so black. The past, never so blindly interpreted. Their elders are narrow-minded, outdated, insensitive, and uninformed. The professional theatre is cowardly and pocket mad. The students haven't been to a really great production since the one they did back in ... At the age of twenty-one, they are reliving the glorious past of an age long ago when they were seventeen. With the assertive and the arrogant is the evidence of power and imagination that is variously expressed.

I was not surprised, then, to discover that the choice of plays in English and American universities is very similar. I agree with the Honorable Anthony Wedgwood Benn who said that statistics always help an argument and that, if he doesn't have them, he makes them up. I haven't made mine up, although, while I have numerous compilations and statistics, their correlation is more intuitive than scientific. There should be, however, a rough justice in the conclusions.

|  | English | American |
|---|---|---|
| By native authors | 60% | 59% |
| By foreign authors | 40% | 31% |
| Musicals | No accurate record | 9% |

About 4% of the English (native) plays are originals usually by student authors; about 10% of the American plays are plays not necessarily by students in residence at the time of production.

Approximately 7% of the productions in English universities are Shakespeare's plays. 10% of the American university productions are of Shakespeare. Shaw, the second most popular dramatist, secures 4½% of all American productions against 2% of those in England.

Shakespeare, Shaw, Fry, Eliot, and Wilde are widely performed in both countries. Philip Johnson, Priestley, Rattigan, and Milne are popular in England while America is more likely to choose Emlyn Williams, Coward, Barrie. Wilde is much more popular in America than in England.

The twenty most frequently produced plays in American college and university theatres during the academic year 1957-1958 were *The Rainmaker, Anastasia, The Crucible, Twelfth Night, Androcles and the Lion, The Glass Menagerie, Macbeth, Caine Mutiny Court Martial, Arms and the Man, The Desperate Hours, The Skin of Our Teeth, My Three Angels, The Importance of Being Earnest, My Sister Eileen, Death of a Salesman, Hedda Gabler, Cradle Song, Our Town, Blithe Spirit* and *Hamlet*. More than half of these titles have been produced by English universities. Approximately a third of the playwrights represented by this list have not yet been produced in English universities but, since these are for the most part authors of plays recently released in America to non-professionals, it is possible that the rights have not yet been released in England.

Few American playwrights are produced in English universities. American colleges and universities agree with the English in the choice of Thornton Wilder, Tennessee Williams, and Arthur Miller. American directors are less likely to choose William Saroyan (a favorite of English universities) or Elmer Rice. They prefer Maxwell Anderson, Eugene O'Neill, N. Richard Nash, Mary Coyle Chase, John Van Druten, and John Patrick.

American and English universities agree in selecting plays of Ibsen and Strindberg from Norway and Sweden; of Chekhov from Russia; of Brecht from Germany; of Pirandello from Italy. Giradoux, Anouilh, Sartre, and Molière are equally popular in both countries but the English universities will include more French authors: Cocteau, Ionesco, Beaumarchais.

In America *Carousel, Finian's Rainbow, Brigadoon,* and *The Mikado* are the most popular of the musicals.

Looking closely at lists and summaries, I conclude that English universities tend to do more English plays written before 1900 and more medieval and Elizabethan plays. American colleges and universities do more contemporary plays and often include a children's play.

Out of five plays, an American college or university will probably do one classic, two contemporary plays, a musical, and either a children's play or an original full length play. In addition, they usually give a number of student-written one-acts.

Tyrone Guthrie, Helen Hayes, Norris Houghton, Elia Kazan, Sean O'Casey, and Cornelia Otis Skinner recently prepared lists of plays they felt should be in a repertory theatre. The following playwrights were mentioned in more than one list: Shaw,

William Shatner
and France Nuyen in
*The World of Suzie Wong*
(Broadhurst)

*U.S.I.S.*

LONDON

Fenella Fielding
and Cleo Laine
in Sandy Wilson's
*Valmouth* (Saville)

*Sim*

Alfred Lynch, Peter O'Toole, Edward Judd, Kenji Takaki and Bryan Pringle
in *The Long and the Short and the Tall*

**ENGLISH STAGE
COMPANY**
(Royal Court, London)

Earle Hyman
and Jacqueline Chan in
*Moon on a Rainbow Shawl*

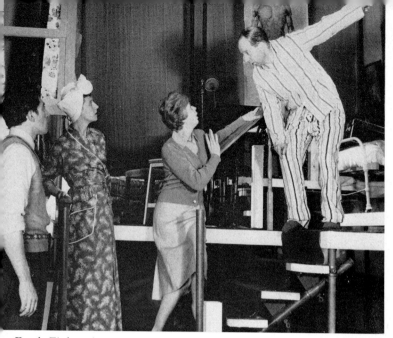

Frank Finlay, Anne Bishop, Margaret Johnston and Toke Townley

'SUGAR IN THE MORNING' (Royal Court, London)

Margaret Johnston and Frank Finlay

*Vickers*

Joan Littlewood          Peter Shaffer

FOUR STARS OF THE LONDON SEASON

Brendan Behan          Shelagh Delaney

*Deakin*

Shakespeare, O'Neill, Wilder, Tennessee Williams, Chekhov, Sheridan, Maxwell Anderson, and Arthur Miller. English and American universities include these playwrights regularly in their production schedules.

And now the 'chuck-hole', that deceptive flaw in the road that jars me back to reality. The quality of the production of plays in the English universities is consistently far below that of American colleges and universities. There are infrequent exceptions but they do not belong to the norm.

The Fourth National Student Drama Festival in association with *The Sunday Times* was presented at the London Student Union, December 29, 1958–January 3, 1959. Institutions belonging to the National Union of Students were eligible to compete. Judges attended productions—sometimes rehearsals—to determine the four plays to be done in London. On Saturday morning after the four performances of plays in the final competition, Harold Hobson, Drama Critic of *The Sunday Times,* evaluated the productions and, with an expert sense of suspense, finally announced the winner. In the 1958-9 competition, it was the Birmingham University Guild Theatre Group's production of Frederick May's translation of *Six Characters in Search of an Author.* This was a consistently fine production of by far the best translation of the Pirandello play that has come to my attention.

Equally effective was *The Crucifixion* from the York Cycle of Mystery Plays, presented by Wadham College, Oxford. This was listed as an experimental production not eligible for the award.

These two productions and those of the Drama Department of the University of Bristol are comparable to the work of American colleges and universities. Certain Oxford, Cambridge, and London University productions grow out of a tradition that implies standards not invariably achieved.

In my opinion, there are a hundred American university drama departments that stage a play better than ninety per cent of the English universities and would equal the finest of the top ten per cent. Judging by the National Student Drama Festival and other student productions I have seen, I would predict that almost no American university production would commit the errors of staging, acting, design, costume, and lighting that characterized most of the performances.

Why should this be? English universities work closely with a carefully chosen few, the ultimate ruling class, who are thought to represent the best minds. The English child who is led to aspire to a university education is conditioned from birth for Oxford or Cambridge or, if he fails, to one of the other fifteen universities. This means an intensive, special program of study and discipline designed for the one purpose of making a good showing in an examination that he takes at the age of eleven plus. If he reaches the highest level, he is permitted to attend a grammar school where he prepares for another set of examinations between the fourteenth and fifteenth year. If he again does well, he goes into the Sixth Form within the grammar school and specialises in two or three subjects upon which he will be examined for entrance into a university. He may then be permitted to take examinations for Oxford or Cambridge. Otherwise he will shop around among the other universities, providing his grades have reached a standard that will make him eligible for a grant to cover his educational costs. Twenty thousand students a year are admitted to universities and, of the total enrollment of 87,000, over 10,000 will be from overseas. The students who are accepted by any university represent a group who have survived a special kind of trial by fire. The assumption is that this method guarantees minds that can be trained to fulfill positions of responsibility in public and professional life; in fact, any one who makes a first (the upper five per cent of a graduating year) should be qualified to excel in any field of human activity. Therefore, why shouldn't this highly selective, precocious group of students do as well as college and university students of America where there is a place for any high school graduate who wishes to continue his education? The standards of American colleges and universities vary, of course, from the severe processing of the universities to the permissive continuation policy of most two year junior colleges.

The reason for this contrast in production standards, I feel, lies in the fact that the untrained student in the theatre will do everything wrong before he does anything right. In the English universities, with the exception of the University of Bristol, the student has no faculty guidance in theatre work. The producer (director) is the student who has persuaded his colleagues he knows most about staging a play. In the City of the Blind, the one-eyed man is King. Except at Bristol, these students will not have had any courses in any aspect of the theatre whatsoever. There are no theatre courses. There is no faculty in Drama. The same lack extends to the physical environment of production. The students will not have a theatre in which to work; the most they can expect is the equivalent of the assembly hall, the auditorium, or some architectural improvisation. The students will have no technical equipment and, should they acquire some, it is very unlikely that there will be anyone qualified to show them how to use it. The question is not why the plays are inadequately done; rather by what miracle are they done at all. More drama often occurs in the wings than on the stage.

The American ought to realize the difference in production procedures; otherwise he will be criticising the English university productions for qualities that are unavoidable in the present dramatic context.

In part the difference must be attributed to contrasting attitudes toward the arts. The English administrations uniformly maintain that the principal justification of drama in the present as it has been in the past, is enjoyment. The student joins a university dramatic society to 'have fun'. If the student wishes to study drama seriously, he must do so against the advice of his tutor and at the sacrifice of his chance for honors at graduation. Serious work in drama must be in spite of his academic obligations, not because of them. No university program may have practical or vocational value; therefore the student will have no training in any technical theatre. The arts are regarded not as a discipline, but as an indulgence, and, while the professional theatre may be subsidised by the Arts Council, private and industrial patronage, municipal subsidy and various gifts and donations, it is still an indulgence, an amusement, a relaxation not to be mentioned in the same breath with classics, mathematics, languages, history, or even the sciences.

The road grows more difficult. I must make an unexpectedly sharp, reverse turn. In America the situation for the most part is completely different.

Virtually every institution of higher learning—meaning colleges and universities as contrasted with high schools and college preparatory schools—will have a faculty responsible for the plays to be performed before a paying audience. Should there be only one instructor, he will still offer in the curriculum a course in acting, in play production, in technical theatre although students in his institution may not select drama as a major. He will have funds for hiring assistants in the technical aspects of production. Students will receive academic credit toward graduation for courses in acting, production, and technical work. The institution will pay salaries and make available production facilities. The actual production cost usually must be paid for by the income from public attendance. In some universities not in or near large cities, the attendance will be predominantly student. In others, near or in large population centers, the student attendance may be as low as 10% with the general public making up the rest of the audience.

From the overworked one man staff, drama departments may expand to an overworked staff of sixty or seventy. In fact, if every person concerned with the operation of the department, including secretaries, typists, departmental librarians, part time assistants, is included, the total figure in some instances will run even higher.

Most of the one hundred and forty universities and seven hundred and fifty liberal arts colleges in America have drama departments of considerable size. There will be various labels: Drama Department, Theatre Arts Department, Speech Department, Department of Speech and Dramatic Art, Department of Communication Arts, School of Drama, School of Speech and Dramatic Art. Certain local conditions influence the size and the emphasis of a department. The University of California, for example, somewhat allocates drama among its nine campuses although all offer drama courses. The University of California at Los Angeles responds to its geographical location by having within the Theatre Arts Department divisions of Motion Picture, Radio and Television, and Theatre.

There are enough educational institutions with substantial drama courses to reconstruct a typical department.

This overworked department—whether the feeling of being overworked is inherent in all theatre or whether it is within the nature of all who go into theatre has never been determined—will have a large enough staff so that there will be personnel of academic rank and standing to teach beginning and advanced acting, stage design, playwriting, literature of the theatre, history of the theatre, aesthetics, research, and criticism. There will be workshop (laboratory) courses in beginning and advanced acting, scene construction, lighting, sound, make-up, painting, and costuming. At the graduate level, there will be playwriting, design, history, literature, criticism, production, acting, and research. In one hundred and eight institutions of higher learning, a student will be able to earn a Master's degree —one year's work after the bachelor's which usually adds up to two years. In nineteen colleges and universities, he may study for the Doctorate in Theatre Arts—three year's work beyond the bachelor's degree that often stretches into five.

This department or school will have between one hundred and seven hundred majors; that is, students concentrating on theatre. About two fifths of the undergraduate's four year course of study will be in theatre subjects. Another two-fifths of his work will be in courses grouped in science, language, English literature, philosophy, art and music, history, and other social sciences. About one-fifth of the total program will be open to the student for free selection. Only the graduate student concentrates all his time on theatre subjects.

This department will give public performances of from six plays annually to the twenty-five plays presented at the three theatres of the University of Washington. Most will add to their major performances, plays that are produced by advanced students as part of their graduate work. There will be a very considerable number of original one-act plays done in conjunction with the writing program. The University of California at Los Angeles, for example, usually produces twelve bills of three manuscript one-act plays each year as well as several original full length plays. The University of Iowa and Yale University will do from three to eight full length student-written plays and many student-written one acts. Major productions will play from four to thirty-six performances depending on the size of the theatre and the extent of the potential audience.

All of these plays will be directed (produced) by members of the faculty, except for those which constitute partial fulfillment of a thesis requirement or a responsibility of an advanced class in play production. A member of the faculty will be responsible for every phase of the production. Students will work the lights, but the lighting will be a faculty obligation. Students will design and make the costumes, but the realisation of the completed costume rests with a member of the faculty.

There is a monumental difference between a student's learning by unsupervised trial and error and a student's learning by working under the direction and control of a qualified member of a university staff.

Faculty supervision results in a high standard in all the aspects of a production. The students put the play on; they do the work; they are the labor force. The production before a paying audience is the laboratory test. Since a faculty member is responsible, however, he will feel that his standing and reputation are at stake. He will make a determined effort for his phase of the production to be good. This will result in an atmosphere where a student learns not by making mistakes but by not making mistakes. There may be a loss of individual initiative, a restriction of personal freedom, but there will be a dedication to make the play a success.

I have never heard—well, I don't remember hearing—an American student say that theatre was 'fun'. It is hard work; it is an art; it is a profession; it is a dedication. Whatever he calls it, he will work with often a grim intensity for the best possible results. Ruskin said, 'Labor without love is sin.' Perhaps the American student feels that labor without a serious purpose is sin.

The return from university productions may be considerable. The box office receipts will be spent for technical equipment, costumes, supplies, and all of the thousand and one items that make for a better production but almost never for faculty salaries or for permanent equipment.

It is likely, too, that the department will have a theatre or theatres over which it will have full and absolute control. An estimated sixty universities have had theatres constructed for them since World War II. Other universities such as Iowa, Yale, Washington, Indiana, Stanford, North Carolina, and Wisconsin had good theatre plants before World War II. There are at least one hundred good physical plants entirely at the disposal of drama departments.

A certain American director may, however, be incompetent and, therefore, his production may suffer for all of his fine equipment and superior acting and production force. Sometimes a mediocre drama department will find funds for an international tour. No system operates to guarantee that America puts its best foot forward dramatically with its overseas productions.

Allowing for margins of error, the American educational theatre productions will be better technically because of faculty responsibility, academic course work, longer periods of time over which a student may work in the theatre, better equipment, longer runs, and many more students upon whom production demands may be made.

ROAD UNDER CONSTRUCTION: PROCEED AT YOUR OWN RISK. I should stop here, treasure the experience of an exploration off the beaten path, and return the way I came. It is impossible, however, not to plunge on.

What is ahead for drama in the English and American universities? The moment has come to add to *drama, the arts,* because the issue now assumes a larger vision. What is said for drama applies to all the arts. The question is not the status of drama but of all artistic expression in relation to an academic setting.

The report of The Committee on the Visual Arts at Harvard (1956) summarised the thinking of many American educators. The Committee exploded the 'myth of the inspired idiot' and explored 'the curious paradox that, highly as the university esteems the work of art, it tends to take a dim view of the artist as an intellectual.'

The report states

One need only think responsibly to realize the absurdity of such a view. When one considers what manual skills, what grasp of composition, what restraint in execution, what capacity for subsuming detail to the integrated whole are needed to produce an authentic work of art, one realises that these are the very highest affirmations of the intellect, and altogether incompatible with any failure of the mind or of the personality. Art is the epitome of order, the very negation of disorder.

The Committee recommends that

It would appear proper for the university to re-examine its relation to the artist. Perhaps the university can offer him ... a continuing and meaningful contact with the best and deepest aspects of the culture ... The hope is that the artist can bring into the university his powers of comprehension, integration, and expression. The hope is that the university can best solve for the artist two of his major problems; one, an environment in which he can work; the other, the cultural stimulation from which his work can achieve content.

Most of the colleges and universities have departments of theatre as well as departments of art and music concerned not only with history and aesthetics but with the practice of the art by both student and faculty. The importance of the Harvard report lies in the fact that Harvard was the last of the great universities to institute a full program in the arts.

The laboratory approach to all the arts is as firmly established in America as the laboratory approach to the sciences. The need for training in technical skills is not vocational but creative. Skills are the ways by which an artist realizes his intention.

The Harvard report continues

The situation of the artist in the university resembles in many ways that of the scientist. At present science occupies a unique position within the university. Other departments of the university are concerned for the most part with contemplating, ordering, and evaluating the activities of others; the scientist himself produces the material of his field of learning. He is both actor and spectator . . .

The scientist in his laboratory presents to the university many of the same problems as the artist in his studio. Successful experimentation in science is permeated with the qualities of intuition and imagination that make it a creative experience. It involves the same interplay of head and hand that goes into the production of a work of art. Just as the scientist differs from his colleagues in the university in being the primary source of his subject, so he differs also in being the only craftsman among university scholars.

The university is the logical place for a well-designed and thoroughly equipped theatre because it is the laboratory without which the theatre cannot grow as an art and a discipline. All artists are craftsmen and, within a university context, they may learn the ways and means of creating truth and beauty.

'The gift which the university has to offer,' said Alfred North Whitehead, 'is the old one of imagination, the lighted torch which passes from hand to hand. It is a dangerous gift which has started many a conflagration. If we are timid as to that danger, the proper course is to shut down the University.'

As far as theatre is concerned, the University of Bristol need have no fear of 'shutting down' because it is 'unwilling to pass the lighted torch from hand to hand.' Vice-Chancellor Sir Philip Morris with wide faculty support, particularly from the shrewd and respected Professors Kitto and Beare in Classics, established a Drama Department in 1947. It is presently under the direction of Dr. Glynne Wickham. The Department of Drama draws upon the Bristol Old Vic Theatre School and The Theatre Royal (The Bristol Old Vic) for technical demonstrations and lectures in the laboratory aspects of the theatre. Many American departments might be visualized if the Bristol Old Vic Theatre School, the Theatre Royal and the Drama Department were all combined under university administration and used exclusively for student work. Here at Bristol are the elements of a university theatre in full swing on a university campus.

I was visiting Fulbright lecturer for the year 1958-59 at Bristol and I availed myself of the privilege of attending all the staff, Arts Board, and Senate meetings. I'm convinced that the theatre has found its proper place on an English university campus. I see no faculty opposition to the presence of a drama department; I am unaware of any weakening of discipline or lowering of standards for drama students. What is most significant of all, however, is the way in which the lighted torch of the imagination is passed from hand to hand, without timidity and without compromise.

In the graduate playwriting, I've participated in a procedure that has brought increased knowledge of writing, a development of personality and social adjustment, and an awakening of the imagination. The intellectual growth has come from within the students, a matter of self-discovery. And the discipline was theirs, not a dogma from outside their natures and their consciousness. Here, I realised, was English education at its best. A limited number of qualified students, a staff always accessible both in and out of tutorial appointments, a Studio Theatre unencumbered by the need for box office (no admission is charged), an informed audience (faculty, public, students and the press are open-hearted to the play and open-minded in critical reaction), a program designed only for the best interests of the writers (no obligation to follow a selection of plays for production announced weeks in advance), a dedication to the freedom of the artist (all theatre instructors are overworked) and the opportunity for the graduate student to devote all his time to playwriting (making it possible for him to pursue his intellectual need wherever it may lead him). The tragedy—it is a tragedy—lies in the fact that this experience is limited to so few when there are so many who are deserving, eager, and capable.

I'm not a guest writing a 'thank you' note to generous and hospitable hosts. The educational, the university theatre, is too important a trust, too sacred a responsibility, to exploit for the purposes of diplomacy. Rather, I want to record a judgment based upon many years of working with students who are in the process of finding themselves creatively in the theatre. Whenever there is the proper opportunity, there is a stirring, an emergence. The growth will vary, of course, and only a few will achieve greatness. Almost all will be better for the experience of working honestly for the theatre in a climate of encouragement, experiment and critical judgment. At the University of Bristol, for the graduate playwriting student, I have observed the finest flowering of these forces in my experience anywhere.

There is, obviously, the overworked staff. Without George Rowell, George Brandt, Iris Brooke, and John Lavendar to assist him, Dr. Wickham would have been only partially successful and many years older.

All of them exist under almost farcical handicaps of lack of space and facilities. I never thought I'd see the day when the office of the Chairman of a department would be housing concurrently three crosses being painted for the production of a passion play at Tewkesbury Abbey, sound equipment being repaired to complete the editing of a film version of *The Pardoner's Tale,* a secretary taking telephone reservations for the performance of Derek Coltman's new play, *Daylight and Champagne* in the Studio Theatre, the page proofs for Dr. Wickham's book on medieval stages awaiting attention, and Iris Brooke fitting the costumes of the three Marys.

Almost all theatre departments in America passed through this pioneering stage. I can remember when my desk was a plank across two sawhorses in the corner of a rehearsal room which was once a temporary army barracks. In the twenties, American college and university administrators had to decide whether to accept the theatre as valid educationally or restrict it to a student social activity. In almost every case, the campus was thrown open to the theatre. 'America is a willingness of heart', F. Scott Fitzgerald said, and this willingness of heart has welcomed drama. The question is not should theatre be on campus but how best to administer it.

ROAD CLOSED TO THROUGH TRAFFIC.

Including stage productions, radio, television, motion pictures, opera, ballet and dance drama, recordings, inventions and contrivances yet to come, the theatre is with us pre-prenatally to the histrionics of our final rites. I cannot imagine an area of human knowledge, a medium of artistic expression, a human activity requiring greater discipline, integrity, courage, and critical and aesthetic judgment. I am inclined, therefore, to suggest that there is no aspect of theatre that is not appropriate, even urgent, to the university. Theatre encompasses and brings to an artistic and visual fulfillment not only the arts but all university disciplines. The theatre arts are with us every living, breathing moment. They shape our minds; they stir our emotions; they articulate and record the dreams by which we live and die. They are international, inter-racial and, I'm certain, interglacial and interspacial.

They are such stuff as universities are made on.

# FOR?

## W. David Sievers

IF my impressions of a six-month tour of European theatres seem rather like Miranda's discovery of a brave new world, it is because to an American the old world is a wonderland of theatre arts in profusion—and at prices unheard of in the States. After playgoing in some fifteen countries and seeing eighty plays, operas and ballets, I realised how much lies ahead of us in creating a truly popular American national theatre. Perhaps the first step, however, is to become aware of what we are missing.

I am referring of course to *professional* theatre. Our non-professional theatre in schools, universities and communities is doing a valiant service in bringing live theatre to the hundred and sixty millions of us who live outside New York. But professional theatre in America, with lamentably few exceptions, is bounded by the waters which circumscribe Manhattan Island. Because of the need to fill this vacuum, university and community theatres in America are, it would be safe to say, ahead of their European counterparts. It could also be established, I believe, that Broadway at its best is the finest theatre in the world for stagecraft and lighting, for the acting of psychological realism, and for the new idiom of musical drama. Having just seen *Compulsion, Look Homeward, Angel, Sunrise at Campobello* and *The Dark at the Top of the Stairs,* I sailed for Europe with a very high standard of theatre as a frame of reference.

But when I stood before the Palais de Chaillot and watched young Parisians buy their tickets to the Théâtre National Populaire for four hundred francs (less than a dollar or seven shillings) to see a brilliant acting company headed by Jean Vilar and Maria Casarès bring to life a classic such as *Phèdre,* I felt a poignant sense of regret that we have no comparable theatre at home.

The T.N.P. is beyond doubt the most invigorating thing to be found on the French theatrical scene, with its simplifications of setting and many reforms on the audience side of the footlights designed to make theatre-going attractive to young people. Its production of *Peer Gynt* on functional, rolling wagons was built around a characterisation of genuine power by Daniel Ivernel in the title role. At the T.N.P. also are to be seen works by major playwrights outside France, which is not the case at the Comédie Française.

The Comédie seems to have some of the same virtues and faults as the Louvre, which displays world treasures as well as many minor works whose primary virtue is that they are by Frenchmen. Standards of scenery and lighting at the house of Molière leave something to be desired, and certainly a mad-cap farce like *An Italian Straw Hat* isn't their dish. But when they come to a major classic such as *The Cid,* then the Comédie Française can give an unforgettable performance in which the emphasis upon tradition suddenly makes sense. The grand old man of the Society, Yonnel, uses his majestic appearance and resonant voice to characterise Don Diègue not as a particular, harassed father but as the very abstraction of all righteous, articulate fathers.

Among the commercial playhouses in Paris, the acting that remains in my memory was that of the fine company headed by Jean Mercure which played *The Caine Mutiny Court-Martial*

Peggy Ashcroft
and Norman Mitchell
in *Shadow of Heroes*
(Piccadilly)

*Sim*

Dulcie Gray
and Michael Denison
in *Let Them Eat Cake*
(Cambridge)

*McBean*

*McBean*

*U.S.I.S.*

Gladys Cooper and Frederick Leister in
*The Bright One* (Winter Garden, London)

Peggy Wood and Imogene Cuca in
*The Girls in 509* (Belasco, New York)

## COMEDY: LONDON AND NEW YORK

Alfred Marks and Naunton Wayne in *A Day in the Life Of ...*
(Savoy, London)

*Boys*

*Parker*

*Parker*

Hermione Baddeley, Dirk Bogarde
and Wendy Hutchinson in Anouilh's *Jezebel*
(Oxford Playhouse)

Christopher Hancock, Natasha Parry,
Ruth Meyers and Michael David
in the world première of William Cooper's
*Prince Genji* (Oxford Playhouse)

Barry Wilsher, Peter Jeffrey, Emrys James,
John Rolfe and Joan Heal in Shaw's
*Captain Brassbound's Conversion* (Bristol Old Vic)

*Tripp*

ENGLISH
PROVINCES

*Thompson*

Anthony Valentine,
Jacqueline Wilson, Frank
Finlay and Charmian Eyre
in Arnold Wesker's
*Chicken Soup with Barley*
(Belgrade, Coventry)

Clifford Parrish
and Ian Richardson in
*Fear Came to Supper*
(Birmingham Repertory)

*Haas*

*Hamlet:* Ian Richardson
with Marigold Sharman
as 'Gertrude'
(Birmingham Repertory)

*Haas*

at the Théâtre en Rond, a tiny playbox similar to many in the United States used by community theatre groups.

France is making a significant effort to bring professional theatre to the people outside Paris, and the Dramatic Centre of the East at Strasbourg is one of five such nuclei. Michel St. Denis, who founded the school at Strasbourg, is no longer there; but his colleague, Pierre Lefevre, is carrying on with a curriculum that is thorough and demanding. Graduates of the school form a Cadet company and give their own productions, while the main troupe of professionals use bus and truck to bring theatre of a high quality to the towns of Alsace and Lorraine. Their schedule of a week at Strasbourg and then seven weeks of one-night stands on the road is fairly gruelling; yet they managed to bring vigor and sprightliness to a performance of *The Marriage of Figaro* which I saw in Metz.

*En route* through the south of France toward Italy I stopped in Vence to pay tribute to the last of the giants of the modern theatre, Gordon Craig. Though ailing and hard of hearing, he was entirely keen and warm in his welcome, talking at length of some trends in the recent theatre, and making the statement, startling considering its source, that 'The actor, after all, is the important thing in the theatre'.

The actor is the important thing at the Piccolo Theatre in Milan, the most forward-looking theatre in a country where operatic spectacle predominates. The repertory of the Piccolo included several new Italian plays, Shakespeare's *Coriolanus*, and an inventive production of Brecht's *The Good Woman of Setzuan*. Among several capable companies playing in Rome, an American would feel most at home at the excellent staging of *Cat on a Hot Tin Roof*, with Lea Padovani as Maggie. (There were only two American 'touches' that would have been out of place in Williams' Southern plantation—a box of Kleenex and a TV set, but they served to show what other nations conceive as most typically American).

Entering West Germany the theatrical traveller is apt to be overwhelmed. There are one hundred and six professional play-houses, each with a permanent company of actors playing gener-ally in repertory (and sometimes on two stages) in cities no larger than our Indianapolis, Pittsburgh or St. Louis (which may have one or two amateur community theatres, a college drama group and four or five road companies a year showing Broadway hits.) It is of course subsidy from city and state governments which make this proliferation and de-centralisation of theatre as well as opera possible.

Although the German theatre is as yet weak in new plays, it seemed to be the best on the continent in stagecraft, lighting and acting. The German-speaking actor articulates as does his English-speaking colleague, so that the traveller who is a bit shaky in his foreign languages will get along better in Germany than in France or Italy, where the tempo of stage speech seems incredibly fast and the actor's art more a verbalisation than a reinforcement of emotion through language, pause and inflec-tion.

The most stunning new theatres in West Germany are the National in Mannheim, where I arrived on Good Friday just in time to see a magnificent *Parsifal* which utilised three pro-jectors, one of them moving, and the Schiller Theatre in Berlin, where Eva-Katharina Schultz was playing a stylish Beatrice in *Much Ado About Nothing*. The finest ensemble of actors was at the end of a long street-car ride in a Berlin suburb, where the Schlosspark Theatre housed a razor-edged performance of *Waltz of the Toreadors* with Roma Bahn as the wife. Brilliant actors are not confined to Berlin, however; in Stuttgart Liese-lotte Rau was creating the role of Sara Melody in O'Neill's

*A Touch of the Poet* (prior to its New York opening) with superb feeling and skill.

The most remarkable actor in West Germany is undoubtedly Gustaf Gründgens, whose Mephistopheles in *Faust I* in Hamburg was incredibly lithe, plastic and ingratiating. In this production the parallel between Faust's medieval alchemy and the devilment of modern nuclear fission was emphasized in scenery, costume and program notes, with a suggestion of an atomium in Faust's laboratory and wild-eyed young existentialists jitterbugging in blue jeans in the Witches' Kitchen scene. Yet this same week these Hamburg actors also gave an absorbing, naturalistic performance of *The Summer of the Seventeenth Doll,* vividly illustrating the advantages of repertory over the long-run system in developing the actor's versatility and resourcefulness.

One of Germany's most inventive directors is Erwin Piscator, who returned after the war and regained his pre-Nazi eminence. His staging of *Mourning Becomes Electra* at Essen utilised distorted columns for the Mannon mansion and portraits of the ancestors projecting from the walls at forced perspective. Other impressive productions in Germany included a 'white-face' version of Marc Connelly's American Negro folk tale from the Bible, *The Green Pastures,* in Frankfurt, an attractively designed and acted *Cymbeline* in the town of Bochum (but why with all the backstage wagons, turntables and elevators do the Germans insist on lowering the curtain and halting the action after each scene in Shakespeare?), and in a commercial theatre in Berlin an engagingly stylised version of *The Importance of Being Earnest*—retitled *Bunbury*—which showed a light touch which the Germans are not supposed to possess, as well as a Lady Bracknell who was a fashion plate rather than an old battle-axe.

After the Continent, the American theatregoer reaches England with a sense of being almost at home. Not only could one understand every word the actors spoke, but there was at last some colored tint in the lighting (a salesman of colored gelatine would go bankrupt on the Continent). If some of the plays in the West End seemed trivial in their content, they were elegant in their mounting and civilised in their acting. Sir John Gielgud demonstrated the virtues of a repertory training by giving a restrained and sensitive performance in *The Potting Shed* and then a week later playing a large-scale, magnificent Wolsey in *Henry VIII* at the Old Vic. Like the T.N.P. in Paris, the Old Vic has found a means of bringing classics to playgoers of modest means, setting a pattern which we in America may someday be wise enough to follow.

The English Stage Company is also making a valuable contribution to the London scene, if not always with a new, experimental play, at least with one of the oldest—*Lysistrata,* an effervescent production that was at once modern without losing its flavor, authentic without being a museum piece, and bawdy without being smutty. Among the new plays, Robert Bolt's *Flowering Cherry* seemed the most absorbing in content, honest in its psychological perceptions and effective as a spring-board for fine acting—in this case the work of Ralph Richardson and Celia Johnson.

The productions of Shakespeare at Stratford are visually more lovely than the Old Vic's and almost as well acted; Dorothy Tutin's Viola remains one of the more pleasant memories of Britain. Any theatrical tour of England should also include Coventry, with its handsome new municipal playhouse, The Belgrade, and Bristol, where the University has a unique Department of Drama which is making a significant pioneer effort to win academic respectability for the theatre, a battle that has largely been won in the States except for such bastions of scholarly conservatism as Harvard. At Bristol, too, in the classes of Duncan Ross at the Old Vic Theatre School is to be found the best instruction in acting of any school I visited in Europe.

By now even the most sceptical would concede that where the people have a will for theatre, a way can be found to give it to them. But if further evidence is needed, it is to be seen in Scandinavia, where both Norway and Sweden have a Riksteatret or professional touring theatre that plays in the most remote villages even during the winter. When I was invited to travel to a small town on a fjord near Oslo to see the Riksteatret perform, I jumped at the opportunity and was amply rewarded with an enchanting musical play for children, *The People and Pirates of Kardemomme Town,* by Thorbjørn Egner. Skilfully acted and inventively staged with portable sets, it was, needless to say, rapturously received by its young audience.

Sweden, which finances its theatre by a national lottery, offered the best example of creative stagecraft and direction which I saw in Europe. While its main stage was being refurbished, the Royal Theatre challenged its resources by playing Almquist's *The Queen's Jewels* on its small stage, using screens, projections, masks, expressionistic movement and all the deviations from realism which first excited Eugene O'Neill's unswerving admiration for the Swedish theatre. Strindberg, Brecht and Thornton Wilder were rolled into one in this ingenious production by Alf Sjöberg. Exactly what the play was about I was never sure—nor was my Swedish interpreter. A girl with a split personality, brilliantly acted by Anita Bjork, apparently won the love of two men and, while dressed as a boy, the love of two women. Almquist was surely a fascinating nineteenth century precursor of Freud, and I look forward to unravelling the implications of *The Queen's Jewels* if a translation can be found.

Stockholm provided another unforgettable theatrical experience at the Drottningholm Court Theatre, where Gluck's *Orpheus and Eurydice* was exquisitely staged in authentic eighteenth century wings and backdrops, which move in view of the audience as the underworld opens up in the Renaissance Italian manner to reveal the Elysian fields.

Nor shall I ever forget sitting at the Pushkin Theatre in Leningrad for a performance of Vishnevsky's *An Optimistic Tragedy*. (I had previously been privileged to watch the Moscow Art Theatre give their affectionate and finely etched performance of *The Cherry Orchard* in London). Vishnevsky's Soviet classic begins as two sailors walk down the aisle from the back of the auditorium talking about the audience. 'They've come to see heroes,' one says, and the other replies with a gesture toward the spectators, 'Let them look at each other'. When the curtain opens on a great revolving stage depicting the deck of a battleship with more than a hundred sailors lined up at attention in immaculate white uniforms, a red flag activated by fans waving overhead and a full symphony orchestra playing in the pit, it is little wonder that the audience applauds. The story then flashes back to the early days of the Revolution when conditions were less disciplined in the Red Navy. A woman commissar is sent to take command of a battleship, and meets with hostility and resistance from the crew. She gradually wins some over and liquidates others (there are a number of scenes of violence including one in which an old peddler woman is thrown overboard). There is also a scene satirising religion, in which a priest comes to lead the men in prayer when it appears they are about to be captured. There is a good deal of broadly burlesqued kneeling and making the sign of the cross, and when the Red Army breaks through and rescues the men, the priest is turned upside down and carried out kicking his feet in the air, accompanied by great laughter and applause from the audience. The woman commissar ultimately leads the men to a final victory which costs her life. An American sitting among these deeply stirred spectators may not condone the content of *An Optimistic Tragedy* and yet may still be aware of the fact that the Soviets are making skilful use of the theatre to mould public opinion, to reinforce official attitudes and to give the people unity and a sense of pride in their history. (We in the States have made a tentative beginning along these lines with outdoor historical pageants at Manteo, Williamsburg and Jamestown, but have not scratched the surface of the theatre's potential as a means of reaffirming our own democratic beliefs.)

If my playgoing thus far seems to be a chain of superlatives, the climaxes were yet to come. As a theatrical capital, Vienna is a triumph of theatre and opera over adversity and privation. Young people begin to queue up at three in the afternoon for standing room at the Opera and the Burg Theater. Perhaps it is only coincidence that the name of Freud comes to mind in Vienna, but in any case the Burg Theater actors attacked their roles in Schiller's *Don Carlos* with a nervous, even neurotic intensity that bordered on frenzy, in contrast with the Comédie Française where all remains controlled and restrained even at moments of crisis. As Don Carlos Walter Reyer was always impressive in his emotional power, and the King was played by a fine old man with piercing eyes, Werner Krauss. When I was shown the opulent lobbies, staircases and galleries of the Burg Theater with its paintings of the great actors who have built a two-hundred year tradition, I said in awe to my guide, an elderly drama critic, 'You know, we have nothing like this in America'. He replied gently, 'You are young'.

Even younger among the democracies is Israel; yet it already has achieved this feeling of theatre hallowed by tradition and cherished by the people. The Habimah occupies this place in the affections of the older generation in Israel. But a younger generation that has no sentimental ties to middle Europe with its legends of *The Dybbuk* and *The Golem* has forced a revolution on the Israeli stage; the old grotesque make-up and expressionistic acting were nowhere in evidence in Habimah's realistic and deeply felt performance of *Hanna Szenesh* which I saw in the little village of Petach-Tikvah. This factual biography by Aharon Meged tells of an Israeli girl who volunteered to be dropped behind Nazi lines in Hungary to rescue Jews, only to be caught and martyred by the Nazis. The title role was played with tragic power by Miriam Zohar, herself a refugee from the Nazis with no formal dramatic training other than skits in a Cyprus internment camp until she was discovered by Harold Clurman and given the opportunity to become the young star of the Israeli stage with her performances in *Caesar and Cleopatra* and *Anna Christie*.

Although national defense and economic expansion are much higher in priority, the state of Israel nonetheless manages to subsidise Habimah to the extent of 100,000 Israeli pounds a year. But Habimah is not the only theatrical group in Israel. With a population of only 363,000, Tel Aviv has three partially subsidised theatres, an opera company, a unique dance troupe called Inbal, a symphony orchestra, and three other semi-professional companies that tour to the collective farms!

By now a theatre-loving American will have developed a severe inferiority complex. If Israeli and Europeans can find a way to enjoy this rich theatrical heritage, then we who can surely better afford it must find a way also. Perhaps when enough Americans discover this brave new world and return as Marco Polos to their countrymen, it will come to pass.

Homeward bound, I ended my survey where the drama began —in Greece. After jostling over winding, narrow roads, stopping overnight at the jewel-like bay of Nauplia, watching Greeks picnicking and folkdancing to accordions among the ruins of the shrine of Asclepius beside the theatre, and remembering the tomb of Agamemnon that had been visited that afternoon at Mycenae as the actor playing this legendary hero strides into the orchestra circle in this magnificent, acoustically perfect theatre of 14,000 seats, I felt that my theatrical pilgrimage had truly reached its climax.

Although Katina Paxinou did not appear in the two *Iphigenia* plays that were scheduled on successive nights, the company of the Greek National Theatre was a distinguished one, achieving an enlarged style commensurate with the size of this great theatre while retaining the inner truth of emotion.

The need for the classic *strophe* and *antistrophe* became clear for the first time as the chorus moved about the circle of this theatre in the three-quarters round, some facing each part of the auditorium, using simple and expressive movement, chant and antiphonal choral speech with telling effect. The Klytemnestra of Aleka Katseli had authority and intensity, and the Iphigenia of Anna Synodinou rose on the second night to such heights of lyric expression that her recognition scene with Orestes drew two rounds of applause. When at the end of *Iphigenia in Tauris* the stage lights dimmed out and the goddess Athena appeared on the roof of the stage in a shaft of white light crowned by the millions of stars above that mountainous and serene Greek valley, I was ready to believe, if not in Athena herself, at least in the eternal and universal purpose of the theatre.

# WORLD PREMIÈRES

*The information given below is gathered from many sources: commercial publications, international bulletins and individual societies and managements throughout the world. The Editor wishes to thank his helpers for their co-operation and to invite organisations to submit information for future issues of the Annual. It is regretted that while every effort is made to ensure the accuracy of this list, neither the Editor nor the Publishers can be responsible for any error it may contain.*

1 May    QUAINT HONOUR, A Play by Roger Gellert.
Arts Theatre, London. Producer: Frank Dunlop; cast: Michael Caridia, John Charlesworth, Roderick McLaren, John Richmond, Philip Waddilove.

2 May    COME AND KISS ME, A play by Lewis Meltzer.
Las Palmas Theatre, Hollywood, U.S.A. Producer: Penrod Dennis; cast: Douglas Henderson, Vikki Dougan, Dee Parker, Thom Carney, Lou Krugman.

3 May    HEIR TO ARDMALLY, A Play by Edna Lamont Stewart.
Pitlochry Festival Theatre, Scotland. Producer: Jordan Lawrence; cast: Brian Hankins, Anne Godley, William Roderick.

5 May    CHARLIE, 22 ANS, TROMPETTE, A Play by Dominique Vincent.
Théâtre d'Aujourd'hui, Paris. Producer: François Maistre; cast: Gérard Blain, Claude Sylvain, Louise Roblin, André Thorent.

5 May    CRIME FICTION, A Thriller by Geraldine and Neville Brian.
Pier Theatre, Hastings, England. Producer: Ray Parry; cast: Keith Lorraine, Patricia Grive, Mark Follett, Mary Gauntlett, Henry Moxon, Anne McPartland.

5 May    ONE MORE RIVER, A Play by Beverley Cross.
New Shakespeare Theatre, Liverpool, England. Producer: Sam Wanamaker; cast: Norman Wooland, Robert Shaw, Dudley Foster, Norman Mitchell.

5 May    THE NEW HOUSE, A Play by Brendan Behan.
Pike Theatre, Dublin. Producer: Alan Simpson; cast: Marcella Grimes, May Ollis, Michael McCabe, Nuala O'Faolain, Charles Roberts.

7 May    SIGN OF WINTER, A Tragedy by Ettore Rella.
Theatre Seventy-Four, New York. Producer: David Amram; cast: Elizabeth Farrar, Lance Cunard, Jay Barney, Bill Gunn, Richard Morse, Joyce Ebert, Michael Ebert.

12 May    THE OFFSHORE ISLAND, A Play by Marghanita Laski.
Cambridge Arts Theatre, England. Producer: Peter Hoar; cast: William Simons, Anneke Willys, Pauline Letts, Meadows White, John McLaren.

12 May    THE GIPSY WARNED ME, A Play by Philip King.
Richmond Theatre, England. Producer: Jack Williams; cast: Max Wall, Avril Angers, Gay Cameron, Edna Petrie.

13 May    THE CURIOUS SAVAGE, A Play by John Patrick.
Birmingham Repertory Theatre, England. Producer: Bernard Hepton; cast: Nancie Jackson, Sonia Fraser, Mark Kingston, Arthur Pentelow.

14 May    COMIC STRIP, A Farce by George Panetta.
Barbizon-Plaza Theatre, New York. Producer: Ruth Rawson; cast: Gary Morgan, Jerry Wimberly, Joey Trent, Tom Pedi, Cliff Norton, Loretta Fury.

15 May    CHELOVEK V OTSTAVKE (The Retired Man), A Play by A. Sofronov.
Mayakovsky Theatre, Moscow. Producer: V. Dudin; cast: A. Khanov, E. Baranova.

15 May    THE SATURDAY NIGHT KID, A Play by Jack Dunphy.
Provincetown Playhouse, U.S.A. Producer: Leonard Barry; cast: Martin Brooks, Nan Martin, Joseph Sullivan.

15 May    ENCRUCIJADA (Crossroads), A Play by Manuel Mendes Ballister.
Tapia Theatre, San Juan, Puerto Rico. Producer: Leopoldo Santiago Lavandero; cast: Roberto Rivera Negron, Ruth Cains, Luis Antonia Rivera.

16 May    DAS TICKENDE HERZ DER ZEIT, A Play by Franz Bauer.
Badisches Staatstheater, Karlsruhe, Germany. Producer: Wilhelm Kappler; cast: Gusti Bayrhammer, Ursula Schindehütte, Ingrid Görres, Wilhelm Kappler, Toni Weidner, Frank Scholze.

17 May    BELLE VISTA, A Play by Thomas Muschamp.
Pitlochry Festival Theatre, Scotland. Producer: Jordan Lawrence; cast: Peter Smallwood, Maurice Jones, William Roderick, Paul Streather, Sheila Keith, Brian Manhins.

19 May    THE HAMLET OF STEPNEY GREEN, A Play by Bernard Kops.
          Oxford Playhouse, England. Producer: Frank Hauser; cast: Harold Lang, John
          Fraser, Joss Ackland, John Barrard, Christopher Hancock, Ruth Meyers.
19 May    THE SCYTHE AND THE SUNSET, A Play by Denis Johnston.
          Abbey Theatre, Dublin. Producer: Ria Mooney; cast: Denis Brennan, Kathleen
          Barrington, Doreen Madden, Edward Golden, T. P. McKenna.
19 May    THE VELVET SHOTGUN, A Play by Christopher Taylor.
          Cambridge Arts Theatre, England. Producer: Frith Banbury; cast: Sarah
          Marshall, Conrad Janis, Anne Firbank, Michael Danvers-Walker, Wynne
          Clarke.
19 May    ORDER TO VIEW, A Play by Reginald Long.
          Connaught Theatre, Worthing, England. Producer: Guy Vaesen; cast: Peter
          Byrne, Gerald Flood, Oliver Fisher, Angela Browne, John Gorrie.
19 May    AS IT HAPPENED, A Play by Sutherland Scott.
          Palmers Green Intimate Theatre, London. Producer: Frederick Tripp; cast:
          James Irwin, Victor Lucas, Margaret Gibson, Joan Lindsay.
19 May    NO LOVE LOST, A Play by Richard Woolley.
          Royal County Theatre, Bedford, England. Producer: Weyman Mackay; cast:
          Elliot Playfair, Elizabeth Alys, Maitland Moss, Iris Gilbert.
21 May    FLESH TO A TIGER, A Play by Barry Reckord.
          Royal Court Theatre, London. Producer: Tony Richardson; cast: Cleo Lane,
          James Clarke, Edgar Wreford, Pearl Prescod, Tamba Allen.
22 May    LA HACIENDA DE LOS CUATROS VIENTOS (House of the Four Winds),
          A Play by Emilio S. Belaval.
          Tapia Theatre, San Juan, Puerto Rico. Producer: Piri Fernandez; cast: Victor
          Arrilaga, Rosaura Andrea, Braulio Castillo.
23 May    OUR GUARDIAN ANGEL, A Comedy by N. Tsiforos and Pol. Vassiliadis.
          Theatre Samartzi, Athens. Producer: Nicos Tsiforos.
24 May    DAS FRAÜLEIN UND DER ZUFALL, A Comedy by August Defresne.
          Lessingtheater, Nurnberg, Germany. Producer: Horst Eisel; cast: Eva Schmitt,
          Georg Kostya, Johannes Sendler, Wilhelm Chandon, Sofie Keeser, Erna Möller.
24 May    V NASHEM DOME (In Our House), A Play by G. Fedorov.
          Drama Theatre, Moscow. Producer: S. Razumov; cast: N. Nikomarov, G.
          Degtyarevskaya.
26 May    HONOUR BRIGHT, A Play by Donald Ogden Stewart.
          New Theatre, Hull, England. Producer: Phil Brown; cast: Richard O'Sullivan,
          David Franks, Richard Palmer, Sally Smith, Peggy Cummins, Patrick Barr,
          Betty Marsden.
27 May    A TASTE OF HONEY, A Play by Shelagh Delaney.
          Theatre Royal, Stratford, London. Producer: Joan Littlewood; cast: Avis
          Bunnage, Frances Cuka, Murray Melvin.
27 May    THE PIER, A Play by James Forsyth.
          Bristol Theatre Royal, England. Producer: John Moody; cast: Valerie Gearon,
          Richard Harris, Emrys James.
29 May    VEJIGANTES, A Play by Francisco Arriva.
          Tapia Theatre, San Juan, Puerto Rico. Producer: Nilda Gonzalez; cast: Lucy
          Boscana, Jose Luis Marrero, Ramon Arbona, Ulpiano Rivera, Mercedes Sicardo.
29 May    A KIND OF HERO, A Play by John Garforth.
          Portcullis Theatre, London. Producer: John Garforth; cast: Gavin Clare,
          Stella Lewis.
30 May    THE WATERFALL FAIRY, A Play by Crinio Pappa.
          Dionyssia Theatre, Athens. Producer: Crinio Pappa; cast: Crinio Pappa, Helectre
          Vahla, Popi Celiyanni, Th. Camenidis, Ant. Xenakis, Panos Xynos.
2 June    THE BOY WITH THE MEAT AXE, A Play by Ray Rigby.
          Guildford Theatre, England. Producer: Jack McNaughton; cast: Edward Kelsey,
          Bernard Kay, Sylvia Francis.
2 June    MR. AND MRS. BLUEBEARD, A Play by Gerald Verner.
          Intimate Theatre, Palmers Green, London. Producer: Frederick Tripp; cast:
          George Gibson, Margaret Gibson, Daphne Riggs.
2 June    COLD WATER CHILD, A Play by Phyllis Kramer.
          Toynbee Hall, London. Producer: Patricia R. Burke; cast: Marian Barrett,
          Lynne Malone, Anthony Stanton, Cyril Stickler.
3 June    UN SIMPLE SOLDAT, A Play by Marcel Dube.
          Comédie Canadienne Theatre, Montreal. Producer: Jean-Paul Fugère; cast:
          Gilles Pelletier, Juliette Huot, Paul Guevremont, Robert Rivard, Jean Duceppe,
          Michelle Rossignol.
5 June    ULYSSES IN NIGHTTOWN, A Play adapted by Burgess Meredith from the
          novel by James Joyce.

Rooftop Theatre, New York. Producer: Burgess Meredith; cast: Zero Mostel, Robert Brown, Pauline Flanagan, Beatrice Arthur.

5 June LES SOLES TRUNCOS (The Maimed Suns), A Play by Rene Marques. Tapia Theatre, San Juan, Puerto Rico. Producer: Victoria Espinosa; cast: Gilda Galan, Madeline Williamson, Myrna Casas.

5 June THE HALLELUJAH CHILD, A Play by Francis Butler. Park Lane Theatre, London. Producer: John Calden; cast: Yvonne Gibbs, Bertram Charles, Malcolm Tanner, Rodney Douglas, Francis Butler, Laurence Barnes.

15 June BIRDS OF THE WILDERNESS, A Play by Bruce Mason. Lyric Theatre, London. Producer: Pat Sandys; cast: Geoffrey Colville, Joan Drummond, Barbara Bolton, Edward Palmer, Gordon Whiting, Kenneth Warren, Prunella Scales.

16 June THE MAN IN THE MIRROR, A Play by Joan Brampton. Palace Theatre, Watford, England. Producer: Ivan Butler; cast: John Clegg, Alan John, Mavis Pugh, Edna Dore, Valerie Newbold.

16 June DOUBLE TAKE (later THREE WAY SWITCH), A Play by Ronald Jeans. Theatre Royal, Windsor, England. Producer: John Counsell; cast: Daphne Anderson, Leslie Phillips, Bryan Forbes, Cyril Raymond.

16 June THERE WAS A CROOKED MAN, A Comedy by Bruce Walker. Royal Court Theatre, Liverpool, England. Producer: John Cervenka; cast: Brian Reece, Gladys Henson, Vic Wise, Harriette Johns, Joyce Mandré.

16 June THE LONDONDERRY HEIR, A Musical Play by Willard Stoker and Ronald Settle. Liverpool Playhouse, England. Producer: Willard Stoker; cast: Valerie Miller, Terence Knapp, Irene Sutcliffe.

19 June TEMPLETON, A Play by Anthony Lock. Arts Theatre, London. Producer: John Gibson; cast: William Russell, Heather Chasen, Oliver Burt, Mary Kenton.

21 June BRIXHAM REGATTA, A Play by Keith Johnstone. Aldeburgh Festival, England. Producer: William Gaskill; cast: David Andrews, Dudley Foster, Tamara Hinchko, Jocelyne Page.

21 June FOR CHILDREN, A Play by Keith Johnstone. Aldeburgh Festival, England. Producer: Ann Jellicoe; cast: Keith Crane, Geraldine Neyle.

23 June THE MOTHER-IN-LAW, A Play by Philip Barrett. Empire Theatre, West Hartlepool, England. Producer: Charles Denville; cast: Valerie Day, Maude Foster, Peter Walker, Victoria Fayne.

23 June TIME IS ALL, A Play by A. B. Paterson. The Byre, St. Andrews, Scotland. Producer: David Forder; cast: Manus Doherty, Graham Roberts, June Watson, Lynn Lamb, Neil Robertson.

23 June THE JOSHUA TREE, A Play by Alec Coppel. Theatre Royal, Newcastle, England. Producer: Allan Davies; cast: Ann Baxter, William Sylvester, Hugh McDermot.

26 June GUESTS OF THE NATION, A Play adapted by Neil McKenzie from the short story by Frank O'Connor. Theatre Marquee, New York. Producer: Neil McKenzie; cast: Tom Clancy, Liam Clancy, Dan Morgan, Tim O'Connor, Alan Davison, Grania O'Malley.

26 June ARIA DA CAPO, A Play by Edna St. Vincent. Theatre Marquee, New York. Producer: Neil McKenzie; cast: Berna Richter, Maurice Edwards, Roscoe Brown, Richard Merrell, Liam Clancy.

28 June A MAN HAS TWO FATHERS, A Play by John McGrath. Oxford Playhouse, England. Producer: Colette King; cast: Patrick Garland, Michael Simpson, Vernon Dobtcheff, Howard Jenkins.

30 June POET AND PHEASANT, A Comedy by Willis Hall and Lewis Jones. Palace Theatre, Watford, England. Producer: Ivan Butler; cast: Mavis Pugh, Valerie Newbold, Robert S. Grant, John Clegg, James Perry.

30 June FIVE FINGER EXERCISE, A Play by Peter Shaffer. Cambridge Arts Theatre, England. Producer: John Gielgud; cast: Roland Culver, Adrianne Allen, Brian Bedford, Michael Bryant, Juliet Mills.

1 July THE MIDNIGHT CALLER and JOHN TURNER DAVIS, Two Plays by Horton Foote. Sheridan Square Playhouse, New York. Producer: Leo Penn; cast: Richard Snyder, Richard Ward, Mary James, Nora Dunfee, Justin Reid, Rebecca Darke, Sidney Lee, Richard Nagel, Mary Jo Davis, Mary Perry, Patricia Frye, Robert Morris.

5 July DER HERR KOMMT AUS BAHIA, A Play by Ulrich Becher. Deutsches Theater in Göttingen, Germany. Producer: Heinz Hilpert; cast: Miriam

Spoerri, Grete Wurm, Martin Hirthe, Karl Walter Diess, Eberhard Müller-Elmau, Günther Ungeheuer.

7 July  AT THE GRAND, A Musical Drama by Luther David, Robert Wright and George Forrest.
Philharmonic Auditorium, Los Angeles. Producer: Albert Marre; cast: Paul Muni, Joan Diener, Cesare Danova, Neile Adams.

7 July  MR. DOLLINGER, A Play by Doris Lessing.
Oxford Playhouse, England. Producer: Andrew Broughton; cast: Rosemarie Dunham, Elaine Wells, David Crosse, Ivor Dean, Annabelle Lee.

7 July  CHICKEN SOUP WITH BARLEY, A Play by Arnold Wesker.
Belgrade Theatre, Coventry, England. Producer: John Dexter; cast: Frank Finlay, Charmian Eyre, Anthony Valentine.

10 July  THE CROWDED ROOM, A Play by Humphrey Tomalin.
Theatre Royal, Margate, England. Producer: Douglas Rye; cast: Reginald Birks, Gillian Francis, John Bromley, Marlene Kaplan.

10 July  ALL ABOUT LOVE, A Comedy by Bruce Brighton.
Drury Lane Summer Theatre, Illinois. Producer: Ramsey Burch; cast: Grace Valentine, Dennis Morgan, Wendy Barrie, Sushelagh Ree, Robert Lansing, Martha Miller.

14 July  A TALE OF TWO SPACEMEN, A Satire by Richard Hamilton.
Repertory Theatre, Dundee, Scotland. Producer: Raymond Westwell; cast; Ken Wynne, Robert McBain, Rowena Cooper, Brian Gilmar.

14 July  ROOM IN THE PARADISE, A Play by Desmond Stewart.
Belgrade Theatre, Coventry, England. Producer: Gerard Dynevor; cast: Leonard White, Ian White.

14 July  DON'T DREAM LILLIAN, A Comedy by Archie Douglass.
Egerton Park Theatre, Bexhill, England. Producer: Richard Burnett; cast: Richard Burnett, Peggy Paige, Kathleen Willis, Pilton Wilson.

14 July  THE PRIVATE PROSECUTOR, A Play by Thomas Wiseman.
Salisbury Playhouse, England. Producer: Derek Benfield; cast: Michael Atkinson, Geoffrey Lumsden, Ian Mullins, Nancie Herrod.

14 July  TOM SAWYER, A Musical Comedy, adapted from the story by Mark Twain, by Edward Reveaux, Richard H. Berger, Frank Gurny and Frank Luther.
Starlight Theatre, Kansas City, U.S.A. Producer: Richard H. Berger; cast: Randy Sparks, Richard France, Virginia Gibson.

21 July  BLOOD AND DUST, A Play by Cedric Richards.
Prince's Theatre, Bradford, England. Producer: Doel Luscombe; cast: Sylvia Melville, David Weller, George Malpas, Austin Steele, Martin Carroll.

22 July  THE THIRD BEST SPORT, A Play by Eleanor and Leo Bayer.
Cape Playhouse, Dennis, U.S.A. Producer: Michael Howard; cast: Celeste Holm, Andrew Duggan, Russell Gaige.

24 July  SWEET AND SOUR, A Play by Florence Lowe and Carolyn Francke.
Edgewater Beach Playhouse, Chicago. Producer: Don Richardson; cast: Melvyn Douglas, Ina Balin, Connie Sawyer, Martha Greenhouse, Leslie Woods.

28 July  DEAR AUGUSTINE, A Comedy by Allison MacLeod.
Royal Court Theatre, London. Producer: Jordan Lawrence; cast: Anne Blake, Kerry Jordan, Derek Martinus, Christine Pollon, Sonia Graham.

30 July  PARDON WIRD NICHT GEGEBEN (No More Forgiveness), A Comedy by Herbert Asmodi.
Kammerspiele, Munich. Producer: Paul Verhoeven; cast: Paula Denk, Arno Assmann, Peter Parsetti, Benno Sterzenbach, Marie Adorf, Hans Magel.

31 July  BROUHAHA, A Comedy by George Tabori.
Theatre Royal, Brighton, England. Producer: Peter Hall; cast: Peter Sellers, Jules Munshin, Leo McKern, Lionel Jeffries.

July  DIE LADY MIT DER LAMPE (The Lady with the Lamp), A Play by Elsie Attenhofer.
Schauspielhaus, Zurich. Producer: Karlheinz Streibing; cast: Rosemarie Gertsenberg, Peter Schuette, Trante Carlsen, Margrit Winter, Richard Muench.

4 August  THE HEART'S A WONDER, A Musical Play adapted by Nuala and Mairin O'Farrell from 'Playboy of the Western World' by Synge.
Gaiety Theatre, Dublin. Producer: Denis Carey; cast: Milo O'Shae, Mick Eustace, Ann O'Dwyer, Charlie Byrne.

4 August  A CHANGE OF MIND, A Play by John O'Donovan.
Queen's Theatre, Dublin. Producer: Ria Mooney; cast: T. P. McKenna, Patrick Layde, Frank Moran, Michael Hennessy, Michael O'Brien, Bill Foley.

4 August  THE UNEXPECTED GUEST, A Play by Agatha Christie.
Bristol Hippodrome, England. Producer: Hubert Gregg; cast: Nigel Stock, Renée Asheron, Violet Farebrother.

5 August  WITWEN (Widows), A Comedy by Ludwig Thoma.

Residenz Theatre, Munich. Producer: Arnulf Schröder; cast: Liesl Karlstadt, Ruth Kappelsberger, Eva Vaitl, Veronika Fitz, Hans Baur, Hans Cossy.

5 August  DAS ZAUBERBETT, A Play by Werner Egk.
Stadtische Buhnen, Frankfurt am Main. Producer: Heinrich Koch; cast: Edda Seippel, Alwin Michael Rueffer.

7 August  A SENSE OF LOSS, A Play by J. W. James.
Library Theatre, Scarborough, England. Producer: Stephen Joseph; cast: Robert Fyfe, Pauline Devaney, Christine Roland, David Sutton.

9 August  EVER SINCE EVE, A Musical Play by Ken Hooper and Ralph Trewelha.
Intimate Theatre, Johannesburg. Cast: Olive Wright, John Boulter, Sheila Holliday.

11 August  THE LANDING PARTY, A Play by R. H. Ward.
Bristol Little Theatre, England. Producer: Ronald Russell; cast: Lockwood West, Frieda Knorr, Celia Ryder, Jane Comfort, Michael Edwards.

11 August  AKIN TO LOVE, A Play by Peggy Simmons.
Salisbury Playhouse, England. Producer: Ronald Magill; cast: Margaret Jones, Geoffrey Lumsden, Ian Mullins, Ann Patrick.

11 August  THE DESERTERS, A Play by Thaddeus Vane.
Royal Court Theatre, Liverpool, England. Producer: Alan Schneider; cast: Elizabeth Sellars, Albert Lieven, Michael Wager, Jeannette Sterke.

14 August  THUNDERSTRUCK, A Play by Ronald Scott Thorn.
Frinton Summer Theatre, England. Producer: James Ottaway; cast: Pauline Murch, Patricia Hicks, John Gill, Jack Watling.

15 August  BOSTON LOVE STORY, A Play by Victor Wolfson.
Bucks County Playhouse, New Hope, U.S.A. Producer: Aaron Frankel; cast: Shirl Conway, Dorothy Sands, Frederick Tozere, Ruth McDevitt.

18 August  LOVE A LA CARTE, A Musical Play by Alan Chester.
Richmond Theatre, England. Producers: Jack Williams and Charles Ross; cast: Pamela Charles, John Morley, Billy Milton, Enid Lowe, Tristram Jellinek, Barbara Joss.

18 August  THE ELDER STATESMAN, A Play by T. S. Eliot.
Theatre Royal, Newcastle, England. Producer: E. Martin Browne; cast: Paul Rogers, Anna Massey, William Squire, Eileen Peel, Alec McGowen.

18 August  SIX DAYS TO LIVE, A Play by James Gordon.
Ivy Tower Playhouse, Spring Lake, U.S.A. Producer: Therese Hayden; cast: Scott Brady, Paul Lilly, Monica Lovett, Carroll Brooks, Paul E. Richards.

25 August  JADA, A Comedy by Paul S. Nathan.
Barter Theatre, Abingdon, U.S.A. Producer: Lyle Dye Jr.; cast: Carolyn Condron, Marcie Hubert.

25 August  A FRENZY OF PEACE AND QUIET, A Play by John D. Hess.
Bucks County Playhouse, New Hope, U.S.A. Producer: John Cromwell; cast: Chester Morris, Signe Hasso.

25 August  EDWIN BOOTH, A Play by Milton Geiger.
La Jolla Playhouse, California, Producer: José Ferrer; cast: José Ferrer, Lorne Greene, Robert Geiringer.

25 August  WEIR OF HERMISTON, A Play by J. B. Sellar.
Gateway Theatre, Edinburgh. Producer: Brian Carey; cast: Tom Fleming, Lennox Milne, Frank Wylie, William Simpson.

26 August  JOSETTE, A Musical Comedy by Jack Reed, S. J. Byrne, and Frances Hall.
Ivar Theatre, Hollywood, U.S.A. Producer: Jack Reed; cast: Josiane Marbais, Hal K. Dawson, Kay Riehl, Constance Simons.

27 August  THE DISCIPLINES OF WAR (later BOYS, IT'S ALL HELL, later THE LONG AND THE SHORT AND THE TALL), A Play by Willis Hall.
Cranston Street Hall, Edinburgh. Producer: Peter Dews; cast: Patrick Garland, Michael Simpson, David Webster.

30 August  15 SCHNÜRE GELD (15 Money Bags), A Play by Gunther Weisenborn.
Thalia-Theater, Hamburg. Producer: Gelmut Geng; cast: Hans Paetsch, Hans Lothar, Heinz Klevenow, Erich Weiher, Erwin Linder.

1 September  THE BONEFIRE, A Play by Gerard McLarnon.
Lyceum Theatre, Edinburgh. Producer: Tyrone Guthrie; cast: Margaret d'Arcy, Maurice O'Callaghan, Denys Hawthorne.

1 September  HANDFUL OF FIRE, A Play by N. Richard Nash.
National Theatre, Washington. Producer: Robert Lewis; cast: Roddy McDowall, James Daly, Kay Medford, Joan Copeland.

1 September  MITSU-RYO (Poaching), A Play by Sasaki Bukan.
Shimbashi Embu-jo Tokyo. Producer: Hodoshima Takeo; cast: Ishii Kan.

1 September  AKA-EBOSHI (Red Cap), A Comedy by Haji Seiji.
Kabuki-za, Tokyo. Producer: Kubota Mantaro; cast: Ichikawa Danshiro, Ichikawa Chusha.

1 September  THE AIMLESS, A Play by André de Launay.
Royal Arch Hall, Edinburgh. Producer: John Duncan; cast: Nicholas Ferguson, John Duncan, Ronald Crowe.

1 September  AUTUMN AFFAIR, A Play by Arthur Watkyn.
Connaught Theatre, Worthing, England. Producer: Guy Vaesen; cast: Patricia Kneak, Gerald Flood, Richard Aylen, Pauline Letts.

2 September  GOLDILOCKS, A Musical Play by Walter and Jean Kerr, Leroy Anderson and Joan Ford.
Erlanger Theatre, Philadelphia. Producer: Walter Kerr; cast: Barry Sullivan, Elaine Stritch, Russell Nype, Pat Stanley, Nathaniel Frey.

2 September  DIE KORREKTUR, A Play by Heiner and Inge Müller.
Maxim Gorki-Theater, Berlin. Producer: Hans Dieter Mäde; cast: Fritz Diez, Albert Hetterle, Kurt Steingraf.

2 September  HOWIE, A Play by Phoebe Ephron.
Wilbur Theatre, Boston, U.S.A. Producer: John Gerstad; cast: Leon Ames, Peggy Conklin, Albert Salmi, Patricia Smith, Patricia Bosworth.

3 September  STRATEGY OF MURDER, A Play by Sonia Brown.
Beverley Hills Playhouse, U.S.A. Producer: William Gass; cast: Jonathan Kidd, Frederic Villani.

3 September  CURLY ON THE RACK, A Play by Ru Pullan.
Elizabethan Theatre, Sydney. Producer: Nigel Lovell; cast: Ken Wayne, Grant Taylor, Stewart Ginn, Max Osbiston.

4 September  BABES IN ARMS, A Play by Patrick Casey.
Roof Garden Theatre, Bognor Regis, England. Producer: Kevin Barry; cast: Mary Fouracres, Piers Stephens, David Grain, Charles Kay, Michael Cox, Jeanne Laffan.

4 September  A SUMMER'S MISCHIEF, A Play by Neville Brian.
Summer Theatre, Hythe, England. Producer: David K. Grant; cast: James Craig, Neville Brian, David K. Grant, Joan Deering, Bridget Wood, Peter Mason.

5 September  IHR BRAEUTIGAM (Her Fiancé), A Play by Fritz Eckhardt.
Theater in der Josefstadt, Vienna. Producer: Hannes Tannert; cast: Willy Birgel, Fritz Eckhardt, Guilo Wieland.

8 September  THE HOLIDAY, A Play by John Hall.
Cambridge Arts Theatre, England. Producer: Frank Dunlop; cast: Sylvia Syms, Peter O'Toole, Mary Hinton.

8 September  A DAY IN THE LIFE OF . . ., A Comedy by Jack Popplewell.
Theatre Royal, Nottingham, England. Producer: Charles Hickman; cast: Alfred Marks, Naunton Wayne, Kenneth Warren, Therese Burton.

8 September  A FIG FOR GLORY, A Play by Jenny Laird, adapted from 'Les Derniers Outrages' by Robert Beauvais.
Royal Court Theatre, Liverpool, England. Producer: John Fernald; cast: Elvi Hale, Derek Farr, Joan Young.

8 September  WOLF'S CLOTHING, A Comedy by Kenneth Horne.
New Theatre, Bromley, England. Producer: David Poulson; cast: Joan Seton, Tony Beckley, Diana Scougall, Robert Hartley.

8 September  A TOUCH OF THE POET, A Play by Eugene O'Neill.
Shubert Theatre, New Haven, U.S.A. Producer: Harold Clurman; cast: Helen Hayes, Eric Portman, Kim Stanley, Betty Field.

8 September  CHRYSANTHEMUM, A Musical Play by Neville Phillips, Robin Chancellor and Robb Stewart.
Opera House, Manchester, England. Producer: Eleanor Fazan; cast: Pat Kirkwood, Hubert Gregg, Robin Gage, Patricia Moore, Raymond Newell, Vivien Grant.

8 September  PERSON UNKNOWN, A Thriller by John Aldridge.
Plaza Theatre, Tynemouth, England. Producer: Douglas Emery; cast Judith Gibson, Rio Fanning, Jean Challis, Drummond Marvin, Claire Bailey.

8 September  PEACOCK IN A DOVECOT, A Comedy by Jack Penycate.
Guildford Theatre, England. Producer: Richard Hayter; cast: Jean Trend, Brenda Barry, Derek Mayhew, Colin Rix, Philip Grout.

9 September  DE PASSAGE À PARIS, A Comedy by Michel André.
Petit Théâtre de Paris, Paris. Producer: Jean Wall; cast: Frank Villard, Guy Pintat, Anna Tonietti.

9 September  CHAPARRAL, A Play by Valgene Massey.
Sheridan Square Playhouse, New York. Producer: Valgene Massey; cast: Rip Torn, Ann Hamilton, Ruth White, Gene Hackman.

10 September  ILS ONT JOUÉ AVEC LES ALLUMETTES, A Tragedy by Marcelle Routier.
Théâtre d'Aujourd'hui, Paris. Producer: José Quaglio; cast: Sami Frey, François Maistre, Pierre Michael, Evelyne Ker.

10 September  LAAHUS (The Train), A Comedy by Lauri Kokkonen.
Tampere Theatre, Tampere, Finland. Producer: Lilli Markkanen; cast: Va-
lyyeri Virmajoki, Yrjo Jarvinen, Elsa Rantalainen, Eeva-Kaarina Volanen,
Helena Haavisto.

10 September  THE GIRLS IN 509, A Play by Howard Teichmann.
Playhouse, Wilmington, U.S.A. Producer: Bretaigne Windust; cast: Peggy
Wood, Imogene Cuca, Laurinda Barrett, King Donovan.

10 September  ICH BIN KEIN CASANOVA (I'm no Casanova), A Play by Otto Bielen.
Kammerspiele, Vienna. Producer: Ilo Janko; cast: Peter Weck, Doris Kirchner,
Elizabeth Berzabohaty.

11 September  RIDIDINE, A Comedy by Alexandre Breffort.
Théâtre de la Fontaine, Paris. Producer: Maurice Vaneau; cast: Mary Renaud,
René Havard, Paul Préboist, Bernard Musson, Pierre Ferval, Huguette Hue,
Rolande Ségur.

11 September  THE WORLD OF SUZIE WONG, A Play by Paul Osborn.
Shubert Theatre, Boston, U.S.A. Producer: Joshua Logan; cast: France Nuyen,
William Shatner, Mary Mon Toy, Ron Randell.

12 September  KIMBERLEY TRAIN, A Play by Lewis Sowden.
Library Theatre, Johannesburg. Cast: Jennifer Grey, Kita Redelinghuys,
Valerie Philip, Bruce Meredith Smith.

12 September  WHO KILLED THE CORPSES?, A Comedy Thriller by Leonard A. Tooke.
St. Peter's Hall, Southsea, England. Cast: Michael Sykes, Joan Ockenden,
Michael T. Harman, Leonard A. Tooke.

14 September  LADY ON THE BAROMETER (later SUGAR IN THE MORNING), A
Play by Donald Howarth.
Royal Court Theatre, London. Producers: Miriam Brickman and Donald
Howarth; cast: Patricia Jessel, Eric Thompson, Jeanne Watts, Anne Bishop,
John Gatrell.

15 September  MOURIR AU SOLEIL, A Tragedy by Jean Primo.
Théâtre de l'Oeuvre, Paris. Producer: Robert de Ribon; cast: Jean Pierre Joris,
Evelyne Rey.

15 September  THAT'S THE SPIRIT. A Comedy by Kenneth Saunders.
Angel Theatre, London. Producer: Kenneth Saunders; cast: Valerie Brooks,
Kenneth Saunders, Gwen Adeler, Harry Brunning, John Evitts.

15 September  TASTE OF FREEDOM, A Play by Rolanda Ronald.
Hovenden Theatre, England. Producer: Jean Black; cast: Mary Quinn, Robert
Hollyman, Charles Hards, Ivan Plowright.

15 September  REWARD IN HEAVEN, A Play by Roger Milner.
The Playhouse, Sheffield, England. Producer: Geoffrey Ost; cast: Ella
Atkinson, Julie Paul, Geraldine Gwyther, Philip Stone, Victor Lucas.

15 September  THE STEPMOTHER, A Play by Warren Chetham-Strode.
Grand Theatre, Leeds, England. Producer: Henry Kaplan; cast: Kate Reid,
Ian Hunter, Tim Seely, Maggie Smith, Joan Newell, David Waller.

15 September  DRINK TO ME ONLY. A Comedy by Abram S. Ginnes and Ira Wallach.
Warren Theatre, Atlantic City, U.S.A. Cast: Tom Poston, Georgann Johnston,
John McGiver, Royal Beal, Cameron Prud'homme, Paul Hartman, Leona
Powers.

16 September  LE LION D'AVIGNON, A Comedy by Jean-Claude Eger.
Théâtre des Arts, Paris. Producer: Christian-Gérard; cast: René Clermont,
Jacques Ciron, Nathalie Nattier, Madeleine Clervanne.

17 September  ONCE MORE WITH FEELING, A Play by Harry Kurnitz.
Shubert Theatre, New Haven, U.S.A. Producer: George Axelrod; cast: Joseph
Cotten, Arlene Francis, Walter Matthau, Leon Belasco, Ralph Bunker.

18 September  FAMILY NEXT DOOR, A Play by Kenneth Alan Taylor.
Ventnor Theatre, Isle of Wight. Producer: Carl Paulsen; cast: Kenneth Alan
Taylor, Maryann Turner, Nona Williams, Gordon Cave.

18 September  HUGHIE, A Play by Eugene O'Neill.
Little Theatre, Stockholm. Producer: Bengt Ekerot; cast: Bengt Eklund, Allan
Edwall, Marik Vos.

18 September  THE YOUNG PROVINCIALS, A Play by Ben Levinson.
Cricket Theatre, New York. Producer: Ben Levinson; cast: Jonne Morton, Luke
Askow, Barbara Pitcher.

19 September  L'ÉTRANGÈRE DANS L'ÎLE, A Play by Georges Soria.
Studio des Champs Élysées, Paris. Producer: Jean Negroni; cast: Bruno Cremer,
Yves Brainville, Philippe Kellerson, Michel Maurette, Jeanine Crispin, Anne
Perez.

20 September  ELDEN (Fire), A Play by Walentin Chorell.
Little Theatre, Helsinki. Producer: Vivica Bandler; cast: Alf Kjellin, Lasse
Poysti, Gunvor Sandkvist, Birgitta Ulfsson, Majlis Granlund.

20 September MARGARET ODER DAS WAHRE LEBEN, A Play by Richard Hey.
Württembergisches Staatstheater, Stuttgart. Producer: Dietrich Haugk; cast: Mila Kopp, Lieselotte Rau, Charles Wirths.

22 September LUCY CROWN, A Play by Jean-Pierre Aumont, from the novel by Irwin Shaw. Théâtre de Paris, Paris. Producer: Pierre Dux; cast: Edwige Feuillère, Bernard Blier, Paul Guers, Jacques Riberolles, Michel Giannou.

22 September SING CUCKOO, A Comedy by A. P. Dearsley.
Leas Pavilion, Folkestone, England. Producer: Julian Herington; cast: Carol Raymont. Jeanette Rae, Patricia Parry, Peter Walter, Martin Bradley, Barry Warren.

22 September STRAW IN THE WIND, A Play by Frank Baker.
Leatherhead Theatre, England. Producer: Alan Judd; cast: Peter Vaughan, Hester Paton Brown, Derek Martinus, Sonia Graham, Edward Harvey.

22 September CANDIDE, A Musical Play by Leonard Bernstein, Lillian Hellman, Richard Wilbur, John Latouche and Dorothy Parker.
Bucks County Playhouse, New Hope, U.S.A. Producer: David Alexander; cast: Martyn Green, Robert Rounseville, Irra Petina, Mary Costa, Lee Bergere, Charles May.

22 September THE RUSSIAN, A Play by Richard Thomas.
Lyric Theatre, Hammersmith, London. Producer: David Ash; cast: Emrys Jones, Esmond Knight, Eleanor Leigh, Peter Prouse.

23 September THERMOPYLAE, A Play by H. C. Branner.
Royal Theatre, Copenhagen. Producer: Anna Borg; cast: Poul Reumert, Poul Reichhardt, Karin Nellemose, Birgitte Price, Kirsten Rolffs.

23 September THE RISEN PEOPLE, A Play by James Plunkett.
Queen's Theatre, Dublin. Producer: Ria Mooney; cast: T. P. McKenna, Maire O'Donnell, Maire Kean, Harry Brogan, Ray McAnally, Doreen Madden.

23 September THE WINGS OF AN EAGLE, A Play by Peter M. Caporn.
Arts Theatre, Nottingham, England. County Theatre Company.

23 September LA HOBEREAUTE, A Play by Jacques Audiberti and Yves Claoue.
Théâtre Vieux-Colombier, Paris. Producer: Jean Le Poulain; cast: Françoise Spira, Daniel Ivernel, Jean Le Poulain.

24 September MAN IN THE DOG-SUIT, A Play by Albert Beich and William H. Wright.
Playhouse, Wilmington, U.S.A. Producer: Ralph Nelson; cast: Jessica Tandy, Hume Cronyn, Cathleen Nesbitt, Carmen Andrews.

24 September MAKE A MILLION, A Play by Norman Barasch and Carroll Moore.
Warren Theatre, Atlantic City, U.S.A. Producer: Esra Stone; cast: Don Wilson, Sam Levene, Ann Wedgworth, Neva Patterson.

26 September JUICIO CONTRA UN SINVERGUENZA (Trial of a Wastrel), A Play by Alfonso Paso.
Reina Victoria Theatre, Madrid. Producer: Fernando Granada; cast: Fernando Granada, Pastora Pena, Antonio Prieto, Ricardo Canales, Alicia Hermida.

26 September JACKNIFE, A Play by Rock Anthony.
Royal Playhouse, New York. Producer: Byrne Piven; cast: Joseph Boley, Dolly Jonah, Rochelle Oliver, Glen Cannon.

26 September ZUR ZEIT DER DISTELBLÜTE, A Play by Hermann Moers.
Schauspielhaus Bochem, Germany. Producer: Hans Schalla; cast: Erwin Kleist, Siegmund Giesecke.

27 September THE MARRIAGE-GO-ROUND, A Play by Leslie Stevens.
Alcazar Theatre, San Francisco. Producer: Joseph Oenslager; cast: Claudette Colbert, Charles Boyer, Julie Newmar, Edmond Ryan.

28 September BIEDERMANN UND DIE HÖLLE, A Play by Max Frisch.
Städtische Bühnen, Frankfurt. Producer: Harry Buckwitz; cast: Ullrich Haupt, Joachim Teege, Wolfgang Schirlitz.

29 September THESE PEOPLE, THOSE BOOKS, A Play by Dodie Smith.
Grand Theatre, Leeds, England. Producer: Richard Mathews; cast: Diana Churchill, Elizabeth Allen, Jack Gwillim, Marie Löhr, Gladys Henson.

29 September HOT SUMMER NIGHT, A Play by Ted Willis.
Pavilion, Bournemouth, England. Producer: Peter Cotes; cast: Joan Miller, John Slater, Andree Melly, Lloyd Reckord, Harold Scott.

29 September FIREWORKS IN THE SUN, A Play by Guy Bolton.
Connaught Theatre, Worthing, England. Producer: Guy Vaesen; cast: Elizabeth Hart, Susannah York, Gerald Flood, Michael Lees, Kenneth Laird.

29 September PACIFIC PARADISE, A Play by Dymphna Cusack.
Colchester Repertory Theatre, England. Producer: Bernard Kelly; cast: Frank Woodfield, Heather Canning, Frederik Paine, Pamela Coles, Peter Baldwin.

30 September A MERY PLAY BETWEEN JOHAN JOHAN, THE HUSBANDE, TYB, HIS WYFE, AND SYR JOHAN, THE PREEST.

Birmingham Repertory Theatre, England. Producer: Bernard Hepton; cast: Christine Low, Terence Lodge, Arthur Pentelow.

**September** TEPER'ILI NIKOGDA (Now or Never), A Play by R. Runinshtein and A. Volobrinskii.
Lenin Komsomol Theatre, Leningrad. Producer: A. Viner

**September** A TRUMPET IN THE STREETS, A Play by James Cheasty.
Studio Theatre, Dublin. Producer: Fergus Cogley; cast: John McGivern, Gerard Kiernan, Eithne O'Neill, Mary Lawlor, Fergus Cogley, Anne Coughlan.

**1 October** MR. VENUS, A Musical Play by Ray Calton, Johnny Speight, Norman Newell, Trevor H. Stanford.
Manchester Opera House, England. Producer: Charles Reading; cast: Anton Diffring, Frankie Howerd, C. Denier Warren, Gavin Gordon, Annette Carell.

**1 October** PLEASURE OF HIS COMPANY, A Play by Samuel Taylor and Cornelia Otis Skinner.
Shubert Theatre, New Haven, U.S.A. Producer: Cyril Ritchard; cast: Cornelia Otis Skinner, George Peppard, Dolores Hart.

**1 October** COMES A DAY, A Play by Speed Lamkin.
Playhouse, Wilmington, U.S.A. Producer: Robert Mulligan; cast: Judith Anderson, Arthur O'Connell, Diane van der Vlis, Brandon de Wilde, George S. Scott, Ruth Hammond, Eileen Ryan.

**2 October** LOS MANOS SON INOCENTES (The Innocent Hands), A Play by José Lopez Rubio.
Maria Guerrero Theatre, Madrid. Producer: Claudio de la Torre; cast: Mari Carmen Diaz de Mendõna, Angel Picazo, Mercedes Munõz Sampedro, A. Povedano.

**3 October** LA BONNE SOUPE, A Comedy by Felicien Marceau.
Théâtre du Gymnase, Paris. Producer: André Barsacq; cast: Armontel, Henri Crémieux, Daniel Ceccaldi, Alfred Adam, Marie Bell, Jeanne Morceau, Mathilde Casadesus.

**3 October** THE THIEF SHOUTS TO FRIGHTEN THE VICTIM, A Comedy by Demetre Psathas.
Cotopouli-Rex, Athens. Producer: Mary Aroni; cast: Mary Aroni, Théano Joannidou, Dinos Héliopoulos, D. Papayannopoulos, D. Kalivocas.

**3 October** REGEN DER INS WASSER FÄLLT, A Comedy by Theo Frisch-Gerlach.
Intimes Theatre, Munich. Producer: Harald Sanders; cast: Theo Frisch-Gerlach, Ernst G. Schiffner, Maria Reiter.

**6 October** HAVEN, A Play by Eric Coxon.
Leas Pavilion, Folkestone, England. Cast: Elizabeth Addyman, Margaret Fry, Carol Raymont, Patricia Parry, Peter Walter, William Hepper.

**6 October** CUCKOO IN CLOVER, A Play by Kate Lindsay.
Scala Theatre, Southport, England. Producer: Vint Graves; cast: Josie Kidd, Donald Pelmear, Jean Alexander.

**6 October** DAYS THAT ARE BRIGHTEST, A Play by Leonard Irwin.
Bolton Hippodrome, England. Producer: Hugh Wallington; cast: Lawrence-Williamson Repertory Players.

**7 October** SHADOW OF HEROES, A Documentary Play by Robert Ardrey.
Piccadilly Theatre, London. Producer: Peter Hall; cast: Peggy Ashcroft, Emlyn Williams, Alan Webb, Mogens Wieth, Stephen Murray, Martin Miller.

**7 October** LA MOISSON DE PILAR, A Play by Myriam Lempereur.
Le Théâtre Rideau, Brussels. Producer: Claude Etienne; cast: Madeleine Barrès, Gysèle Oudart, Denyse Berger, Serge Christian.

**8 October** FARVÄL TILL KARLEKEN (Good-bye to Love), Three one-act plays by Herbert Grevenius.
Municipal Theatre, Hälsingborg, Sweden. Producer: Johan Falck.

**8 October** CRAZY OCTOBER, A Play by James Leo Herlihy.
Shubert Theatre, New Haven, U.S.A. Producer: James Leo Herlihy; cast: Tallulah Bankhead, Joan Blondell, Estelle Winwood, Jack Weston.

**9 October** DEATHWATCH, A Play by Jean Genet.
Theatre East, New York. Producer: Leo Garen; cast: Vic Morrow, George Maharis, Harold Scott, Stefan Gierasch.

**10 October** SERENITY, A Play by Nestor Matsas.
Kyvelis Theatre, Athens. Producer: Greg Tallas; cast: Aliki Miranda, Anne Bratson, P. Santorinaiou, G. Glinos, Hel. Stamatiou, D. Starenios.

**12 October** THE WAVING LAUREL, A Play by Charles C. Gairdner.
Perth Theatre, Scotland. Producer: Maurice Winton; cast: Alexander Reid, Graham Fulton, Geoffrey Forrest.

**14 October** THE HOSTAGE, A Comic Tragedy by Brendan Behan.
Theatre Royal, Stratford, London. Producer: Joan Littlewood; cast: Murray

Melvin, Avis Bunnage, Howard Goorney, Dudley Sutton, Celia Salkeld, Robin Chapman, Eileen Kennally.

14 October    DIE ZWÖLF GESCHWORENEN, A Play by Horst Budjuhn.
Kammerspiele, Munich. Producer: Hans Schweikart; cast: Kurt Meisel, Banno Sterzenbach, Mario Adorf, Friedrich Domin.

17 October    MÄNNER, FRAUEN UND TÖCHTER (Man, Woman and Daughters), A Play by Charlotte Frances.
Thalia-Theater, Hamburg. Producer: Hans Paetch; cast: Freca-Renate Bortfeldt, Dorit Fischer, Erwin Linder, Michael Toost.

17 October    NO GOOD FRIDAY, A Play by Athol Fugard.
Darragh Hall, Johannesburg. Cast: Stephen Moloi, Gladys Sibisi, Daniel Poho, Bloke Modisane, Connie Mabasa.

20 October    MAKE IT MURDER, A Play by Jack Last.
Bromley New Theatre, England. Producer: David Poulson; cast: Hazel Coppen, Anthony Howard, Angela Crow, Peter Goss, Robert Hartley.

20 October    MATILDA SHOUTED FIRE, A Thriller by Janet Green.
New Theatre, Oxford, England. Producer: Charles Hickman; cast: Perlita Neilson, Kieron Moore, Moira Redmond, Christine Roberts, Philip Lennard, John Carson, Peter Bayliss, Patrick Connor.

20 October    LET'S LIVE A LITTLE, A Play by David Curtis.
The Palace, Westcliffe, England. Producer: Donald B. Edwards; cast: George Cormack, Lois Penson, Jeane Stenning, Anthony Beaumont, William Treacher, Alan Curtis, Valerie Dunlop.

21 October    FEAR CAME TO SUPPER, A Play by Rosemary Anne Sisson.
Birmingham Repertory Theatre, England. Producer: Bernard Hepton; cast: Marigold Sharman, Clifford Parrish, Ian Richardson.

22 October    LA GUERRE BLONDE, A Comedy by Roger Boussinot.
Ranelagh Theatre, Paris. Producers: Fabiène Mai and Pierre Arnaudeau; cast: Jean-Marie Fertey, Serge Lhorca.

25 October    THE GOLDEN SIX, A Play by Maxwell Anderson.
York Playhouse, New York. Producer: Warner Le Roy; cast: Viveca Landfors, Alvin Epstein, Thayer David, Roger Evan Boxhill.

27 October    THE GRASS IS GREENER, A Comedy by Hugh and Margaret Williams.
Theatre Royal, Brighton, England. Producer: Jack Minster; cast: Celia Johnson, Joan Greenwood, Hugh Williams, Edward Underdown, Moray Watson.

27 October    GWENDOLINE, A Play by Geoffrey Lumsden.
Playhouse, Salisbury, England. Producer: Oliver Gordon; cast: Graham Armitage, Gay Cameron, Geottrey Lumsden, Ronald Magill, Derek Smee.

27 October    A RIGHT ROSE TREE, A Play by M. J. Molloy.
Queen's Theatre, Dublin. Producer: Ria Mooney; cast: Maire ni Chathain, Maire ni Dhomnaill, Brid ni Loinsigh, T. P. McKenna, Ray McAnally.

27 October    MOON ON A RAINBOW SHAWL, A Play by Errol John.
Manchester Opera House, England. Producer: Frith Banbury; cast: Earle Hyman, Vinette Carroll, John Bouie, Soraya Rafat.

27 October    THE CITY CHAP, A Play by Leigh Pennington.
Wimbledon Theatre, England. Producer: John Hussey; cast: Ruth Porcher, Veronica Hurst, Peter Haddon, Donald Price, Barrie Gosney.

27 October    FLOWER DRUM SONG, A Musical Play by Rogers and Hammerstein.
Shubert Theatre, Boston, U.S.A. Producer: Gene Kelly; cast: Ed Kenny, Juanita Hall, Miyoshi Umeki, Larry Storch, Arabella Hong, Conrad Yama.

27 October    THE NIGHT CIRCUS, A Play by Michael V. Gazzo.
Shubert Theatre, Detroit, U.S.A. Producer: Frank Corsaro; cast: Ben Gazzara, Janice Rule.

28 October    LE CHINOIS, A Musical Comedy by Barillet and Gredy, and Michel Emer.
Théâtre de la Bruyère, Paris. Producer: Georges Vitaly; cast: Jacques Dufilho, Michel Galabru, Jacqueline Maillan.

28 October    KRAPP'S LAST TAPE, A Play by Samuel Beckett.
Royal Court Theatre, London. Producer: Donald McWhinnie; cast: Patrick Magee.

28 October    WHO DONE HUGH DUNNETT?, A Comedy Thriller by Clifford Davies.
Victory Theatre, Portsmouth, England. HMS 'Victory' Drama Group.

29 October    L'HOMME DE GUERRE, A Play by François Ponthier.
Comédie de Paris, Paris. Producer: Marcelle Tassencourt; cast: Gérard Buhr, Jean Davy, Roland Rodier, Lucien Nat, Françoise Delille.

29 October    THE DISENCHANTED, A Play by Budd Schulberg and Harvey Breit.
Shubert Theatre, New Haven, U.S.A. Producer: David Pressman; cast: Jason Robards Jr., Rosemary Harris.

29 October    THE WARM PENINSULA, A Play by Joe Masteroff.
Playhouse, Wilmington, U.S.A. Producer: Warrren Enters; cast: Julie Harris.

29 October    UN TRAPEZIO PER LISISTRATA (A Trapeze for Lysistrata), A Musical
              Comedy by Garinei and Giovannini.
              Sistina Theatre, Rome. Producers: Garinei and Giovannini; cast: Delia Scala,
              Mario Carotenuto, Paolo Panelli.
30 October    LESKET (The Widows), A Farce by Walentin Chorell.
              National Theatre of Finland, Helsinki. Producer: Jack Witikka; cast: Pentti
              Siimes, Vilbo Siivola, Kyllikki Forsell, Pia Hattara.
30 October    LE PAIN DES JULES, A Play by Ange Bastiani and Raoul Stucky.
              Arts Theatre, Paris. Producer: Jean Le Poulain; cast: Charles Moulin, Claude
              Castaing, Yves Massard, Jean-Marie Rivière, Georgette Anys.
31 October    CALL ME NOT NAOMI, A Play by Ruth Messinger.
              Unity Theatre, London. Producer: Bernard Goldman; cast: Isobel Shelley, Louis
              Raynes, Norman Allen, Sara Randall.
31 October    VAIN IHMISIÄ (Just Men), A Play by Reino Lahtinen.
              Little Theatre, Helsinki. Producer: Vivica Bandler; cast: Lasse Pöysti, Elvi
              Saarnio, Eila Pahkonen.
31 October    OVERSÄTTNING (Transposition), A Play by Mary Mandelin.
              Little Theatre, Helsinki. Producer: Vivica Bandler; cast: Lasse Pöysti, Staffen
              Aspelin, Gunvor Sandkvist.
 1 November   THE REMNANTS, A Play by Alain Germoz.
              Koninklijke Nederlandse Schouwburg, Antwerp. Producer: Fred Engelen; cast:
              Gaston Vandermeulen, Jan Cammans, Fanny Winkeler, Ketty van de Poel.
 2 November   THE WHOLE WORLD OVER, A Play by Laurence Dobie and Robert Sloman.
              Wyndham's Theatre, London. Producer: Nancy Poultney; cast: Robert James,
              Jessica Spencer, Charles Leno, Kathleen Helme.
 3 November   LOVE OR MONEY, A Comedy by Peter Thwaites and Charles Cowper.
              Grand Theatre, Leeds, England. Producer: Charles Ross; cast: Basil Lord,
              Hugh Latimer, Howard Pays, Rowena Gregory, Vivian Pickles, Janet Morrison.
 3 November   MEET THE COUSIN, A Comedy by Alan Haines and Al Nesor.
              Lyceum Theatre, Edinburgh. Producer: Andre van Gyseghem; cast: Noelle
              Middleton, Lisa Gastoni, Jack Watling, Richard Hart, Claude Hulbert, Olga
              Lowe.
 3 November   RIVER IN A HIGH PLACE, A Play by Robert G. Armstrong.
              Circle Theatre, Los Angeles. Producer: Alex Nicol; cast: Stan Young, Jack
              Jones, Robert Karnes, June White.
 4 November   EVERY DOG HAS HIS, A Play by Hyam Gilbert.
              Park Lane Theatre, London. Producer: Francis Butler; cast: Peter Bawfon
              Dawson, Bobby Bernard, Francis Mexwell, Pat Joliffe, John Calden, Robert
              Heginbotham.
 4 November   FERDINAND THE MATADOR, A Musical Play by Christopher Whelen, and
              Leo Lehman.
              Belgrade Theatre, Coventry, England. Producer: Bryan Bailey; cast: Oscar
              Quitak, Diana Coupland, Audrey Nicholson, Cherry Morris, Gerald Deacon.
 4 November   THE COLD WIND AND THE WARM, A Play by S. N. Behrman.
              Locust Street Theatre, Philadelphia. Producer: Harold Clurman; cast: Eli
              Wallach, Maureen Stapleton, Sanford Meisner, Morris Carnovsky.
 4 November   PENELOPE'S WEB, A Play by Sheridan Gibney.
              Margo Jones Theatre 58, Dallas, U.S.A. Producer: Aaron Frankel; cast: Henry
              Barnard, Ruthe Elliot, Benneye Gatteys.
 5 November   ISÄ JA POIKA (Father and Son), A Play by Ilmari Turja.
              National Theatre of Finland, Helsinki. Producer: Wilho Ilmari; cast: Tauno
              Palo, Martti Romppanen, Maikki Länsiö, Tyyne Haarla.
 5 November   LA CATHÉDRALE DE CENDRES, A Tragedy by Berta Dominguez.
              Théâtre d'Aujourd'hui, Paris. Producer: Abel Gance; cast: Tony Taffin, Giani
              Esposito, Antoine Balpêtré, Lucie Arnold, Tania Balachova.
 5 November   CUE FOR PASSION, A Play by Elmer Rice.
              Shubert Theatre, New Haven, U.S.A. Producer: Elmer Rice; cast: Diana
              Wynyard, John Kerr.
 6 November   NO CONCERN OF MINE, A Comedy by Jeremy Kingston.
              Westminster, London. Producer: Adrian Brown; cast: John Fraser, Judith
              Stott, Alan Dobie, Lally Bowers.
 7 November   PAUVRE EDOUARD, A Comedy by Marc Camoletti.
              Comédie Wagram, Paris. Producer: Michel de Ré; cast: Henri Vilbert, Maxime-
              Fabert, Jacques Sommet, Jean-Marie Proslier, Anne Carrière, Claude Emy.
 7 November   A NIGHT ON THE MEDITERRANEAN, A Play by Anghelos Terzakis.
              Greek National Theatre, Athens. Producer: Costis Michaelidis; cast: Jenny
              Karezi, Despo Diamantidou, Vera Deliyanni, Alecos Alexandrakis, Nicos
              Tzoyas.
10 November   WHO'S YOUR FATHER?, A Comedy by Denis Cannan.

Theatre Royal, Brighton, England. Producer: Peter Wood; cast: Donald Sinden, Maurice Denham, Maureen Swanson, Newton Blick.

10 November GILT AND GINGERBREAD, A Play by Lionel Hale.
Theatre Royal, Newcastle, England. Producer: Harold French; cast: Kay Hammond, John Clements, Ralph Michael, Nicholas Hannen.

10 November I SAW HIM DIE, A Play by William Douglas.
Derby Playhouse, England. Producer: Leslie Twelvetrees; cast: William Douglas, Mary Laine.

10 November THE INFORMER, A Play by Micheál MacLiammóir, adapted from the novel by Liam O'Flaherty.
Olympia Theatre, Dublin. Producer: Hilton Edwards; cast: Micheál MacLiammóir, Maureen Potter, Laurie Morton.

10 November THE WILL TO KILL, A Play by George I. Ross.
Queen's Theatre, Hornchurch, England. Producer: Clifford Williams; cast: Keith Marsh, David Nettheim, Gary Watson, Lala Lloyd.

10 November BLOOD ORANGE, A Play by Hugh Hastings.
Colchester Repertory Theatre, England. Producer: Bernard Kelly; cast: David Jarrett, James McInnes, Heather Canning, Arthur Cox, Virginia Stride.

10 November WHOOP-UP, A Musical Play by Norman Gimbel, Moose Charlap, Freuer and Martin.
Shubert Theatre, Philadelphia. Producer: Freuer; cast: Susan Johnston, Paul Ford, Ralph Young, Romo Vincent, Sylvia Syms, Danny Meehan.

11 November PACIFICO, A Play by Jo Moutet and Paul Nivoix.
Théâtre Porte-Saint-Martin, Paris. Producer: Max Revol; cast: Georges Guetary, André Bourvil, Camille François, Robert Chabrier, Pierrette Bruno, Corinne Marchand, Marcel Journet.

12 November DON JUAN, A Comedy by Henry de Montherlant.
Théâtre de l'Athénée, Paris. Producer: Georges Vitaly; cast: Pierre Brasseur, Lucien Baroux, Françoise Guérin, Suzanne Dehelly.

12 November THE GAZEBO, A Play by Alec Coppel.
Playhouse, Wilmington, U.S.A. Producer: Reginald Denham; cast: Walter Slezak, Jayne Meadows, Edward Andrews.

14 November DAS HAUS ERINNERUNG, A Play by Erich Kästner.
Kammerspiele, Munich. Producer: Hans Schweikart; cast: Heinrich Wildberg, Peter Paul, Benno Sterzenbach, Heini Göbel, Robert Graf, Heinz Kargus.

14 November PASTORALE, A Play by Wolfgang Hildesheimer.
Kammerspiele, Munich. Producer: August Everding; cast: Paul Verhoeven, Robert Graf, Maria Nicklish, Arno Assmann, Benno Sterzenbach, Renate Grosser, Herbert Bötticher.

14 November LE SAINT VALENTIN, A Play by Raymond Vincy.
Théâtre de la Renaissance, Paris. Producer: Pasquali; cast: Jean Raymand, Robert Murzeau, Pasquali, Jane Sourza, Simone Paris, Gisèle Grandpré.

15 November DE LAATSTE VERLOFGANGER (Ashes of Tjiparan), A Play by Jan Staal.
Stadsschouwburg, Arnhem, Netherlands. Producer: Johan Walhain; cast: Hetty Beck, Marise Crefcoeur, Elise Hoomans, Elly van Stekelenburg, Anne de Lange, Annie Langenaken.

16 November ICH SELBST UND KEIN ENGEL (I Myself and No Angel), A Play by Thomas Christoph.
Theater in der Kongresshalle, Berlin. Producer: Konrad Swinarski; cast: Claudia Brodzinska, Barbara Morawiecz, Ethel Reschke, Armin Stahl, Helmut Ahner.

16 November DIE FESTUNG (The Fortress), A Play by Claude Hubalek.
Theater am Kurfürstendamm, Berlin. Producer: Harry Meyen; cast: Hans Nielsen, Paul Edwin Roth, Paul Bösiger, Horst Keitel, Alexander Engel, Horst Hans Jochmann.

17 November HAPPY DAYS, A Play by Walter Greenwood.
Coliseum, Oldham, England. Producer: Harry Lomax; cast: Thora Hird.

17 November LOVE AT LAW, A Comedy by Harold Brooke and Kay Bannerman.
Theatre Royal, Windsor, England. Producer: John Counsell; cast: Mary Kerrige, Francis Matthews, Jennifer Wright, Malcolm Russell.

17 November GOLD IN THE FIRE, A Play by Philip Weathers.
Connaught Theatre, Worthing, England. Producer: Guy Vaesen; cast: Irene Sutcliffe, Oliver Fisher, Elizabeth Hart, Rosamunde Burne.

17 November ET PUIS . . . VINT LE JOUR, A Play by Vincent Rigoir and Alain Robert-Yves.
Coliseum Theatre, Paris. Producer: Lucien Carey; cast: Michel Salina, Jacques Dancour, Gisèle Grant, Sophie Perrault.

18 November LES TROIS COUPS DE MINUIT, A Play by André Obey.
Théâtre de l'Oeuvre, Paris. Producer: Pierre Dux; cast: Fernand Ledoux, Palau, Daniel Dancourt, Maria Daems.

19 November  DER AUFHALTSAME AUFSTIEG DES ARTURO UI (The Reckless Career of Arturo Ui), A Play by Bertolt Brecht.
Württembergisches Staatstheater, Stuttgart.  Producer: Peter Palitzsch; cast: Wolfgang Kieling, H. H. Dickow, Herbert Steinmetz.

20 November  CHÉRIE NOIRE, A Comedy by François Campaux.
Théâtre Michel, Paris.  Producer: Jacques Charon; cast: Jean-Jacques, Paul Demange, Marcel Darvey, Jean Sylvère, Marthe Mercadier, Yoko Tani.

20 November  MELOCOTÓN EN ALMIBAR (Peach in Syrup), A Play by Miguel Mihura.
Infanta Isabel Theatre, Madrid.  Producer: Miguel Mihura; cast: Isabel Garcès, Julia G. Caba, Luisa Rodrigo, José Orjas, Antonia Gandia, Emilio Rodriguez, Angel Lafuente.

21 November  THE MAN WHO NEVER DIED, A Play by Barrie Stavis.
Jan Hus Theatre, New York.  Producer: Robert Mayberry; cast: Mark Gordon, John Graham, Kermit Murdock, Stephen Gray.

22 November  DAMALS 18/19, A Play by Wera and Claus Küchenmeister.
Theater der Freundschaft, Berlin.  Producer. Lothar Bellag; cast: Hermann Eckhardt, Peter Groeger, Hansjürgen Gruner.

23 November  SUIKER (Sugar), A Play by Hugo Claus.
Rotterdamse Schouwburg, Rotterdam.  Producer: Ton Lutz; cast: Ina van Faassen, Jan Lemaire Sr., Ton Lutz, Pim Dikkers, Leo de Hartogh.

24 November  THE BRIGHT ONE, A Comedy by J. M. Fulton.
Theatre Royal, Brighton, England.  Producer: Rex Harrison; cast: Gladys Cooper, Kay Kendall, Michael Gwynn, Hugh McDermott, Frederick Leister.

24 November  SEVEN AGAINST THE SUN, A. Play by James Ambrose Brown.
Springs Municipal Theatre, Springs.  Cast: Michael Turner, Bill Brewer, Pieter Geldenhuys, David Herbert.

24 November  BLOOMSDAY, A Play by Allen McClelland, adapted from the novel 'Ulysses', by James Joyce.
Oxford Playhouse, England.  Producers: John McGrath and Michael Simpson; cast: David Webster, Roland MacLeod, Roger Smith, Elizabeth MacLennan.

24 November  EIGHTY IN THE SHADE, A Play by Clemence Dane.
Theatre Royal, Newcastle, England.  Producer: Lionel Harris; cast: Sybil Thorndike, Robert Flemyng, Valerie Taylor, Lewis Casson.

24 November  THE EDGE, A Play by Richard Dellar.
Guildford Theatre, England.  Producer: Richard Hayter; cast: Brendan Barry, Jean Trend, Edna Landor, Michael Ellison, Geoffrey Wearing.

24 November  FAREWELL MY FANCY, A Musical Play by Michael Wild, based on the novel 'The Trumpet Major', by Thomas Hardy.
Everyman Theatre, Reading, England.  Producer: Michael Wild; cast: Dennis Inwards, Sylvia Moss.

24 November  J. B., A Play by Archibald MacLeish.
National Theatre, Washington.  Producer: Elia Kazan; cast: Pat Hingle, Christopher Plummer, Raymond Massey, Nan Martin.

25 November  TEA TIME, A Play by Jan Christiaens.
Keldertheater ARCA, Ghent.  Cast: Dan Decock, W. Cornelis, N. de Jonge, L. Premer.

26 November  DE KLEUPRACKER, A Comedy by Karl Bunje.
Oldenburgisches Staatstheater, Oldenburg, Germany.  Cast: Carl Hinrichs, Karla Krause, Ursel Tammen.

26 November  TACO, A Play by Herman Teirlinck.
Rotterdamse Schouwburg, Rotterdam.  Producer: Jo Dua; cast: Wies Anderson, Dora van der Broen, Cyriel van Gent, Jeannine Bernaus.

26 November  JOURNEY WITH STRANGERS, A Play by Richard Lortz.
Greenwich Mews Theatre, New York.  Producer: Adrian Hall; cast: Mary Sinclair, Michael Ray, Lois Holmes.

27 November  LUMISOTA (Snowball Fight), A Play by Hagar Olsson.
Jyväskylä Theatre, Finland.  Producer: Laure Kuorti.

29 November  BALLYHOO, A Comedy by Philip McHale.
Crescent Theatre, Birmingham, England.  Producer: Barbara Morgan; cast: Brian J. Burton, Michael LeCocq, Patricia Hancock, Bill Willetts, George Deeley.

30 November  MORE LIKE STRANGERS (later DISPLACED AFFECTIONS), A Play by George Hulme.
Royal Court Theatre, London.  Producer: Phil Brown; cast: Vivian Matalon, Valerie White, Leo Ciceri.

1 December  PATTES DE MOUCHE, A Comedy by Marcel Franck.
Théâtre de Capucines, Paris.  Producer: Henri Soubeyran; cast: Jean-Paul Thomas, Bernard Lavalette, Anna Gaylor, Maria Pacome.

2 December  L'ANNÉE DU BAC, A Comedy by Jose-André Lacour.

Théâtre Edouard VII, Paris. Producer: Yves Robert; cast: René Lefèvre, André Valmy, Sami Frey, Francis Nani, Roger Dumas, Jacques Perrin.

2 December   VINGT-ET-UN SCÈNES DE COMÉDIE, A Satire by Alain.
Théâtre Lutèce, Paris. Producer: François Maistre; cast: Paul Crauchet, François Maistre, André Thorent.

2 December   TO KILL OR CURE, A Play by George Walsh.
Brighton Pavilion, England. Producer: Tristram Butt; cast: Maureen Luke, Michael Fry, John Dawson.

3 December   NAKED IN EDEN, A Play by Richard Reich and Alden Nash.
Studio Theatre, Hollywood. Producer: James F. Collier; cast: June Vincent, Yvette Vickers.

4 December   SCHLEUSE, A Play by Wolfgang Altendorf.
Theater der Stadt Trier, Germany. Producer: Lothar Michael Schmidt; cast: Wilhelm Meyer-Ottens, Erich Will, Eva-Maria Lahl.

5 December   HAY ALGUIEN DETRÁS DE LA PUERTA (Someone behind the Door). A Play by Alfonso Paso.
Recoletos Theatre, Madrid. Producer: Benitez Sanchez Cortes; cast: Mari Carillo, Guillermo Marin, Carlos Muñoz.

6 December   SUCHEN SIE MAGDALENA?, A Play by Werner Sprenger.
Städtische Buhnen, Frankfurt. Producer: Heinrich Koch; cast: Wolfgang Schirlitz, Sigfrit Steiner.

7 December   EH' DIE BRÜCHEN VERBRENNEN, A Play by Gert Weymann.
Lessingtheater, Nurnberg, Germany. Producer: Hesso Huber; cast: Adolf Gerstung, Lothar Diettriech, Walter Ueding, Hertha Schwarz, Klara Klotz, Heinrich Cornway.

8 December   TEDDY BOYS' PICNIC, A Play by William Barrow.
Theatre Royal, Portsmouth, England. Producer: Patrick Barton; cast: Hector Ross, Dudley Stevens, Allan Barnes, Joan Cooper, Joan Scott.

8 December   ROGUE PRINCE, A Play by Lyndon Brook.
Salisbury Playhouse, England. Producer: Oliver Gordon, cast: Michael Atkinson, Nancie Herrod, Derek Smee, Tim West.

8 December   THE SQUARE TRIANGLE, A Play by Michele Carpenter.
Grand Theatre, Southampton, England. Producer: Ian Cunningham; cast: Jean Kent, Lennard Pearce, David Kerr, Peter Bovet.

8 December   OFF THE RAILS, A Farce by John Waterhouse.
Prince's Theatre, Bradford, England. Producer: Doel Luscombe; cast: Doel Luscombe, Austin Steele, Sylvia Melville.

8 December   FRIEND OF THE FAMILY, A Play by Peter Stone.
Crystal Palace, St. Louis, U.S.A. Producer: Theodore J. Flicker; cast: Theodore J. Flicker, Thomas Aldrege, Janice Meshkoff.

10 December  SOMETHING ABOUT A SAILOR, A Play by Earle Couttie.
Connaught Theatre, Worthing, England. Producer: Alan Bridges; cast: Barry Sinclair, Ian Holme, Peter Byrne, Peggy Sinclair.

12 December  LES PORTES CLAQUENT, A Comedy by Michel Fermand.
Théâtre Danou, Paris. Producer: Christian-Gérard; cast: Pierre Jourdan, Jean-Claude Brialy, Yvonne Clech, Hélène Dieudonné.

12 December  ESTA NOCHE ES LA VISPERA (Night of Vigil), A Play by Victor Ruiz Iriarte.
Goya Theatre. Madrid. Producer: Manuel Benitez Sanchez Cortès; cast: Maria Asquerino, Luisa Sala, Mary Campos, José Maria Rodero, Carlos Casaravilla, José-Luis Heredia.

14 December  WILKKARENGAS (The Ring around the Ankle), A Play by Arttuti Leinonen.
Finnish Theatre of Vaasa, Finland. Producer: Veikko Manninen; cast: Seppo Karjalainen, Ahti Halja-Liisa Ahlgren.

15 December  ALWAYS FRIDAY NIGHT, A Play by Peter Hogben and Cecil Widdows.
Palace Theatre, Watford, England. Producer: Ivan Butler; cast: Penelope Charteris, Jessie Ball, David Butler, Robert S. Grant, John Clegg, Valerie Newbold.

15 December  LE PRINCE DE PAPIER, A Play by Jean Davray.
Théâtre des Mathurins, Paris. Producer: Jacques Charon; cast: Jean-Louis Trintignant, Jean Payen, Marcelle Praince, Madeleine Lambert, Francine Bergé, Claudine Coster.

16 December  LA BAGATELLE, A Comedy by Marcel Achard.
Théâtre des Bouffes-Parisiens, Paris. Producer: Jean Meyer; cast: Pierre Mondy, Yves Robert, Danièle Delorme.

17 December  THE ROYAL ASTROLOGERS, A Play by Willis Hall.
Birmingham Repertory Theatre, England. Producer: Bernard Hepton; cast: Arthur Pentelow, Hilary Hardiman.

17 December  LET YOUR HAIR DOWN, A Musical Play by Adam Leslie.

Intimate Theatre, Johannesburg. Cast: Joan Blake, Hilda Kriseman, Robert Wilson, Eric Micklewood.

18 December  UN SOÑADOR PARA UN PUEBLO (Dreamer for a Nation), A Play by Antonio Buero.
Espagnol Theatre, Madrid. Producer: José Tamayo; cast: Carlos Lemos, Asunción Sancho, Ana Maria Noé, José Bruguera.

18 December  THE LOCAL POSTMAN, A Comedy by Panayotis Kayas.
Municipal Theatre, The Piraeus, Greece. Producer: D. Rondiris; cast: Anne Kyriakou, D. Zeza, V. Charialou, S. Katsarou, A. Proussalis, N. Dendrinos.

20 December  KLEIST, A Play by Hans Rehberg.
Oldenburgisches Staatstheater, Oldenburg, Germany. Cast: Günther Amberger, Sonja Weckemann, Irmgard Tiletzek.

22 December  REDHEAD, A Musical Play by Herbert and Dorothy Fields, Sidney Sheldon, David Shaw and Albert Hague.
Shubert Theatre, New Haven, U.S.A. Producer: Bob Fosse; cast: Gwen Verdon, Richard Kiley, Leonard Stone, Doris Rich.

22 December  RING OF ROSES, A Comedy by David Campton.
The Library Theatre, Scarborough, England. Producer: Stephen Joseph; cast: Dona Martyn, David Sutton, Faynia Jeffery.

25 December  THE AMERICAN SIXTH FLEET, A Comedy by A. Sakeliarios and Chr. Yannakopoulos.
Photopoulos Theatre, Athens. Producer: A. Sakellarios; cast: M. Krevvata, X. Kalogeropoulos, P. Lazou, Z. Phytoussi, D. Photopoulos, K. Naos.

26 December  FORT CHRISTINA, A Musical Comedy by Hendrik Lundblom.
Municipal Theatre, Upsala-Gävle, Sweden. Producer: Ellen Bergman.

29 December  PERIOD OF ADJUSTMENT, A Play by Tennessee Williams.
Coconut Grove Playhouse, Miami, U.S.A. Producers: Tennessee Williams and Owen Philips; cast: James Daly, Barbara Baxley, Robert Webber, Martine Bartlett.

31 December  PRAIRIE-SALOON, A Play by Heinz Wunderlich.
Das Junge Theatre, Hamburg. Producer: Hans Richter; cast: Maria Martinsen, Dorothea Moritz, Papperitz Verena Wiet.

31 December  FRAGEN SIE ONKEL ERNST (Ask Uncle Ernest), A Comedy by Pierre Bürki.
Zimmer Theatre, Aachen, Germany. Producers: Wilhelm Wiegand and S. Willi Thomas; cast: Anja Rau, Sabine Rohde, Ildegard Fein, Liselotte Kuschnitzky, Susanne David.

December  YUHREI WA KOKO NI IRU (The Ghost is Here), A Satirical Comedy by Abe Kobo.
Haiyù Theatre, Tokyo. Producer: Senda Koreya; cast: Tanaka Kunie, Mishima Masao.

December  BARA TO KAIZOKU (Rose and Pirate), A Play by Mishima Yukio.
Daiichi Seimei Hall, Tokyo. Producer: Matsuura Takeo; cast: Akutagawa Hiroshi, Sugimmura Haruko.

2 January  TO SOME A PERFUME, A Play by Mary Antony.
Philbeach Hall, London. Producer: George Rawlins; cast: Stella Lewis, Bill Gaunt, Cherry Dennis, Basdeo Pandy.

5 January  THE SINGING DOLPHIN, A Play by Beverley Cross.
Oxford Playhouse, England. Producer: David Buxton; cast: Edmund Bailey, Gilbert Vernon, Christopher Hancock, Ruth Meyers.

9 January  TALL STORY, A Comedy by Howard Lindsay and Russel Crouse.
Locust Street Theatre, Philadelphia. Producer: Herman Shumlin; cast: Marian Winters, Nina Wilcox, Robert Wright, Mason Adams.

9 January  CODETTA FOR STARLINGS, A Play by an anonymous author.
Celtic Ballet Theatre, Glasgow. Producer: Gerard Slevin; cast: Peter Stuart-Smith, Alex McAvoy, Robert Baird, Toni McGettigan, Frank Wylie.

11 January  JUDGMENT IN SUNLIGHT, A Play by Michael Kelly.
Strand Theatre, London. Producer: Nigel Stock; cast: Pamela Abbott, Frederick Treves, John Crocker, Michael Golden.

11 January  DIE HERZOGIN VON LANGEAIS, A Play by Jean Giraudoux.
Residenztheater, Munich. Producer: Axel von Ambesser; cast: Agnes Fink, Anne Kersten, Klausjurgen Wussow.

12 January  A MAJORITY OF ONE, A Comedy by Leonard Spigelgrass.
Forrest Theatre, Philadelphia, U.S.A. Producer: Dore Schary; cast: Gertrude Berg, Cedric Hardwicke, Ina Balin, Michael Tolan.

16 January  THE POKER GAME, A Comedy by George Panetta.
Shubert Theatre, Washington. Producer: Ruth Dawson; cast: Aline MacMahon, J. Carrol Naish, Doretta Morrow, Kay Medford.

18 January  DIE TAT, A Play by Peter Kissener.

Städtische Bühnen, Bielefeld, Germany. Producer: Harry Niemann; cast: Toni Berger, Michael Noss, Curth A. Tichy.

19 January   LA FOLIE, A Comedy by Louis Ducreux and André Popp.
Théâtre de la Madeleine, Paris. Producer: Louis Ducreux; cast: Claude Dauphin, Albert Medina, Jacques Verlier, Pierre Gay, Elina Labourdette.

19 January   THE NIGHT OF THE SHOOT, A Thriller by Edwin Evans.
Harrogate Opera House, England. Producer: Sonia Dresdel; cast: Campbell Barr, Edwin Quayle, Joan Clevedon, Alethea Charlton.

21 January   A RAISIN IN THE SUN, A Play by Lorraine Hansberry.
Shubert Theatre, New Haven, U.S.A. Producer: Lloyd Richards; cast: Sidney Poitier, Claudia McNeil, Ruby Dee, Diana Sands, Ivan Dixon, John Fiedler, Glynn Turman, Louis Gosset.

21 January   NO, A Play by Joaquin Calvo Sotelo.
Reina Victoria Theatre, Madrid. Producer: Rafael Rivelles; cast: Rafael Rivelles, Francisco Pierra, Enrique Closas, Luis Casal, Amparo Marti, Lolita Crespo.

22 January   THE WOMAN ON THE STAIR, A Play by James Parish.
Westminster Theatre, London. Producer: Jack Minster; cast: Gwen Watford, Raymond Huntley.

24 January   JUGEND 44, A Play by Ernst Bürger.
Kreistheater, Crimmitschau, Germany. Producer: Siegfried Meyer; cast: Rudolfe Grabbe, Wolfgang Bölling, Gisela Kretzschmar.

26 January   SEVEN MOONS TO MIDNIGHT, A Play by Herbert Davies.
Cardiff Little Theatre, Wales. Producer: Herbert Davies; cast: Joan Hobbs, Jack Broad, Harry Collins.

26 January   PRINCE GENJI, A Play by William Cooper.
Oxford Playhouse, England. Producer: Frank Hauser; cast: Michael David, Natasha Parry, Ruth Meyers, Julian Somers, Edmund Bailey, David Cameron, Gwen Nelson, Christopher Hancock.

26 January   THE COAST OF COROMANDEL, A Play by J. M. Sadler.
Theatre Royal, Brighton, England. Producer: John Fernald; cast: Peggy Ashcroft, Molly Urquhart, Alan Webb, Eric Porter.

27 January   RASHOMON, A Play by Fay and Michael Kanin, based on stories by Ryunosuke Akutagawa.
Music Box Theatre, New York. Producer: Peter Glenville; cast: Claire Bloom, Rod Steiger, Akim Tamiroff, Oscar Homolka, Noel Willman.

27 January   TRY FOR WHITE, A Play by Basil Warner.
Hofmeyr Theatre, Cape Town. Cast: Michael Turner, Marjorie Gordon, Zoe Randall, Minna Millsten.

28 January   TCHIN-TCHIN, A Comedy by François Billetdoux.
Poche-Montparnasse Theatre, Paris. Producer: François Darbon; cast: François Billetdoux, Claude Berri, Katherina Renn.

28 January   LE DESSOUS DES CARTES, A Play by André Gillois.
Théâtre Hébertot, Paris. Producer: Jacques Hébertot; cast: Jean Leuvrais, Pierre Tabard, Frank Estrange, Etienne de Swarte, Michel Salina, Huguette Hue, Claude Pasquier.

28 January   THE AGE OF THE NIGHT, A Play by Jacques Campannellis.
Arts Theatre, Athens. Producer: Ch. Koun; cast: Yania Savoppulou, Angelika Capellari, C. Bakas.

29 January   LES POSSÉDÉS, A Play by Albert Camus after the novel by Dostoievsky.
Théâtre Antoine, Paris. Producer: Albert Camus; cast: Pierre Blanchard, Marc Eyraud, Pierre Vaneck, Michel Bouquet, Tania Balachova, Nadine Basile.

29 January   MADAME DE . . ., A Play by Jean Anouilh from a story by Louise de Vilmorin.
Arts Theatre, London. Producer: Peter Hall; cast: Elizabeth Sellars, John Warner, Douglas Wilmer, Geoffrey Keen.

30 January   PUERTO FRANCO, A Play by Leonard Peck.
Unity Theatre, London. Producer: Anne Dyson; cast: Bernard Forrest, Margery Shaw, Michael Hannan, Louis Raynes.

30 January   UN JEUNE HOMME EN HABIT, A Fantastic Tragedy by Armand Lanoux, Gerard Calvi and Alexandre Tansman.
Tertre Theatre, Paris. Producer: Gabriel Garran; cast: Gérard Blain, Jean-Marie Robain, Edgar Bischoff, Gaston Vacchia, Raymond Jourdan, Jacqueline Lanno.

31 January   KEINE ZEIT FÜR HEILIGE, A Play by Joachim Wichmann.
Deutsches Theater in Göttingen, Germany. Producer: Claus Leininger.

2 February   GOODBYE WORLD, A Play by Bernard Kops.
Guildford Theatre, England. Producer: Richard Hayter; cast: Philip Grout,

John Charlesworth, Phyllis Montefiore, Alfred Hoffman, Aimee Delamain, Chip Coveney, James McLoughlin.

2 February    A NIGHT ON THE ISLAND, A Comedy-Thriller by Leslie Halliwell.
Little Theatre, Bristol, England. Producer: Peggy Ann Wood; cast: Michael Edwards, Anthony Collin, Anthony Brown, Gwerfyl Hamer, Elizabeth Boxer.

2 February    JULIAN THE APOSTATE, A Tragedy by Nicos Kazantzakis.
National Theatre, Athens. Producer: Costis Michailidis; cast: Nelly Anghélidou, Gelly Mavropoulou, Rita Myrat, Qt. Vocivic, N. Paraskevas.

2 February    TREASURE IN EARTH, A Play by Keith Gardner.
Empire Theatre, Cleethorpes, England. Producer: Frank Marlborough; cast: Bill Weisener, Frank Marlborough, Jean Rimmer, Merry Legge.

2 February    FIRST IMPRESSIONS, A Musical Play by Helen Jerome, based on the novel 'Pride and Prejudice' by Jane Austen.
Shubert Theatre, New Haven. U.S.A.   Producer: Abe Burrows; cast: Polly Bergen, Farley Granger, Hermione Gingold.

2 February    THE SAINTLINESS OF MARGERY KEMP, A Comedy by John Wulp.
York Playhouse, New York. Producer: James Price; cast: Francis Sternhagen, Thomas Barbour, Charles Nelson Reilly.

2 February    KING KONG, A Musical Play by Harry Bloom and Todd Matshikiza.
Great Hall, University of the Witwatersrand, Johannesburg.   Cast: Nathal Mdledle, Joe Mogotsi, Miriam Makeba.

3 February    MON ANGE, A Comedy by Solange Terac.
Comédie Wagram, Paris. Producer: René Clément; cast: Gérard Séty, Maxime-Fabert, Michel François, Jacqueline Gautier.

4 February    LA MAISON DES SOEURS GOMEZ, A Play by Geneviève Bailac.
Théâtre de l'Athénée, Paris. Producers: Geneviève Bailac and Bernard Bimont; cast: Mario Pilar, Inès Nazaris, Odile Mallet.

5 February    L'HURLUBERLU OU LE RÉACTIONNAIRE AMOUREUX, A Comedy by Jean Anouilh.
Comédie des Champs-Élysées, Paris. Producer: Roland Pietri; cast: Paul Meurisse, Roland Pietri, Camille Guérini, Jean Claudio, Hubert Deschamps, Marie-José Martel.

6 February    LES CHOUTES, A Comedy by Barillet and Gredy.
Théâtre des Nouveautés, Paris. Producer: Jean Wall; cast: Guy Trjan, Claude Rich, Michel Gonzalès, Brigitte Auber, Maire Deams, Dany Saval, Jeanne Fusier-Gir.

7 February    PROGRESS TO THE PARK, A Play by Alun Owen.
Royal Court Theatre, London. Producer: Lindsay Anderson; cast: Harry H. Corbett, Margaret Tyzack, Tom Bell, Donal Donnelly, Keith Smith, Gerard Dynevour.

7 February    THE RIVALRY, A Play by Norman Corwin.
Bijou Theatre, New York. Producer: Norman Corwin; cast: Nancy Kelly, Martin Gabel, Richard Boone.

7 February    KEINE ZEIT FÜR HEILIGE, A Play by J. Wichmann.
Studio des Deutschen Theater Göttingen, Germany. Producer: Claus Leininger; cast: Alwin Westhoff, K. Behrendt, Aldona Ehret.

9 February    THE ROVING BOY, A Play by Joe Corrie.
The Citizen's Theatre, Glasgow, Scotland. Producer: Callum Mill; cast: Ewan Hooper, Iain Cuthbertson, Roddy MacMillan, Irene Sunters, Frank Wylie.

9 February    L'ENFANT DU DIMANCHE, A Comedy by Pierre Brasseur.
Théâtre de Paris, Paris. Producer: Pierre Valde; cast: Pierre Brasseur, Maurice Sarfatti, Jacqueline Porel, Marguerite Pierry, Anne Wartel.

9 February    THE LEGEND OF LIZZIE, A Play by Reginald Lawrence.
Fifty-fourth Street Theatre, New York. Producer: Hartney Arthur; cast: Douglass Montgomery, Anne Meacham.

10 February   SWEET BIRD OF YOUTH, A Play by Tennessee Williams.
Locust Street Theatre, Philadelphia, U.S.A. Producer: Elia Kazan; cast: Geraldine Page, Paul Newman, Madeleine Sherwood, Diana Hyland.

12 February   MAUVAISE SEMENCE, A Play by Paul Vadenberghe and T. Mihalakeas.
Théâtre des Arts, Paris. Producer: Fred Pasquali; cast: Tony Taffin, André Reybaz, Germaine Kerjean, Marie Valsamaki.

16 February   WOLF'S CLOTHING, A Comedy by Kenneth Horne.
Theatre Royal, Brighton, England. Producer: Anthony Sharp; cast: Muriel Pavlow, Derek Farr, Elspeth Gray, Patrick Cargill.

16 February   STRANGE HANDS AT TABLE, A Play by Dudley Stevens.
Castle Theatre, Farnham, England. Producer: Peter Jackson; cast: Dorothy Edwards, Sheila Reid, Richard Brooks, C. Lethbridge Baker.

16 February   NOT ENOUGH TRAGEDY, A Play by Val Gielgud.
Colchester Repertory Theatre, England. Producer: Bernard Kelly; cast: Arthur

Cox, James McInnes, Virginia Stride, Heather Canning, Richard Sothcott.

16 February MRS. HOWARD'S HUSBAND, A Play by Seamus de Burca.
Gate Theatre, Dublin. Producer: Maureen O'Sullivan; cast: Maureen O'Sullivan, Maura Wylie, Maureen Foley, Oliver Bradley, Sally Jennings, Mignon Byrne, Bernard Frawley, Val Kiely, Tom Nolan.

16 February IN THE RED, A Comedy by Madeleine Bingham.
Shakespeare Memorial Theatre, Stratford-on-Avon, England. Producer: Richard Bird; cast: Peter Jones, Lally Bowers, Peter Myers, John Boxer, Patricia Heneghan, Robertson Hare.

17 February FINGS AINT WOT THEY USED T'BE, A Musical Play by Frank Norman.
Theatre Royal, Stratford, London. Producer: Joan Littlewood; cast: Glynn Edwards, Eileen Kennally, Richard Harris, James Booth, Howard Goorney.

18 February ONE WHO WORKS MIRACLES, A Play by Anatol Stern.
Nowy Theatre, Lodz, Poland. Producer: Kazimierz Deimek; cast: Tadeusz Minc, Hanna Bedrynska, Barbara Horawianka.

21 February KLÄVEMANN SPEELT LEWEMANN, A Play by Erich Schiff.
Oldenburgisches Staatstheater, Germany. Producer: Gussy Schnittker; cast: Carl Hinrichs, Heinz Schnittker, Anneliese Bülow, Ursel Tammen.

21 February THE GOLD SPIDER, A Comedy by Et. Fotiadis. Cotopouli-Rex Theatre, Athens. Producer: M. Aroni; cast: Mary Aroni, Th. Ionnidou, E. Apergi, Dinos Heliopoulos.

22 February SINGAPORE 67, A Comedy by Krzystof Gruszxzynski.
Dramatzczny Theatre, Wroclaw, Poland. Producer: Arthur Mioduicki; cast: Mirian Wisniowski, Adam Dzieduszynski.

23 February FOOL'S PARADISE, A Comedy by Peter Coke.
Grand Theatre, Wolverhampton, England. Producer: Allan Davis; cast: Cicely Courtneidge, Nora Swinburne, Guy Dehy, Agnes Laughlan, Jennifer Daniel, Ronald Wilson.

23 February LA COPIE DE MADAME AUPIC, A Play by Albert Husson.
Théâtre de la Fontaine, Paris. Producer: Daniel Ceccaldi; cast: Jean Martinelli, Robert Bazil, Jean Galland, Madeleine Robinson, Jacqueline Jehanneuf.

24 February LA RÉPÉTITION GÉNÉRALE, A Comedy by André Frère.
Théâtre de l'Oeuvre, Paris. Produced and acted by the author.

25 February THE SPARROW'S FALL, A Play by Patricia O'Connor.
Ulster Theatre Group Theatre, Belfast, Northern Ireland. Producer: R. H. McCandless; cast: Doreen Hepburn, Irene Bingham.

25 February TRESOR-PARTY, A Comedy Thriller by Bernard Regnier from the novel by P. G. Wodehouse.
Théâtre de la Bruyère, Paris. Producer: Christian-Gérard; cast: Jean-Roger Caussimon, Henri Giguel, Jacques Ciron, Jean-Paul Belmondo, Georges Audobert.

25 February THE GOLD PRISON, A Comedy by Sotiris Patatzis.
Photopoulou Theatre, Athens. Producer: Pelos Catsélis; cast: Popi Lazou, Marica Crevata, Xenia Calogeropoulou, Mimis Photopoulos.

26 February LOVELY STAR, GOOD NIGHT. A Play by Sigmund Miller.
Shubert Theatre, New Haven, U.S.A. Producer: Warren Enters; cast: Cloris Leachman, Mark Richman, Donald Cook, Glenda Farrell.

27 February TUEUR SANS GAGES, A Play by Eugène Ionesco.
Théâtre Récamier, Paris. Producer: José Quaglio; cast: Claude Nicot, Jean-Marie Serreau, Nicolas Bataille.

28 February MYOSOTIS, A Comedy by Maecel van Roey.
Koninklijke Nederlandse Schouwburg, Antwerp. Producer: Luc Philips; cast: Fanny Winkeler, Jet Naessens, Frans van den Brande, Maurits Goossens.

2 March MAN FOR THE JOB, A Play by Dennis Driscoll.
Theatre Royal, York, England. Producer: Ralph Jago; cast: Jean Alexander, James Beck, Jeffrey Dench, Jill Johnson, Dennis Spencer, June Barry, Cherry Crest.

2 March MONEY TALKS, A Comedy by Archel McCaw.
Empire Theatre, Cleethorpes, England. Producer: Frank Marlborough; cast: Merry Legge, Bill Weisner, Derek Tobias, Ronald McPhee, Eunice Mann.

2 March GOODWILL AMBASSADOR, A Comedy by Harry F. Tarvin.
Olympia Theatre, Dublin. Producer: Harald Bromley; cast: Denis King, Martyn Green, Cyril Cusack, Peter Donat, Alexander Szabo, Rita Vale.

3 March LOOK AFTER LULU, A Comedy by Noel Coward, adapted from the play by Feydeau.
Henry Miller Theatre, New York. Producer: Cyril Ritchard; cast: Roddy McDowell, Tammy Grimes, George Baker.

6 March CIRCLE OF WHEELS, A Comedy by Arthur Ross.

Horton Theatre, Hollywood. Producer: Joseph Sargent; cast: Gene Saks, Phyllis Coates.

7 March   FRANK V, A Play by Friedrich Dürrenmatt.
Schauspielhaus Zürich, Switzerland. Producer: Oscar Wälterlin; cast: Kurt Horwitz, Therese Giese, Maria Becker, Gustav Knuth, Ernst Schröder.

7 March   ST. GIGLIN, A Comedy by Claude Schnerb.
Comédie de Paris, Paris. Producer: René Clermont; cast: Jacques Jouanneau, Yves Furet, Annie Noel, Denise Clair.

8 March   IT IS HARD TO BE A JEW, A Comedy by Szelem Alekchem.
Zydowski Theatre, Warsaw. Producer: Chewel Buzgan; cast: Chewel Buzgan, Bywka Szyler, Zofia Skrezszewsk.

9 March   THE GIMMICK, A Comedy by Joseph Julian.
Grand Theatre, Leeds, England. Producer: Charles Ross; cast: Bernard Braden, Barbara Kelly.

9 March   OUT OF THIN AIR, A Comedy by Derek Benfield.
Salisbury Playhouse, England. Producer: Oliver Gordon; cast: Jacqueline Hussey, Nancie Herrod, Graham Armitage, Geoffrey Lumsden, Robert McBain.

9 March   HOW SAY YOU?, A Comedy by Harold Brooke and Kay Bannerman.
Lyceum Theatre, Edinburgh. Producer: John Counsell; cast: A. E. Matthews, Kathleen Harrison, Leslie Dwyer, Ann Firbank, Francis Matthews, Duncan Lewis, Malcolm Russell.

9 March   THE TATOOED LADY, A Play by Edgar K. Bruce.
Plaza Theatre, Tynemouth, England. Producer: Douglas Emery; cast: Edgar K. Bruce, Elizabeth Warde, Ian Cullen, Ursula Smith.

9 March   HIDDEN RIVER, A Play by Ruth and Augustus Goetz.
Theatre Royal, Brighton, England. Producer: Dennis Arundell; cast: Catherine Lacey, Leo Genn, Ralph Michael, John Stratton, Alan MacNaughton, Marianne Benet.

9 March   JUNO, A Musical Play by Joseph Stein and Marc Blitzstein, based on 'Juno and the Paycock' by Sean O'Casey.
Winter Garden Theatre, New York. Producer: José Ferrer; cast: Shirley Booth, Melvyn Douglas, Jack MacGowran.

9 March   MEMBERS ONLY, A Play by G. C. Chambers.
Guildford Theatre, England. Producer: Colin Gordon; cast: Colin Gordon, Cicely Paget-Bowman, William Abney, Richard Burrell, George Cormack, Colin Rix.

11 March   THE SLAUGHTER OF ST. THERESA'S DAY, A Play by Peter Kenna.
Elizabethan Theatre, Sydney. Producer: Robin Lovejoy; cast: Neva Carr-Glyn, Grant Taylor, Patricia Conolly, Dinah Shearing.

12 March   AN EINEM TAG WIE HEUTE, A Play by Tilde Ondra.
Städtische Bühnen, Bielefeld, Germany. Cast: Margret Grammerstorff, Brigitte Otto, Carlheinz Emmerich, Michael Noss.

12 March   THE BUSKERS, A Play by Kenneth Jupp.
Arts Theatre, London. Producer: Toby Robertson; cast: Patricia Jessel, Patrick Magee, Gordon Gostelow, Neil McCallum.

14 March   OF GRASS AND BEARS, A Play by Michael du Barry.
Invicta Road Institute, Blackheath, London. Producer: Michael du Barry; cast: Mary Hamilton, Roger Coombs, Colleen Francis, Anne Walker, Christine Spragg, Kathleen Wilson, Jane Atkinson.

16 March   SPARK IN JUDEA, A Play by R. F. Delderfield.
Parish Church of St. Mary, Newington, London. Producer: Peter M. Elrington; cast: Ian Wallace, Pamela Harrington, Michell Tregarthen, Frances Guthrie.

16 March   BEGINNING AND END, A Play by David Shellan.
Bromley Little Theatre, England. Producer: Victor Thornton; cast: Betty Pinchard, Raymond Collett, Betty Breden, Michael Ward.

16 March   THE CAPTIVES, A Play by Charlotte Hastings.
Connaught Theatre, Worthing, England. Producer: Guy Vaesen; cast: Ronald Lewis, Irene Sutcliffe, Michael Lees.

16 March   NO MONUMENT FOR MARK, A Comedy by Kate Lindsay.
Scala, Southport, England. Producer: Vint Graves; cast: Michael Hughes, Jean Lockhart, Josie Kidd, Eliane Formby, Peter Lawrence.

16 March   MR. FOX OF VENICE, A Play by Frederick Knott.
Lyceum Theatre, Edinburgh. Producer: Denis Carey; cast: Paul Rogers, Marian Spencer, Jeremy Brett, Carl Bernard, Newton Blick, Andreas Malandrinos.

16 March   MASQUERADE, A Play by Sigmund Miller.
John Golden Theatre, New York. Producer: Warren Enters; cast: Donald Cook, Glenda Farrell, Cloris Leachman.

| | |
|---|---|
| 17 March | KAMELIADAMEN (The Lady of the Camelias), A Play by Kjeld Abell after the novel by Alexandre Dumas.<br>Det Ny Teater, Copenhagen. Producer: Sam Besekow; cast: Mogens Wieth, Erik Mork, Olaf Nordgreen, Bodil Kjer, Inge Hvid Moller, Vera Stricker. |
| 20 March | FOUR O'CLOCK NOON, A Play by Peter Godfrey.<br>Springs Municipal Theatre, Springs, South Africa. Cast: Molly Seftel, Gabriel Bayman. |
| 23 March | STOLEN WATERS, A Play by Lionel Brown.<br>Harrogate Opera House, England. Producer: Sonia Dresdel; cast: Alethea Charlton, Don Hill, Elizabeth Friis, Joan Clevedon. |
| 24 March | DESERT INCIDENT, A Play by Pearl S. Buck.<br>John Golden Theatre, New York. Producer: Tad Danielewski; cast: Shepperd Strudwick, Sylvia Daneel, Paul Roebling, Cameron Prud'Homme. |
| 26 March | WIE ZIJN DE MOORDENAARS? (Who are the Murderers?), A Thriller by Gaston Martens.<br>Koninklijke Vlaamse Schouwburg, Brussels. Producer: Jo Dua; cast: Greta Lens, Lia Lee, Senne Rouffaer, Vic. Moeremans. |
| 30 March | ALL ENDS UP, A Farce by Richard Wilding.<br>Colchester Repertory Theatre, England. Producer: Bernard Kelly; cast: James McInnes, Pamela Coles, Heather Canning, Peter Baldwin, Gillian Phelps. |
| 31 March | KATAKI, A Play by Shimon Wincelberg.<br>Walnut Street Theatre, Philadelphia. Producer: Alan Schneider; cast: Sessue Hayakawa, Ben Piazza. |
| 2 April | LE TIR CLARA, A Play by Jean-Louis Roncoroni.<br>Théâtre du Palais-Royal, Paris. Producer: Jean-Louis Barrault; cast: William Sabatier, Rosy Varte, Roland Rodier, Maurice Sarfati, Pierre Pernet, Henry Gaultier. |
| 5 April | JOURNEY BY TRAIN, A Play by Aubrey Colin.<br>Hovenden Theatre, England. Producer: Valery Hovenden; cast: Jennifer Lautrec, Irene Barry, Frederick Pryce. |
| 5 April | NIGHT WITHOUT SLEEP, A Play by Scott Holman.<br>Wyndham's Theatre, London. Producer: André Van Gyseghem; cast: John Arnatt, Margaret Diamond, Michael Ely, Leonard Fenton, Kathleen Helme. |
| 6 April | MAYORS EAT OATS, A Play by Stanford and Timothy Home.<br>Harrogate Opera House, England. Producer: Sonia Dresdel; cast: Frank Tregear, Alethea Charlton, Joan Clevedon, Elizabeth Friis, Alec Wallis. |
| 6 April | UNDER THE LIGHT, A Play by Iain Crawford.<br>Citizen's Theatre, Glasgow. Producer: Peter Duguid; cast: Iain Cuthbertson, Ewan Hooper, Annette Crosbie, Harry Walker, Anne Kristen. |
| 8 April | AU BORD DE LA SCÈNE, A Comedy by Guy Gaurey.<br>Théâtre Gramont, Paris. Producer: Christian-Gérard; cast: Christian-Gérard, Jacques Ciron, Georges Audoubert, Rosine Favrey. |
| 13 April | BEDTIME FOR JONAH, A Play by John Ormerod.<br>Theatre Royal, Lincoln, England. Producer: K. V. Moore; cast: Michael Griffiths, Judith Harte, John Ronane. |
| 13 April | BRIDGE OF SIGHS, A Play by Thomas Muschamp.<br>Belgrade Theatre, Coventry, England. Producer: James Roose Evans; cast: Richard Martin, Charles Kay, Alan Howard, Jacqueline Wilson, Terry Wale, Cherry Morris, Peter Palmer. |
| 13 April | CHANGE OF TUNE, A Comedy by Alan Melville.<br>Lyceum Theatre, Edinburgh. Producer: Vida Hope; cast: Geraldine McEwan, Michael Goodliffe, Hugh Latimer, Dilys Laye, John Glyn-Jones, Hope Jackman. |
| 14 April | A PAPER ARK, A Play by John English.<br>Highbury Little Theatre, Sutton Coldfield, England. Producer: John English; cast: Doreen Cross, Diana Daggett, Edward Dodd, Lilian Fletcher, Michael Butler, Frank Williams. |
| 14 April | THE WORLD OF PAUL SLICKEY, A Musical Comedy by John Osborne and Christopher Whelen. Producer: John Osborne; cast: Dennis Lotis, Adrienne Corri, Marie Lohr, Jack Watling, Harry Welchman. |
| 14 April | DARK HALO, A Play by Sylvia Leigh.<br>Arts Theatre, London. Producer: Clifford Williams; cast: Mary Ellis, Sheila Burrell, Betty McDowall, Edgar Wreford, Larry Cross. |
| 16 April | SINGLE MAN AT A PARTY, A Play by Richard Kayne.<br>Off-Broadway Little Theatre Marquee, New York. Cast: Constance Carpenter, Ron McNeil. |
| 18 April | DE ZWANEN VAN DE THEEMS (The Thames Swans), A Play by Cees Nooteboom.<br>Stadsschouwburg, Amsterdam. Producer: Han Bentz van den Berg. |
| 18 April | SPELL MY NAME RIGHT, A Play by Ken Marshall. |

Salisbury, Rhodesia. Producer: John Poremba Brumer; cast: Ken Marshall, Moira Winslow, George Yeatman, Campbell Hastie, Peter Robins, Morag Pearson.

18 April     DIE UHREN and DER SCHIEFE TURM VON PISA, Two one-act plays by Wolfgang Hildesheimer. Producer: Hannes Razum; cast: Hilde Heinrich, Hans Pabst.

20 April     FAREWELL YESTERDAY, A Play by Ted Willis.
Connaught Theatre, Worthing, England. Producer: Guy Vaesen; cast: Rosamunde Woodward, Joe Hicks, Jill Hyem, Michael Lees.

26 April     THE TRIAL OF COB AND LEACH, A News-Play by Christopher Logue.
Royal Court Theatre, London. Producer: Lindsay Anderson; cast: Shani Wallis, George Rose, Shirley Cameron, Harry Gwyn Davis, Barbara Hicks, Ronald Fraser, Bryan Pringle.

26 April     GOLDHAUPT, A Play by Paul Claudel.
Städtische Bühnen, Essen, Germany. Producer: Erich Schumacher; cast: Fritz Lichtenhahn, Günther Tabor, Marie-Luise Etzel.

27 April     LET THEM EAT CAKE, A Comedy by Frederick Lonsdale.
New Theatre, Oxford, England. Producer: Wallace Douglas; cast: Michael Denison, Dulcie Gray, Eunice Gayson, Cyril Raymond, Phyllis Neilson-Terry, Guy Middleton, Henry Kendall, Claude Hulbert, Patricia Burke.

27 April     WHAT CAN WE DO ABOUT AUNTIE?, A Comedy by Philip King and Parnell Bradbury.
New Theatre, Bromley, England. Producer: Alexander Doré; cast: Bill Maynard, Alec Ross, Robin Ray, Patricia Webster, Barbara Bolton, George Lee.

27 April     BEWARE OF ANGELS, A Play by Audrey Erskine Lindop and Dudley Leslie.
New Theatre, Hull, England. Producer: Geoffrey Edwards; cast: Ruth Dunning, Lyndon Brook, Wendy Hutchinson.

29 April     PIQUE-NIQUE EN CAMPAGNE, A Comedy by Arrabal.
Théâtre Lutèce, Paris. Producer: Jean-Marie Serreau; cast: Philippe Kellerson, André Gille, Michael Goldmann.

30 April     DIE HEILIGE JOHANNA DER SCHLACHTHÖFE, A Play by Bertolt Brecht.
Deutsches Schauspielhaus, Hamburg. Producer: Gustav Gründgens; cast: Hanne Hiob, Hermann Schomberg.

# THEATRICAL OBITUARY

*May 1958*
Thorpe Bates (75), actor
Paul Bernard (65), actor
Francis Carco, playwright
Ronald Colman (67), actor
Aubrey Dexter (60), actor
Richard Dornseiff (71), manager
Moses Feder (67), actor
Norman Bel Geddes (65), designer/producer
Ann Gerlette (45), actress/producer
Harry Green (68), actor
Sylvia Grey (92), actress
F. Hugh Herbert (60), playwright
Martha Leavitt (49), actress
Robert A McNeil (70), manager
Frank McNellis (67), actor
Leo Mittler, producer/playwright
John C. Phelps (55), manager
Ainslie Pryor (37), actor
Lionel Shapiro (50), playwright
Mary Welch (35), actress

*June*
Raoul Aslan (72), actor/director
Robert Donat (53), actor
Evelyn Ellis (64), actress
Harry Fontana (64), manager
James Garrow (83), actor
Lloyd Hughes (60), actor
Mike Morgan (29), actor
Alfred Noyes (77), playwright
Maude Nugent (85), actress
Virginia Pearson (70), actress
Edward P. Riley (78), playwright
Adeline Adler Victorson (76), actress

*July*
Karol Adwentowicz (84), actor
Harold Brighouse (75), playwright
Julian Courtville, actor/producer
Rachel Crothers (80), playwright
Elfrida Derwent, actress
John Gobau (67), actor
Raymond Hackett (55), actor
Richard Herndon (85), producer
George Hubbard (73), actor
W. P. Lipscomb (70), playwright/actor
Ruth C. Mueller, actress
Franklin Pangborn (65), actor
Antonio Pasco (82), playwright
Irene Rooke (80), actress
Gordon Sandison (45), General Secretary of *Equity*
George Seibel (85), critic
Leonard R. Smith (69), actor
Evelyn Varden (63), actress
Eric Vivian (78), manager
George Carlton Wallace (86), actor/manager/playwright
Wilfrid Walter (77), actor/playwright
Ragna Wettergren (92), actress
Victor G. Wood (43), actor
Charles Young (63), actor

*August*
Barbara Bennett (50), actress

Rosie Boote (Marchioness of Headfort), (80), actress
Leslie Burgess (60), playwright
Bessie Burke (64), actress
Sydney W. Carroll (81), manager/critic
Harry C. Chakers (77), manager
Bonar Colleano (35), actor
Wolcott Gibbs (56), critic/playwright
Helen Jerome, actress
F. Tennyson Jesse (69), playwright
Kurt Katch (62), actor
Joseph McEvoy (64), playwright
Jacob Mestel (74), actor/producer
Enrice Pea (77), playwright
Charles Quartermaine, actor
Vasco Santana (68), actor
L. A. G. Strong (62), playwright
Harry Warburton (69), manager
Gayne Whitman (68), actor

*September*
Yvonne Arnaud (65), actress
Claire Bender (53), actress
Lawrence Bolton (60), actor/producer
Carl Brisson (62), actor
Frederick W. Brunelle (60), manager
Edward Dunstan (73), actor/manager
Lulu Glaser (84), actress
N. M. Gorchakov (60), actor/producer
Nancy Hornsby (48), actress
Gertrude Jennings (81), playwright
Doris Johnstone, teacher/actress
Charles O'Brien Kennedy (79), actor
Cecil King (83), manager
Aladar Laszlo (59), playwright
John Myers, producer
Victor W. Nixon (70), manager
Marie Price (Maire Nic Hiubhlaigh), actress/Founder of Irish National Theatre
Mary Roberts Rinehart (82), playwright
Lena Sandford Roberts (74), actress
Sydney Palethorpe Stather, manager
James Wesley (89), actor
Joshua Plumpton Wilson (79), actor

*October*
Zoe Akins (71), playwright
Gustav Berger (48), actor
Edwina Boyde (63), actress
Harry W. Crull (79), manager
Hamilton Deane, actor/manager/playwright
Mae Dix (63), soubrette
Polly Emery (83), actress
Canon Louis A. Ewart (77), chaplain/actor/magician
John Hamilton (71), actor
Merton Hodge (54), playwright/critic
John Roland Hogue (76), actor
Douglas G. Hubbard (35), actor
Jerome Jordan (54), actor/producer
Nugent Monck (81), producer/Founder of Maddermarket Theatre, Norwich.
Bessie Osborne, actress
Hubert Osborne (77), actor/playwright
Albert van Rempert, actor
Lennox Robinson (72), playwright/producer/critic

Philip Ryder, actor
Margaret Scudamore (73), actress
Leonard Sharp (68), actor
Karl Skraup (60), actor
Jessie Welburn (84), actress

*November*
Samuel Hopkins Adams (87), playwright
Wilmer H. Bentley (81), actor/producer
Robert F. Boda (71), manager
Ethel Buckley (79), actress
Coralie Carmichael (55), actress
Lotta W. Donaghy (83), actress
Cecil Frederick, actor
Henry Forbes (70), producer
John Goldin (63), producer/manager
George Higgs, manager
Doty Hobart (72), playwright
Gareth Jones (35), actor
Grace P. Katz, manager
Charles J. Lammers (82), actor
Johnston McCulley (75), playwright
W. F. McDermott (67), critic
Maurice Meldon (32), playwright
Bruce Moir (56), actor
Robles Monteiro (70), actor/manager
Grace D. Nile, actress
Henriette Payton (81), actress
Tyrone Power (44), actor
Reginald Sellick (59), actor/manager
Max Siegel (57), manager/producer
Claud Snelling, actor
Ronald Squire (72), actor
Hans von Twardowski (60), actor/
    producer/playwright
Ida Wuest (74), actress

*December*
Ferdinand Bruckner (67), playwright
Jose Collins (71), actress
Leon Feuchtwanger (74), playwright
Fyodor Gladkov (75), playwright
Carleton Guy (81), actor/producer/
    playwright
Ben Heater (80), actor/producer
Jack Kemp (78), producer
Jean Stirling Mackinlay (76), diseuse
Cameron Matthews (74), actor
Edwin F. Melvin (64), critic
Harry Moore (70), actor
Thomas King Moylan (73), playwright
James S. Powers (63), manager
Elizabeth Risdon (71), actress
Edward Runkle (56), manager
Homer Saint-Gaudens (79), producer
Florence Salkeld (78), playwright
Jack Sheehan (67), actor
Sir John Squire (74), playwright/critic
H. B. Warner (82), actor

*January 1959*
Muriel Barnby (79), actress
Clifford Brooks, manager
Dudley Edmunds (65), manager
Lillian Elliot (84), actress
MacGregor Gibb (52), actor
Harold Gordon (40), actor
Malcolm Graham (62), actor
Molly Pearson Hales (83), actress

Herbert Higgin (88), manager
Lee K. Holland (62), producer/manager
Hilda Knight (41), producer
Boris Lavrenev (67), playwright
Dionysius MacDuffy (John Woulfe
    Flanagan), actor/translator
William MacIntosh (60), manager
Else Mauhs (74), actress
Marie Montrose (88), actress
Susan Richmond (64), actress
R. W. Ross-Crawford (55), manager
Sara Perry Stainach (87), actress
Michael Thompson (34), actor/manager
Philip Tonge (61), actor
Frances Williams (57), actress

*February*
Kathryn Adams (65), actress
Maxwell Anderson (70), playwright
Nell Ballantyne, actress
Evelyn Shannon Clyndes (78), actress/
    manager
John C. Darlinson (93), actor/manager
Irving Fisher (73), actor
Laurence Housman (93), playwright
Stanley Howlett (74), actor
Matilde Moreno (84), actress
Una O'Connor (66), actress
Grace Palotta, actress
Bertrand Robinson (70), actor/playwright
Yvonne Rorie (51), actress
Enid Sass (70), actress
Frank Connolly Shannon (84), actor
Julius Steger, actor
John Wildberg (55), producer
Pat Woodings (51), actor/producer
Arthur Young (60), actor
Harold Young (59), actor/producer

*March*
Eric Blore (71), actor
Fan (Francis) Bourke (68), actress
Williard Bowman (85), actor
Georgina Carhart (93), actress
Olga Knipper-Chekhova (90), actress
Douglas Clarke-Smith (70), actor
Anne Croft (62), actress/manager
Shalva Nikolaevitch Dadiani (84),
    playwright/actor
Owen Fellowes (65), actor
T. C. Murray (85), playwright
Marie Olivette (67), actress
Fred Andrew Stone (85), actor
W. G. Thomas (55), manager
*April*
Amy Augarde (90), actress
Ulrich Bettac (61), actor/producer
Jefferson Clifford (66), actor
Irving Cummings (70), actor
Louis van Gimberg (79), actor
H. M. Harwood (85), playwright/manager
Rosalind Ivan (75), actress
Michael Lynd (37), actor
Edie Macklin (Mrs. Harry Lundon) (93),
    actress
Peter Marwoode (55), manager
Evelyn Williams, British Council Deputy
    Director of Drama
Cecilia Willman, actress